YANKEES '98

BEST EVER!

SPORTS PUBLISHING INC.
www.SportsPublishingInc.com

ACKNOWLEDGMENTS

When the 1998 New York Yankees wrapped up the franchise's 24th World Series Championship in San Diego, the *Daily News* was busy putting together its 24th Yankees Championship edition. As always, the *Daily News* provided world championship coverage worthy of the new World Champions.

There are literally hundreds of people at the *Daily News* whose hard work and dedication throughout this magical season have made this book possible. The efforts of the many reporters, columnists, editors, executives, and photographers were all essential in bringing the Yankees' record-setting year to the pages of the newspaper every day. A few of those who were instrumental in assisting us in this project were Ed Fay, Les Goodstein, John Polizano, Lenore Schlossberg, Angela Troisi, Eric Meskauskas, and Lori Comassar. From the *Daily News* sports pages, we specifically want to acknowledge the contributions of Barry Werner, Bill Madden, Mike Lupica, Peter Botte, Rafael Hermoso, Linda Cataffo, Gerald Herbert, Keith Torrie, Howard Simmons, and Mike Albans.

Space limitations preclude us from thanking all the other writers and photographers whose work appears in this book. However, wherever available, we have preserved the writers' bylines and the photographers' credits to ensure proper attribution for their work.

Sports Publishing Inc.

Sports Publishing Inc. staff: Joseph J. Bannon, Jr., Thomas H. Bast, Michael G. Pearson, Joanna Wright, Terrence C. Miltner, Victoria J. Parrillo
Editor: Susan M. McKinney
Interior design: Terry N. Hayden
Book Layout: Terry N. Hayden, Susan M. McKinney, Jennifer L. Polson and Erin J. Prescher
Dustjacket Design: Terry N. Hayden

ISBN: 1-58261-030-4
Library of Congress Number: 98-89120

Printed in the United States.

SPORTS PUBLISHING INC.
804 North Neil Street
Champaign, IL 61821
www.SportsPublishingInc.com

TABLE OF CONTENTS

INTRODUCTION

FANS LOVE THEIR CLASSY CHAMPS

OCTOBER 25, 1998

By Chris N. Karalekas

Generations ago it was said that rooting for the New York Yankees was like rooting for U.S. Steel. You just didn't do it. Generations later, one of the uniquely remarkable attributes of the 1998 Yankees is that fans all across America rooted for this group, or at the very least liked and respected them.

Fans admired and appreciated their excellence and their virtue. As fans, and as parents, we keep waiting for the inevitable mindless behavior so inherent in our athletes today.

Visions of Mark Jackson and his broom; Moses Malone and his infamous fo, fo, fo; Dennis Rodman, Mike Tyson and the like, in all their self-serving pomposity have not surfaced with these Yankees.

Instead, on the heels of winning the World Series in four straight games, Derek Jeter, Paul O'Neill, Scott Brosius and their teammates answered postgame interviews with humility and class. They showed respect for themselves, their audience, and the institution of this wonderful game.

What a marvelous example to project to children across the landscape of America. We didn't have to worry about what or how they said it. Kids of all ages were hearing and seeing a special group of men who epitomized the seemingly lost art of professionalism.

This year's Yankees have entered the pantheon of elite baseball teams. Their glorious 114-win regular season is testament to the talent, work ethic, character and selflessness that has distinguished their team. Until this season, no team in baseball history had ever won an astonishing 125 games in a year. Not the '75 Reds. Not the Athletics of the early '70s. We can hope that, in addition to this new standard of baseball excellence, the '98 Yankees have re-introduced class, respect, and humility into our lexicon.

How wonderfully compelling a summer it was for all New Yorkers to witness this charming superstarless team. The manner in which they went about their work was their greatest quality. There were no public gripes; no egos; no I; no me; just what we can do.

Take nothing away from the individual accomplishments of Mark McGwire and Sammy Sosa, but to win 114 games in this me-first millionaire era says volumes about this special collection of men who have methodically and yes, lovingly (there, I've said it) focused on their craft in a masterful way. By intrinsically putting money, ego, and commercial interferences aside, they have re-established the concept of team.

Remember these '98 Yankees and this mythical baseball season as they seem to be from another era.

Indelibly etched in our memories will be the symmetry of their spirit as they personified class and professionalism to a new generation of baseball fans. It seems the only thing exceeding their talent, dedication and work ethic was their humanity. Remember the way these '98 Yankees have played. They seemed to good to be true.

1998 SPRING TRAINING

LEGENDS FIELD—TAMPA

TORRE SADDLED WITH THE BOSS

MARCH 25, 1998

By Ian O'Connor, Daily News Sports Writer

George Steinbrenner was talking the other day about horses—the kind you ride during World Series victories, not after them. He was saying he likes his stable of pitchers and catchers, slappers and sluggers. Not enough for any guarantee, mind you, but enough to put a fresh signature on a law as old as his land.

For $72 million, the Pope would grumble over a wild-card entry and division series exit. How, then, could those prices and results sate the most impetuous owner in sports?

"When I was a football coach at Northwestern, we had no materials and couldn't do a thing," Steinbrenner said. "When I was at Purdue we had Lenny Dawson, other horses, and won. Now we've given Joe Torre the horses."

Including one aimed at sunset.

Torre has taken 188 regular-season games in

Yankees pitcher Andy Pettitte during the first workout with pitchers and catchers.

DAILY NEWS Linda Cataffo

two years. He shows off a ring, two playoff appearances and a clubhouse full of stars granting him their affection and respect. Book and movie folks bought his story, pudgy kid from Brooklyn to champion of the world.

Yet a week from today, in Anaheim, Torre begins fighting for his job. It's an absurd notion. To date, the man couldn't have done finer work. One feels embarrassed even asking him the what-ifs and what-nexts.

They're asked, anyway, as a matter of necessity. In the Bronx, genius is measured in nine-inning shifts. If Steinbrenner is slightly gentler, slightly kinder, he will remain a most demanding employer for however long he owns this team.

He has the highest payroll and loudest

Spring Training ● Tampa

1

lineup. In good health, the Yankees are capable of winning 100 games. But one David Cone twinge here, another Andy Pettitte spasm there, and the Yankees could just as easily miss the playoffs.

No matter what, Torre should be fire-proof, protected better than a pit bull's lunch. Asked if his manager would be retained all season, regardless of record, Steinbrenner said, "Sure. Yes. Yes."

Torre knows the history of those words. He also knows the terms of his employment. Take the Yankee job, proceed at your own peril.

He has a team worth the gross national product of Portugal. Can those tens of millions in wages actually represent a swell problem to have?

"You're damn right," Torre said. "At least when you get fired here, you had a chance to win. When I got fired in St. Louis, I was told I needed to do more of this and that. Of course, it came down to the fact we didn't have the team.

"That bothered me. Here, you're going to get a better than honest chance because George isn't playing for second place."

This year, George might have to settle for just that. Huge contracts only assure an owner one thing: reporters and fans will forever use them to gauge his team's performance.

Juiced by the constant reminders of his largess, Steinbrenner might feel justified in trading managers if the Yankees fail to reach the World Series. For now, all we have is his word. He insisted Torre should go about his business burden-free.

"I hope Joe doesn't feel pressure because nothing has

Derek Jeter

changed," Steinbrenner said. "Look at our payroll last year and there was no pressure. My relationship with Joe might be the best I've had with a manager.

"Joe will do his best and I'll go to the bank with him. If his best isn't quite enough, I'll understand because a lot of things happen in a season. We're in the toughest division in baseball. We're just another team right now."

But one Torre vows to savor. Whether it comes across or not, the manager declared he's loose as can be.

He tried the hard-guy routine last year and it didn't fly. Months after his dream came true, Torre was afraid people would think the title extinguished his fire.

"Then I had lunch with my wife last May and she said, 'Who are you? I don't recognize you,' " Torre said. "She said, 'Why do you care what people think?' So I started having fun again."

Enjoy while you can. Sound advice everywhere else, a mandate here.

Torre said when Steinbrenner marches into his office, "I never tense up." He talks to his boss the way he couldn't to Ted Turner and August Busch.

If these chats can't stop Steinbrenner from going to the bullpen, they at least will make him think twice. The owner said he admires Torre's Brooklyn moxie. Called him a tough SOB.

"When we hired Joe," Steinbrenner reminded, "everyone said, 'What the hell are you doing? This guy's a loser.'"

DAILY NEWS Linda Cataffo

Reggie Jackson assisted the Yankees during Spring Training.

Torre spit tobacco all over that. And yet a week away from Year 3, his record offers little in the way of security.

"I think this is the hardest I've ever worked to put together a team," Steinbrenner said.

The Boss doesn't like his work or cash going to waste. Joe Torre understood when he signed up.

He wanted the horses and now he has them, strong, fast, and ready to roll. The manager knows the trails. This way to another championship, that way to another job.

YANKEE PROFILE

CHUCK KNOBLAUCH

NEW YANK LOOKS LIKE OLD ROSE

FEBRUARY 10, 1998

By Peter Botte, Daily News Sports Writer

As a teenager, he was a member of a Mickey Mantle team that won a national championship. As a young adult, he was an All-America shortstop at Texas A&M and a participant in the College World Series. At just 23, he was the starting second baseman for the 1991 World Series champion Twins, while capturing the American League Rookie of the Year award.

Success was all Chuck Knoblauch ever had known, and George Steinbrenner's latest catch wasn't about to apologize yesterday if he left more than a few clubhouse feathers ruffled by begging out near the end of six straight sub-.500 seasons in Minnesota.

"I play to win and hate to lose and I'll never, ever, get used to losing," the newest member of the Yankees' All-Star brigade said at the Stadium, a few moments after Joe Torre helped him try on pinstriped uniform No. 11 for the first time.

"Obviously I wasn't too happy there because of the losing. I take my profession seriously. I'm in this to win. Winning creates happiness. That's why I'm so happy today. I know I'm in a situation to win."

Knoblauch, acquired last week for four minor leaguers and $3 million, punctuated his anticipated arrival in the Bronx by suggesting the one player he most patterned his game after was "definitely" Pete Rose.

He termed Rose's infamous steamrolling of catcher Ray Fosse in the 1970 All-Star Game as "the epitome of intensity."

And although 5-9, 170-pound Knoblauch added, "I'm not big enough to run over anybody," the early comparison to baseball's banned all-time hits leader actually is more accurate than one would think.

Rose, who also originally came up as a scrappy, undersized second baseman, compiled a .306 average in his first seven seasons.

David Wells congratulates Chuck Knoblauch after a home run.

DAILY NEWS Howard Simmons

2B

Chuck Knoblauch

Knoblauch's average through his first seven seasons is only two points lower.

Beyond his reputation as a surly clubhouse presence, this is the kind of performer New York is getting:

A Gold Glove middle infielder to pair with Derek Jeter at the keystone for years to come. And a supreme catalyst to place atop what he already called "a very exciting lineup that was hell to defend against," even before he came on board.

DAILY NEWS   Linda Cataffo

Chuck Knoblauch is interviewed as he arrives at Spring Training.

"This sure feels good. I have chills putting on this uniform," the 29-year-old Knoblauch said. "I'm excited. I can't believe I'm a Yankee, and it feels great saying that. I can't wait to have a chance to win every night."

Which brings us, of course, to Knoblauch's eventual desire to have the remaining four years and $24 million on his contract reworked, a matter both sides still

insisted would not become a factor anytime soon.

"The effort to get Chuck traded to a competitive environment — and the Yankees certainly satisfy that — supersedes everything," Knoblauch's agent, Alan Hendricks, said. "After all the effort to get him to New York, that is the furthest thing from our mind."

Chuck Knoblauch Stats

1998 REGULAR SEASON

AVG.	G	AB	R	H	TB	2B	3B	HR	RBI	BB	SO	SB	CS	SH	SF	HP	SLG%	OBP%
.266	149	602	116	160	244	25	4	17	64	74	70	30	12	2	7	18	.405	.359

GAME OF THE WEEK

APRIL 1, 1998 VS. ANAHEIM ANGELS

WEEK 1 ● APRIL 1-4

NOT DANDY

Pettitte Falls to Finley, Angels

APRIL 2, 1998

By Peter Botte, Daily News Sports Writer

No matter what George Steinbrenner had half-jokingly mandated, not even his $72 million Yankees were about to win 162 games this season. But that doesn't make how they lost the first one any more acceptable.

Playing like a team that had not faced a major-league caliber pitcher in four days—and playing like a team that perhaps read one too many press clippings—the high-octane Yankees began the 1998 season of great expectations precisely in a manner Joe Torre had to fear more than any other.

The result was a yawner against Chuck Finley and the Angels, a sluggish 4-1 defeat last night at sold-out and soggy Edison International Field.

Torre and his collection of superstar charges, of course, have preached all spring how games are not played nor won on paper. They generally aren't played nor won in a quagmire, either, but the Yankees are not 0-1 because of El Niño.

They lost last night primarily because their top-to-bottom wrecking crew of a lineup could barely cash in on seven walks and five hits

against Finley and two relievers, going hitless in seven at-bats with runners in scoring position. New $9.8 million DH Chili Davis was the biggest culprit, going 0-for-3 in such situations.

After the start was delayed 56 minutes by rain, the Disney people finally got to blast all

Andy Pettitte

DAILY NEWS   Linda Cataffo

their fireworks, and hauled out former Angel stars Reggie Jackson, Rod Carew, Bobby Grich and Jim Fregosi — joined by ailing former majority owner Gene Autry — to throw out the ceremonial first pitch.

By the time Finley tossed the real first pitch to Chuck Knoblauch, however, it was time for Letterman and Leno back east. The game-time thermometer reading was 53 degrees. And the vaunted Knoblauch/Derek Jeter combo atop the Yankees lineup started out in meek fashion, with the new second baseman tapping out to second and the teen-idol shortstop striking out on a pitch in the soggy dirt in the first.

Pettitte (6.0 IP, 4 ER, 9H) fanned the first two batters he faced before allowing a single by Dave Hollins, which died before reaching Bernie Williams (three hits) in the center-field quagmire, and a walk to Tim Salmon.

Former Yankee Cecil Fielder then worked a 10-pitch walk to load the bases, before Pettitte fanned Garret Anderson to complete his 27-pitch first frame of the season.

In the Yankee second, Davis walked with one out, but was cut down attempting to steal second, if you could call it that, as either Davis or Chad Curtis missed a hit-and-run sign.

For good measure, Curtis followed with a walk, but also was caught stealing by catcher Matt Walbeck.

The lock-and-load Yankees lineup, which averaged

6.8 runs and batted a collective .314 over 31 exhibition games, actually could not muster a hit against Finley until Paul O'Neill singled up the middle leading off the fourth. Williams followed O'Neill with another single to center, but Finley whiffed Tino Martinez and Davis before inducing Curtis to tap to third to end the inning.

The Angels broke through for a four-spot against Pettitte in the fourth. Fielder (two hits) singled past Jeter, and chugged around to third when Norberto Martin followed one out later with a double down the line in right.

Walbeck plated both runs with a water-aided triple to left-center as the ball scooted and splashed past a sprawling Williams. Gary DiSarcina then whistled a double past Scott Brosius at third for another run, which was followed by Darin Erstad's single to right to extend the lead to 4-0.

Even when the Yankees finally scored, they did so in unimpressive fashion. The Yanks had runners on first and third with no outs after Williams and Martinez had singled to open the sixth. Martin ranged behind second base, however, and executed a diving backhand stab of Davis' grounder to start a highlight-reel double-play while Williams crossed the plate with the Yanks' first run of the season.

Preparations at Yankee Stadium for the opening home game on Friday. Veteran groundskeeper Tommy Fyfe checks the field.

DAILY NEWS   Linda Cataffo

REST OF THE WEEK

APR 1	WED	at Anaheim Angels	1-4	L
APR 2	THU	at Anaheim Angels	2-10	L
APR 3	FRI	at Oakland Athletics	PPD	
APR 4	SAT	at Oakland Athletics	3-7	L

> "Torre is the perfect manager for this team. He's a New York guy. He knows how tall the buildings are. He understands how important it is for the owner to be inviting people to his private box."
>
> —Vic Ziegel

TORRE, YANKEES PERFECT FIT

By Vic Ziegel, Daily News Sports Writer
April 1, 1998

Maybe anybody can push the buttons for this Yankee team. Maybe Joe Torre will never re-create the incredible story that was the 1996 Yankees. Maybe the $72 million George Steinbrenner spent to put together this club will buy a few too many headaches for the manager.

I don't think so. Torre is the perfect manager for this team. He's a New York guy. He knows how tall the buildings are. He understands how important it is for the owner to be inviting people to his private box in October.

"New York is not the easiest place to play," Torre said. When he came into town with the Braves or Cardinals, "It was always a hassle for me." He spent 30 years, more than 4,000 games, in the other league, playing and managing. Made it into one playoff series, for all the good it did him.

October, for him, was never more than the month before November.

"You have to find pockets of pride," he said. He mentioned his first managing job, five years with terrible Met teams. "It probably sounds trite, but we never lost 100 games. And believe me, we had the ability to do that." One season, at the start of the last week, they had lost 99. "We had to win six in a row and we did. I was proud of that."

When the Yankees called Torre, he was 55 years old and thought he was done showering with strangers.

George Steinbrenner's new manager — those might be the four toughest words in baseball. "What the hell am I doing here?" he said. "I had no connection with the Yankees. But I made up my mind I was gonna enjoy it."

If you watch him on TV, sitting in the dugout, the jacket buttoned all the way up, a look on his face that

Joe Torre

DAILY NEWS   Gerald Herbert

suggests an aspirin commercial, you couldn't possibly think this man was enjoying himself. Think again.

He likes his team. Likes it too much to even say how much he likes it. The lineup is strong and the infield defense will be better than last year. They will steal more bases, hit more home runs. The pitchers make him nervous, but that's what they always do to managers. He's glad to have so many experienced players. "You can have more conversations" with them, he says. "Instead of me dictating and mandating."

Torre gave his players the team rules yesterday and they had 24 hours to tell him, or the general manager, if being treated like a college swimming team was going to bother these millionaires.

No golf clubs on trips. No playing of radios, tapes or CDs without headphones. No jeans or sneakers on flights. No shorts or thongs or T-shirts in the hotel lobby. Mustaches are permitted, but nothing can grow below the lip. Only one chain or necklace beneath the uniform shirt. No earrings. No agents in the clubhouse. The fine for being late is $250. It doubles the next time and every time. My favorite: the Stairmaster must be wiped down for the next user.

When he started with the Mets, he let the players drink in the hotel bar. "For a month," he said, "they were there until closing. I finally had to tell them, 'Just one beer.'"

Don Zimmer (left) and The Boss, George Steinbrenner.

DAILY NEWS   Linda Cataffo

The manager made his Opening Day speech yesterday—and the players voted on their World Series shares (joke)—because he wanted to get it out of the way. Distractions distract him. The grumpiest I have ever seen him is when Hideki Irabu was or wasn't coming to the Bronx last season. It was a continuing mystery, and that made it a distraction.

The year before that, when the owner told him the club would bring up Darryl Strawberry right after the All-Star Game, Torre said to make the promotion the Sunday before the game. They had Baltimore after the break. He didn't want a Strawberry distraction in a big series. "He made it easy for me," said a grateful Strawberry.

"A manager's job is to get the players to play," he says. "A manager's job is to convince himself he can win."

Torre is convinced, but he has these 162 games to worry about. "Opening Day," he says. "I started thinking this morning about getting nervous."

He's sitting in the visitor's dugout, watching his impressive team work out. It's cold. No sun at all. His jacket is buttoned all the way up. "Everything's really good," he says. "It makes you wonder if it's supposed to be really good all the time."

He doesn't forget it took him 30 seasons to get here.

STANDINGS AT THE END OF WEEK 1

American League East	W.	L.	PCT.	G.B.
Baltimore Orioles	4	1	.800	-
Tampa Bay Devil Rays	3	2	.600	1
Boston Red Sox	2	2	.500	1.5
Toronto Blue Jays	2	2	.500	1.5
NEW YORK YANKEES	0	3	.000	3

GAME OF THE WEEK

APRIL 10, 1998 VS. OAKLAND ATHLETICS

BROSIUS, GIRARDI IMPROVE BOTTOM LINE

Girardi and Brosius bring up the bottom in a lineup

APRIL 11, 1998

By Rafael Hermoso, Daily News Sports Writer

WEEK 2 ● APRIL 5-11

Scott Brosius and Joe Girardi could have been passing each other in a revolving door. One is coming in, the other going out.

For a day, at least, they were in unison, slapping hits from the bottom of the lineup in the Yankees' marathon 17-13 win over the A's in their home opener.

Girardi and Brosius bring up the bottom in a lineup that has been hyped to be a modern-day Murderers Row. Neither had an RBI before yesterday.

Both busted out yesterday. Girardi tied a career high with four hits and added two RBI. Brosius went 2-for-4 with four RBI against his old team.

"The fact it was Oakland made it OK, but I don't think that means much more," said Brosius, who was traded from the A's for Kenny Rogers.

Fans wait outside the stadium in the cold for the players to arrive.

DAILY NEWS Linda Cataffo

Brosius, the new third baseman who made his third error yesterday, claims he wasn't worried about the boos Rogers endured as a Yankee.

"It's what you make of it. You know coming in what to expect," Brosius said. "That's just part of playing in New York. The expectations are high, and they should be."

Girardi was booed at the Yankee Fan Fest two years ago after replacing popular Mike Stanley as the Yankees' catcher. By that October, Girardi helped the Yankees win the World Series.

Now he is just trying to win back his job. Jorge Posada started the last four games of the Yankees' West Coast trip.

"I don't put a whole lot of stock in fast starts, slow starts," Girardi said. "It's just a whole lot of fun to contribute. You want to be part of the wins."

Joe Torre complimented Girardi this week for his professionalism in helping Posada. "He's a friend more than he is a teammate," Posada said.

"I understood it and I was fine with it," Girardi said. "When I'm on the bench I root like crazy, and when I'm in the game I root like crazy."

Torre, who alternated Wade Boggs and Charlie Hayes at third base into last season's playoffs, hasn't outlined how he will use Girardi and Posada.

"I believe there's a lot of at-bats for both of us," Girardi said. "We're going to have pitchers who are better matchups for me and better matchups for Jorgie. Joe is very good at recognizing that. It's a friendly competition that I think will make us both better. That's what we both need."

FINAL
NEW YORK YANKEES 17, AT OAKLAND A'S 13

OAKLAND	ab	r	h	rbi	NEW YORK	ab	r	h	rbi
Henderson lf	5	1	1	0	Knoblauch 2b	6	0	1	2
Mcdonald cf	4	2	1	2	Jeter ss	5	1	0	0
Grieve rf	4	2	2	2	O'Neill rf	4	2	0	0
Stairs dh	6	1	2	3	B Williams cf	3	4	2	0
Giambi 1b	6	1	3	2	T Martinez 1b	4	4	3	5
Magadan 3b	4	1	2	1	Strawberry dh	3	2	2	3
a-Voigt ph-3b	2	0	0	0	b-Spencer ph	0	0	0	0
Spiezio 2b	4	1	0	1	Curtis lf	2	4	2	1
Hinch c	4	2	3	1	Brosius 3b	4	0	2	4
Bournigal ss	4	2	2	1	Girardi c	5	0	4	2
Totals	43	13	16	13	Totals	36	17	16	17

a-flied to center for Magadan in the 7th.
b-pinch-hit for Strawberry in the 9th.

Oakland	050 080 000	—	13
NY Yankees	025 540 10X	—	17

OAKLAND	ip	h	r	er	bb	so	hr	era
J Haynes	2 1/3	3	6	6	5	0	1	9.72
Small	1	4	6	5	4	0	0	13.50
Dougherty L	1 1/3	5	4	4	2	0	0	10.80
Tj Mathews	1	1	0	0	1	0	0	4.50
Groom	2 1/3	3	1	1	0	1	0	2.25

NY YANKEES	ip	h	r	er	bb	so	hr	era
Cone	4 1/3	11	9	9	3	4	0	14.90
Holmes	0	2	3	3	0	0	0	13.50
Buddie W	1 1/3	2	1	0	1	1	0	11.25
Lloyd H	1 2/3	0	0	0	0	1	0	4.50
Nelson	1 2/3	1	0	0	2	1	0	4.05

Holmes pitched to 3 batters in the 5th.

DAILY NEWS Linda Cataffo

"It's what you make of it. You know coming in what to expect. That's just part of playing in New York. The expectations are high, and they should be."
—Scott Brosius

Preparations at Yankee Stadium for the opening home game on Friday. The field is ready.

REST OF THE WEEK

APR 5	SUN	at Oakland Athletics	7-9	W
APR 6	MON	at Seattle Mariners	8-0	L
APR 7	TUES	at Seattle Mariners	7-13	W
APR 8	WED	at Seattle Mariners	3-4	W
APR 10	FRI	Oakland Athletics	17-13	W
APR 11	SAT	Oakland Athletics	3-1	W

> "I'm a litle late getting down here. So many people upstairs today. They wanted some baseball stories. I told them I had at least a few to tell."
> —Joe DiMaggio

GOLDEN OPPORTUNITY FOR JOLT FROM JOE

By Mike Lupica, Daily News Sportswriter
April 11, 1998

Mike Lupica

Chuck Knoblauch talked about walking the blue line. He had used the same entrance at Yankee Stadium he had always used when he was with the Twins, walked down the stairs. There in front of him was the same sign everybody sees. Left for the visitor's clubhouse. Follow the red line. Right was a blue arrow, a blue line. He went right this time. Knoblauch was already a Yankee before yesterday. Walking the blue line meant he was finally a Yankee here.

A couple of hours before the game, before another baseball season came home to the Stadium, Knoblauch stood in front of his locker, across from David Cone's.

"I always wondered what it would be like to take this walk," Knoblauch said.

He smiled and said, "Walking the blue line makes it official."

Now it was after 1 o'clock at the Stadium, maybe 10 minutes from Cone's first pitch at the Stadium, maybe twice that from when Knoblauch would lead off the bottom of the first. Here came Joe DiMaggio out of the elevator, ready to follow the blue line himself. He came after Babe Ruth at Yankee Stadium, played with both Lou Gehrig and Mickey Mantle. He will be 84 in November. He walked slowly toward another season. The line that Knoblauch officially joined yesterday, Joe DiMaggio is in front.

"I'm a little late getting down here," he said. "So many people upstairs today. They wanted some baseball stories. I told them I had at least a few to tell."

He walked down the long hallway past the press room, took a left and walked past the back door to the Yankee clubhouse. It was 1:10. He was supposed to be on the field any time now to throw out the first pitch. He had a baseball in his right hand.

At the bottom of the runway leading to the Yankee dugout, Joe DiMaggio said, "Anybody want to warm me up?"

One of the guys with him stepped back a few feet. DiMaggio tossed him the ball. The man came over, handed the ball back to him, asked if he wanted to throw a few more. The old man smiled and said, "I'm as loose as I'm going to get."

He poked a head inside the Yankee clubhouse, which was completely remodeled over the winter.

"Everything's new today, isn't it?" he said.

Everything except the great DiMaggio. He came here for the first time in 1936 and after that only became one of the magic names in the history of this place, and baseball, and American sport.

When they called for him he walked up the runway and into the sun and heard another April welcome from the Stadium and threw a strike to Joe Girardi, waved to the crowd with both hands. It is a gesture, a snapshot,

12

that has become part of the ceremonies of the day. DiMaggio was out of breath when he came back down the runway.

"That's the most exercise I'll get all year," he said.

He walked back on the blue line and when he came to the elevator that would take him back upstairs, he suddenly found himself in the middle of all the young women from the U.S. women's hockey team that won a gold medal in Nagano. Most of them were born 25 years after DiMaggio last played a game of baseball. But when he came around the corner, all conversation stopped, all laughter. There was a new kind of excitement to the day.

Here was Joe DiMaggio, here with them. And they felt as if they were part of the line, too.

Joe DiMaggio is honored at Yankee Stadium.

DAILY NEWS Linda Cataffo

Katie King, one of the players, introduced herself and said, "Our coach always used your name to motivate us, Mr. DiMaggio."

He asked how that was so, and King said, "Before our games leading up to the Olympics, when we'd go from city to city, he'd always tell us to make sure to have a 'Joe DiMaggio day.'"

The old man grinned. "And what exactly is a 'Joe DiMaggio day?'"

The young woman said, "He said that one time, late in the season after the Yankees clinched the pennant, somebody wanted to know why you'd played so hard that day, in a game that really didn't mean anything. And you said there might be people in the ballpark that day who might only ever see you play once, and you owed them your best."

DiMaggio said, "It was against the St. Louis Browns."

He posed for a picture with Cammi Granato, the team captain. He signed Yankee caps. One of the players leaned up and kissed him. He seemed in no hurry to go anywhere.

Sixty-two years after his first April at Yankee Stadium, here was another one. He never let go of the baseball. At the head of the blue line at the Stadium, one more Joe DiMaggio day. For everyone.

STANDINGS AT THE END OF WEEK 2

American League East	W.	L.	PCT.	G.B.
Baltimore Orioles	8	2	.800	-
NEW YORK YANKEES	5	4	.556	2.5
Tampa Bay Devil Rays	5	4	.556	2.5
Boston Red Sox	5	5	.500	3
Toronto Blue Jays	4	6	.400	4

YANKEE PROFILE

TINO MARTINEZ

TINO HIM IS TO LOVE HIM

MARCH 6, 1998

By Ian O'Connor, Daily News Sports Writer

1B

Tino Martinez

If he did not occasionally rise to wiggle a bat or straighten his cap, one would swear Tino Martinez was an extension of his chair, a prop to ignore. Players pass him on the way to a shave and shower, reporters pass him on the way to richer quotes. The man delivered 44 home runs and 141 RBI in 1997, the kind of season chiseled into Yankee stone, and yet few care to stop and reminisce.

Martinez said the other day not a single New York reporter covering spring training had asked him a question about himself. A little Chuck Knoblauch here, a little murderous lineup there, no Tino Martinez anywhere. This was neither the cry of a self-absorbed ballplayer or an indictment of the hard-working folks who cover him.

"Tino Martinez," David Cone said, "is definitely the heart and soul of this team."

Then the heart and soul resides in the deepest, quietest corner of the clubhouse. If there's a commotion around Martinez, it's

Tino Martinez

DAILY NEWS Linda Cataffo

usually because teammates are tripping over each other on the food line beyond his stall.

Cone is director of public relations, chiefly responsible for fibbing about his injuries. Bernie Williams is gambling with high-roller chips. David Wells is a living, breathing incident. No matter how lame his performance, Irabu draws attention with those magical, mystery magnets attached to his wayward arm.

With their profiles high and their salaries higher, Martinez remains about the best deal George Steinbrenner made this decade. If it didn't look that way when Steinbrenner cut it, trading Russ Davis and Sterling Hitchcock to Seattle and awkwardly nudging Don Mattingly out the door, it sure does now.

In two seasons, Martinez has hit 69 homers and driven in 258 runs. Those are Mattingly numbers from the mid-'80s, Gehrig numbers from the mid-'30s. That they happen to represent the only interesting angle of Martinez' story should not make him part of the furniture.

No, he isn't the most provocative interview. But he also remembers first names and offers thanks when one holds the door. Out of the belching, barfing world of baseball, out of a culture that tolerates coach-chokers and wife-beaters, this alone merits consideration for a Noble Prize.

Martinez is good people doing great work. A Tampa native, a Yankee fan as a kid, he sharpened his stroke by forever driving baseballs into the chain fence in his backyard, eventually blowing holes through the link.

That stroke carried the Yankees across turbulent times last year, through weeks it appeared they might not even secure the wild card. Between then and now, Martinez has been approached in restaurants, stopped on the street. Fans have congratulated him on a career season. It's not quite what the slugger wants to hear.

"I know I can do it again," Martinez said. "Actually, I want to do better. If I get off to a good start, I can do it. It bothers me a little that people think it was a fluke. I don't know how many home runs or RBI I'll get, but I do know I can have another big year."

Toward that end, Martinez added seven or eight pounds of muscle in the winter. He didn't appreciate the fact Mark McGwire and Ken Griffey Jr. dusted him at season's end, reducing a three-man pursuit of history by one. McGwire pumps iron at a Schwarzenegger pace, so, Martinez thought, "Why shouldn't I give it a try?"

DAILY NEWS GERALD HERBERT

Tino Martinez hits a grand slam in Game 1 of the World Series.

"The key last year was having a good April, hitting three homers in one game, and then the swing just being perfect for a long time," he said. "It seemed every mistake a pitcher made I got a good swing on and hit it out."

Much as Martinez kept sending liners over the right-field wall, he made his most profound impact the year before. The loudest sound then was the sound of silence.

He had a miserable start in the Bronx, trying in vain to quell the Mattingly chants. Suddenly, Martinez closed his ears and opened his eyes. The curves started looking like beachballs again, and the fans were ready to make their peace at first base.

"It's an amazing feat that he's been able to make people stop the Mattingly comparisons," Cone said. "To have them say, 'Tino is Tino and we're happy to have him.' Tino defused the Mattingly thing almost immediately, a stunning achievement that snuck by people.

"But Tino is actually a lot like Mattingly. Same intensity. Ready to play every day. A lot of Mattingly leadership qualities."

Like speaking softly and carrying a very big stick. In the middle of a five-year, $20 million deal, Martinez is the best bargain in baseball.

He's also the important deal Steinbrenner has made in years. In the deepest, quietest corner of Yankeedom, that makes Martinez one fascinating prop.

Tino Martinez Stats

1998 REGULAR SEASON

AVG.	G	AB	R	H	TB	2B	3B	HR	RBI	BB	SO	SB	CS	SH	SF	HP	SLG%	OBP%
.282	141	529	92	149	268	33	1	28	123	61	82	2	1	0	10	6	.507	.356

GAME OF THE WEEK

APRIL 15, 1998 VS. ANAHEIM ANGELS

YANKS SHEA HEY FOR DAY

Visit to Flushing Goes Smoothly

APRIL 16, 1998

By Peter Botte, Daily News Sports Writer

WEEK 3 ● APRIL 12-18

One by one they straggled into their country club of a clubhouse. It was barely 7 a.m. yesterday when the Yankees would gather at the Stadium before heading off to Shea and their temporary home away from home.

Several hours later, after a tidy 6-3 victory over the Angels, their caravan landed back on their side of the Triborough and they filed right back into that same country club of a clubhouse.

Only this time, they were a baseball team again. Whole. It mattered little where they had just played. It only mattered that they did. The Crumble in the Bronx was behind them.

"Once we started the game, it was baseball, and that was exactly what I was hoping for," Joe Torre said back in the Bronx as the Yankees began their wait for their fallen Stadium's eventual reopening with the convincing landmark victory before 40,743 at Shea Stadium.

The Yankees now will move on to Detroit for three more rescheduled games this weekend with their first six-game winning streak in Torre's two-plus years managing them.

Two days of relative inactivity may have wreaked havoc on their daily routines, but it evidently has done little to affect the Yankees' mettle or their steamrolling prowess.

"I couldn't believe the support we had. Just great," said George Steinbrenner, who sat with Mayor Giuliani in the field box next to the third-base Yankee dugout the entire game. "Forty thousand people on a 12-noon makeup game, and just shoving a game in there.

"I was proud of the way our guys played. There's a lot to be said for this team, the way they've come through this. They've remained focused through all of it."

Two sets of two buses didn't depart Yankee Stadium, both via police escort over the Triborough Bridge, until 8:30 and 9:15 a.m, respectively.

When the Yankees had completed the

Yankee manager Joe Torre brings out the line-up.

DAILY NEWS Linda Cataffo

eight-mile interborough trek to Flushing, jerseys belonging to the Cubs hung from the locker stalls in the visiting clubhouse.

With the knowledge the Mets and Cubs were awaiting their turns to take the field last night, there also was rain falling when the Yankees arrived.

Still, David Wells (2-1) threw the historic first pitch on time at 12:06 p.m., on his way toward cruising through the first six innings pitching shutout ball in the Yanks' first regular-season game at Shea since Sept. 28, 1975.

"Fifty years from now people will say, 'Wow, you pitched that game at Shea?'" said Wells, who faced the minimum batters through six one-hit innings but allowed three late solo homers before giving way to Jeff Nelson in the ninth. "But I can't get caught up in any of this stuff. . . . I have a job to do. We all do."

Wells, who had attended a Sister Hazel concert at Irving Plaza the night before, permitted a solo home run to Darin Erstad leading off the seventh, and one each in the eighth and ninth. By that time, however, the Yankees had staked him to an early 6-0 lead.

Tino Martinez, who has 11 RBI in his last four games, knocked in two with run-scoring doubles in the first and third. Paul O'Neill went for 3-for-4 (all extra-base hits) with two RBI and now has seven hits in his last nine at-bats following yesterday's 3-for-4.

And the ever-resurgent Darryl Strawberry, who had three more hits in his first game back at Shea in nearly five years to raise his batting average to .400, belted his fourth homer of the season, a solo blast, to extend the lead to 6-0 in the fifth. The former Met has hit more home runs (127) than any player in Shea Stadium history.

"We were just happy and anxious to get into some kind of rhythm. It's been a real choppy start to the season with the weather and the stadium," O'Neill said. "We're playing pretty well and just have to keep battling through. This team has overcome a lot of adversity. It doesn't really matter where we play."

FINAL

ANAHEIM ANGELS 3, AT NEW YORK YANKEES 6

ANAHEIM	ab	r	h	rbi	NEW YORK	ab	r	h	rbi
Erstad 1b	3	1	1	1	Knoblauch 2b	4	1	2	0
D Hollins 3b	4	0	0	0	Jeter ss	3	1	1	0
Salmon rf	4	0	0	0	O'Neill rf	4	2	3	2
Fielder dh	4	0	0	0	B Williams cf	3	0	0	0
Edmonds cf	3	0	1	0	T Martinez 1b	4	0	2	2
Nevin c	3	1	1	1	Strawberry dh	4	1	3	1
G Anderson lf	3	0	0	0	Curtis lf	4	0	1	0
N Martin 2b	3	0	0	0	J Posada c	4	1	1	0
Disarcina ss	3	1	1	1	Sveum 3b	4	0	0	0
Totals	30	3	4	3	Totals	34	6	13	5

HR - Erstad, Nevin, Disarcina.   HR - Strawberry.

Anaheim	000 000 111	—	3
NY Yankees	201 210 00X	—	6

Anaheim	ip	h	r	er	bb	so	hr	era
K Hill L	4	10	5	5	1	2	0	2.50
Olivares	2	2	1	1	0	1	1	5.06
Hasegawa	1/3	0	0	0	0	0	0	9.00
M James	1 2/3	1	0	0	1	1	0	1.29
NY Yankees	ip	h	r	er	bb	so	hr	era
Wells W	8	4	3	3	1	8	3	5.40
Nelson S	1	0	0	0	0	0	0	3.12

Wells pitched to 2 batters in the 9th.

DAILY NEWS   Linda Cataffo

Darryl Strawberry hits a homer at Shea for the first time as a Yankee.

APR 12	SUN	Oakland Athletics	7-5	W
APR 13	MON	Anaheim Angels	PPD	
APR 14	TUES	Anaheim Angels	PPD	
APR 15	WED	Anaheim Angels	6-3	W
APR 17	FRI	at Detroit Tigers	2-11	W
APR 18	SAT	at Detroit Tigers	3-8	W

"I walked out to Monument Park to pay my regards like I do every time we come here, and on the way back I heard this tremendous bang. I looked over and saw this big puff of smoke and chunks of concrete everywhere."

—Angels team masseur Bill Lesuer

THE HOUSE THAT A ROOF CLOSED

Yankee stadium shut down for now

By Leo Standora, Daily News Sports Writer
April 14, 1998

The city closed Yankee Stadium yesterday after a 500-pound steel beam plunged 40 feet from the upper deck and smashed into the stands — forcing postponement of last night's game and throwing this week's schedule into disarray.

Luckily, the stands in the House That Ruth Built were empty when the 75-year-old connecting beam crashed into a left field loge seat — along with a shower of cement chunks — at about 3 p.m.

"If someone had been sitting there when that beam came down, that person would be dead," Mayor Giuliani said, as engineers deemed the fourth-oldest ballpark in the Major Leagues unsafe.

The chilling incident came 4 1/2 hours before last night's game was to start — and three days after a sellout crowd of more than 57,000 packed the historic park for the Yankees home opener.

It also spurred renewed speculation about whether Yankees owner George Steinbrenner will keep the team in the Bronx, or seek new digs in Manhattan or New Jersey.

The damage forced officials to call off games set for The Stadium yesterday and today against the Anaheim Angels so engineers could begin what could be up to three days of inspections.

But the Bronx Bombers will face the Angels tomorrow — at Shea Stadium in Queens — and possibly even at Yankee Stadium.

Deputy Commissioner Richard Visconti of the Buildings Department said the Metropolitan Transportation Authority is fashioning a replacement beam that could be in place as early as this morning.

If the replacement piece and the rest of The Stadium pass muster — and the inspection runs ahead of schedule — it'll be Play Ball in the Bronx again tomorrow.

The plummeting piece of metal that caused the trouble was a connecting beam — two slabs of 3-foot-square steel bolted together — which is used to join two vertical support beams, officials said.

The faulty joint beam was part of the original stadium construction in 1923 — and wasn't replaced when the ballpark was overhauled in the mid-1970s, officials said.

Angels team masseur Bill Lesuer apparently was the only witness to the incident, which came without warning.

"I walked out to Monument Park to pay my regards like I do every time we come here, and on the way back I heard this tremendous bang," he said. "I looked over and saw this big puff of smoke and chunks of concrete everywhere.

"I think the steel went right through the seat," he said, referring to Seat 7, Box A, in Section 20. "I thought the stadium was falling down."

Giuliani, who hot-footed to the Bronx for an up-close look, said: "There's no question something's wrong here. We just don't know the extent of it."

Giuliani said The Stadium likely would be closed for three days. Inspectors said holes would be punched in ceilings and walls in an effort to learn how many other such connecting beams could be faulty.

Through a spokesman, Steinbrenner called the incident "a shocker" — but declined to comment further until he sees what the inspection turns up.

The decision to hoist the NO GAME TODAY sign came just as the gates were opening to let ticket holders in to watch batting practice. More than 20,000 fans were expected.

Nearly 120 cops were rushed to The Stadium in case things got ugly, but there were no incidents.

Yankee Stadium tickets will be honored at Shea — if a game is played there tomorrow. The Mets would then host the Chicago Cubs tomorrow night.

If The Stadium is found unsafe after a closer examination, Giuliani said, the Yankees' three-game weekend set with the Detroit Tigers would also be played at Shea, while the Mets are on the road.

But the long-range outlook is unclear — and even a little scary.

After a beam collapsed in Montreal's Olympic Stadium in 1991, that ballpark was shuttered for 77 days and the Expos were forced to play their final 13 home games on the road. Three years later, the Seattle Mariners canceled their final 15 home games and played them elsewhere after ceiling tiles dropped from the Kingdome roof.

The possibilty of the Yankees playing some or the rest of their home games on the road made for many unhappy campers at Yankee Stadium last night.

"This is a big slap in the face to the fans," said Michael Famularo, 32, of the Bronx, who has rooted for the Bombers since he was 7. "They spend millions on players, but they don't look after the stadium or the safety of the people who buy tickets."

The stadium shutdown comes as Steinbrenner is thinking hard about abandoning the Bronx for new Manhattan digs — or fleeing to New Jersey. He has complained The Stadium needs more parking and better amenities.

On the table are proposals for a multi-million-dollar renovation as well as a new Yankee Stadium on Manhattan's West Side with a price tag of $1 billion. New Jersey also has been wooing the Yanks with the promise of an old-fashioned 55,000-seat arena.

A Yankee Stadium seat on the loge level was crushed when a 500-pound steel beam fell from the roof resulting in the game being cancelled and the Stadium being closed. Here, consultant for the city, Michael Muganga, takes pictures and notes of damage.

STANDINGS AT THE END OF WEEK 3

American League East	W.	L.	PCT.	G.B.
Baltimore Orioloes	11	5	.688	-
NEW YORK YANKEES	9	4	.692	.5
Boston Red Sox	10	6	.625	1
Tampa Bay Devil Rays	9	6	.600	1.5
Toronto Blue Jays	7	9	.438	4

GAME OF THE WEEK
APRIL 22, 1998 VS. TORONTO BLUE JAYS

BLASTING OFF
Bombers pound Rocket for sweep

APRIL 23, 1998

By Peter Botte, Daily News Sports Writer

WEEK 4 ● APRIL 19-25

Consistent defense and an occasional big hit. If you had asked anyone associated with the Yankees what type of performance they would have deemed acceptable from Scott Brosius in 1998, those answers were typical concerning the player for whom it took only Kenny Rogers and a few million Boss Bucks to acquire.

Brosius' defense has been far better than simply consistent all season, and his bat managed at least two significant knocks last night.

The Yankees' new everyday third baseman had three hits and five two-out RBI against Roger Clemens while Andy Pettitte allowed one unearned run for a complete-game victory to lead the Yanks to a 9-1 pounding and series sweep of the Blue Jays at SkyDome.

"The thing I like about the type of team we have here," Brosius said, "is I kind of can go about my business unnoticed."

The attention assuredly will follow, however, should the former Oakland infielder continue to help the Yankees distance themselves from the third-base quandary they possessed with Wade Boggs and Charlie Hayes in 1997.

Pettitte's six-hit gem marked his third straight win and 10th career complete game. It

Andy Pettitte

DAILY NEWS Linda Cataffo

also provided the Yanks their fifth victory in six games on this road trip.

Joe Torre's troops have played 13 of their first 17 games away from the Bronx, and return this weekend. They have won three in a row and 11 of 12. Their 12-5 record — despite a long-forgotten 1-4 start — represents their best season opening since also beginning 12-5 in 1988.

"I was very comfortable watching Andy right from the start. . . . The ball was jumping out of his hand," Torre said. "He's been walking around here very quiet the last couple of days. . . . I know he was pumped up about pitching against Roger."

While Pettitte (3-2, 2.86) was posting early zeroes, Clemens — the four-time AL Cy Young winner and Pettitte's childhood pitching influence in Texas — was pasted for a career-high-tying nine runs (six earned) before departing with two outs in the seventh.

Brosius' two-run fisted single started the onslaught in the second.

"That first base hit was huge for us. It relaxed us a little bit and gave us a chance to go after Roger," Torre said. "Eight of our nine runs were scored with two outs. Brosius was the main culprit."

Two Alex Gonzalez errors and a walk loaded the bases with two outs in the sixth. Brosius, who entered with a career .071 (1-for-14) mark against Clemens, followed with a double that scooted past center fielder Jose Cruz and scored three for a 5-0 lead before the Yanks added four more in the seventh.

The 31-year-old Brosius, who has made enough spectacular picks at third this season that Torre even casually compared his lateral quickness with that of Brooks Robinson late last week, raised his average to .283 with his 3-for-5 showing. The five RBI also tied a career high.

"Scott is unbelievable. He's already made some incredible plays this year," Pettitte said. "He's definitely the best third baseman I've played with since I've been here."

Of course, Pettitte should not be overlooked in the accolade department.

FINAL

NEW YORK YANKEES 9, AT TORONTO BLUE JAYS 1

NEW YORK	ab	r	h	rbi	TORONTO	ab	r	h	rbi
Knoblauch 2b	3	1	0	0	Stewart lf	2	0	1	0
a Bush ph 2b	1	0	1	0	Fernandez 2b	4	0	1	0
Jeter ss	5	0	1	0	Green rf	4	0	1	0
O'Neill rf	4	1	0	0	Canseco dh	4	0	0	0
Martinez 1b	3	1	1	1	Stanley 1b	4	0	0	0
b Sveum ph 1b	1	0	0	0	Sprague 3b	4	0	0	0
B. Williams cf	4	2	0	0	Gonzalez ss	3	1	1	0
Raines dh	4	3	2	2	Cruz Jr.cf	3	0	1	0
Curtis lf	5	1	2	1	Fletcher c	2	0	1	0
Brosius 3b	5	0	3	5					
Girardi c	3	0	0	0					
Totals	38	9	10	9	Totals	30	1	6	4

a singled for Knoblach in the 8th;b grounded out for Martinez in the 9th.

NY Yankees	020	003	400	—	9
Anaheim	000	000	100	—	1

NY Yankees	ip	h	r	er	bb	so
Pettitte W	9	6	1	0	1	6

Toronto	ip	h	r	er	bb	so
Clemens L	62/3	7	9	6	4	6
Risley	11/3	2	0	0	0	3
Almanzar	1	1	0	0	1	0

Scott Brosius

REST OF THE WEEK

APR 19	SUN	at Detroit Tigers	1-2	L
APR 20	MON	at Toronto Blue Jays	3-2	W
APR 21	TUES	at Toronto Blue Jays	5-3	W
APR 22	WED	at Toronto Blue Jays	9-1	W
APR 24	FRI	Detroit Tigers	8-4	W
APR 25	SAT	Detroit Tigers	5-4	W

Linda Ruth Tosetti, granddaughter of The Babe, says her grandfather "would be just devastated" to learn of Steinbrenner's plans to move the Yankees out of Yankee Stadium.

BABE'S KIN: MOVE TALK A NO-HITTER

By Mark Kriegel, Daily News Sports Writer
April 24, 1998

The way Genevieve Herrlein figures things, the House That Ruth Built ought to stay right where Ruth built it. The problem is, this game of stadium moving feels like it's been rigged.

"I think it's a done deal," says Herrlein, speaking of the Yankees' eventual exodus from the Bronx. "I think it's been that way for a while now."

A first-grader, Bryan Velez of Public School 86 in Bushwick, Brooklyn, ambles over with a biography of Babe Ruth, one of a series called "Childhood of Famous Americans." Herrlein is only too happy to grant his request for an autograph.

Herrlein, of Warwick, N.Y., speaks with the authority vested in her as a taxpayer and a baseball fan.

But more than that, in a culture that values fame first, Herrlein speaks as the descendant of the man who was as much fable as flesh. She has her grandfather's broad face and big easy smile, and they only make you wonder what the Babe himself would think of this.

"It's very sad," she says. "I mean, you don't think they'll really move to Jersey, do you?"

There's no evidence to suggest a plan so preposterous as a stadium for the New Jersey Yankees.

"Well, then, who signed on to Giuliani's plan to move it?"

Giuliani. George Steinbrenner. In this case, the mayor and the Boss are like the same guy. They seem to think that nobody will ever go to the Bronx.

Obviously, they have not seen all the nobodies who make Jimmy's Bronx Cafe the hottest joint in town. Nor have they seen all those nobodies at the Botanical Garden and all the nobodies at the Bronx Zoo.

But they can imagine those very important somebodies who'll buy skybox subscriptions for a new corporate castle in Manhattan.

"This isn't about the real die-hard fans, is it?" Herrlein asks. "I guess they want, what-do-you-call-it, the celebrity types."

Actually, Genevieve Herrlein and her sister, Linda Ruth Tosetti, were imported as celebrity types for yesterday's small ceremony at 345 W. 88th St.

Babe Ruth moved into an 11-room apartment on the seventh floor April 17, 1929, the day of his marriage to his second wife, Claire. Herrlein and Tosetti's mother, Dorothy, Ruth's child by a previous relationship, moved in with them. The family stayed there for 14 years.

Yesterday, the Historic Landmarks Preservation Center unveiled a terra cotta plaque signifying Babe's old building for posterity.

It's strange to think that an old apartment building where Ruth used to live is being treated more graciously than the House He Built.

Barbaralee Diamonstein-Spielvogel, chairwoman of the Landmarks Preservation Center, wouldn't disagree. But she also understands that something as grand as the Stadium doesn't need a plaque to confirm its place in history.

"Yankee Stadium doesn't have to be designated as anything," she said.

Sports historian Ray Robinson, author of the newly published Yankee Stadium: 75 Years of Drama, Glamour and Glory, says the Ruthian fable is the Stadium's seminal story. "I talk to people around the country, and one of the first things they ask is, 'Isn't it true that Babe Ruth is buried there?'"

He's not. But the idea that he is poses a more interesting question: "Is Yankee Stadium more history than myth, or more myth than history?"

For Genevieve Herrlein and Linda Ruth Tosetti, myth and history are indivisible. For them, Yankee Stadium is something to be preserved, not something

Yankees line up for the singing of the National Anthem.

to abandon.

"I think it's a travesty," said Linda Ruth Tosetti.

She said her grandfather "would be just devastated" to learn of Mayor Steinbrenner's plans. "He would have been the first to say, 'What? No Way!' He'd be getting the fans together to storm the Stadium."

Now there's a thought, all those nobodies storming the Stadium. It sure beats putting up a plaque by the superstore where the Stadium used to be.

STANDINGS AT THE END OF WEEK 4

American League East	W.	L.	PCT.	G.B.
NEW YORK YANKEES	14	5	.737	.5
Boston Red Sox	16	6	.727	-
Baltimore Orioles	13	9	.591	3
Tampa Bay Devil Rays	11	10	.524	4.5
Toronto Blue Jays	9	13	.409	7

O'NEILL SKIPS DRAMATICS

Forget pact, play's the thing

FEBRUARY 22, 1998

By Peter Botte, Daily News Sports Writer

Paul O'Neill ⚾ OF

He is an All-Star outfielder and a renowned slugger for the New York Yankees. And his status looms as one of the most important decisions facing George Steinbrenner next winter.

Yet no one ever asks the man to Bernie Williams' left about contract deadlines. No one ever asks the man Steinbrenner has labeled "warrior" about being distracted. No one ever asks the man with the fifth-highest batting average in team history about the Arizona Diamondbacks.

His name is Paul O'Neill and nary a word has been written about the fact that he, like Williams, will be eligible for free agency following the 1998 season.

Still, Paul O'Neill clearly prefers it that way.

"I was very happy to see that Bernie's situation got settled, but that has absolutely nothing to do with me," O'Neill said before yesterday's workout at Legends Field. "I'm not even worried about (my contract). Those things always seem to take care of themselves. Especially with this team."

O'Neill will turn 35 Tuesday and over the

Paul O'Neill grits his teeth, not happy with his swing.

DAILY NEWS Roca

last couple of years, has flirted with thoughts of early retirement.

Yesterday, however, O'Neill indicated he has no imminent plans to hang 'em up, not as long as the Yankees continue to provide him with opportunities to get back to the World Series. And not as long as he is able to sustain the on-field excellence he has exhibited the past several years.

"I haven't given that much thought in a while," he said. "Not with as much fun as I'm having now."

A career .259 hitter when obtained from the Reds for Roberto Kelly in November of 1992, O'Neill has evolved into one of the game's most professional lefthanded bats.

His .317 mark in his five seasons in pinstripes — including the AL batting title (.359) in the strike-shortened 1994 season — leave him looking up on the Yankees all-time list only at the great names of Ruth, Gehrig, Combs and

24

DiMaggio.

O'Neill, who has averaged 21 homers and 91 RBI in his five seasons in New York, also led the AL in batting with runners in scoring position (.428) last season while compiling a career-high 117 RBI.

In last fall's brief postseason title defense, O'Neill also was the Yankees' most notable player. He batted .417 in the five-game AL Division Series loss to the Indians and took defeat as hard as anyone, all of which led to The Boss' famed "warrior" tag.

Add it up, and O'Neill, entering the final year of a four-year, $20 million contract, figures to be the latest Yankee to enter the $8 million to $9 million neighborhood.

"I haven't given it that much thought. Maybe we'll talk and maybe we won't. But it won't affect me either way," O'Neill said when asked if he would be amenable to discussing an extension if either new GM Brian Cashman or Steinbrenner approached him or his agent, Joe Bick.

"There's just no need for it to happen now. I prefer to be able to come to the park and play baseball. When you add other things in, I think you're taking your mind off the game.

DAILY NEWS Howard Simmons

Paul O'Neill is up-ended after snagging a fly ball.

"I really like New York and have enjoyed my years here. I came at a time when this team was turning it around. It's hard to describe, because I didn't know what to expect.

"But with this team, and the management here, we're always going to have an opportunity to win. Shoot, I want to be a part of that.

"This offseason was so frustrating for me, probably more so than any other. When you win the World Series one year, you feel like the same things are going to happen. I'm hoping I get a few more chances here to get back there."

Paul O'Neill Stats

1998 REGULAR SEASON

AVG.	G	AB	R	H	TB	2B	3B	HR	RBI	BB	SO	SB	CS	SH	SF	HP	SLG%	OBP%
.317	151	600	95	190	306	40	2	24	115	57	103	15	1	0	11	2	.510	.372

GAME OF THE WEEK

APRIL 27, 1998 VS. TORONTO BLUE JAYS

ANDY, YANKS DODGE ROGER

Pettitte, Yankee pen trip Rocket

APRIL 28, 1998

By Ralph Vacchiano, Daily News Sports Writer

WEEK 5 ● APRIL 26 - MAY 2

Joe Torre was right: The Yankees couldn't rock the Rocket two games in a row. Last night they didn't need to.

Five days after getting lit up by the Yankees in Toronto, Blue Jays ace Roger Clemens held them to just three hits in seven strong innings at the Stadium. But he was outdueled by lefty Andy Pettitte and company as the Yankees held on for a 1-0 win.

The victory, courtesy of Pettitte's 5 2/3 shutout innings and near-flawless relief work by Jeff Nelson, Mike Stanton and Mariano Rivera, was the Yankees' sixth in a row and

Derek Jeter leaps to snag a line drive against the Jays.

DAILY NEWS Gerald Herbert

improved their record to 7-0 at home. They've also won 14 of their last 15 games — their best stretch since August 1985.

And for that they can thank Pettitte (4-2), who gave up seven hits, walked none and struck out seven in front of 17,863.

"One run has to be enough against Clemens," Torre said. "He's a great pitcher and

he gets tough when he needs to get tough."

Clemens (2-3) certainly was tough, striking out eight in seven innings. But he did walk six.

"I think Clemens pitched better than Pettitte," Blue Jays manager Tim Johnson said.

He was certainly better than he was last Wednesday, when the Yanks battered him for seven hits and nine runs (six earned) in 6 2/3 innings. This time, after giving up the lone run in the third, Clemens retired 15 of the next 17 batters he faced.

And even that one run came at the end of an impressive escape. In the home third, the Yanks loaded the bases on two walks and a single with the meat of the order coming up. That's when Tino Martinez crushed a sacrifice fly to the warning track to score Chuck Knoblauch from third.

But with runners at the corners and still only one out, the Yanks couldn't do any more damage as Clemens got Bernie Williams swinging and Tim Raines looking at strike three.

Pettitte's only bump came in the fourth,

courtesy of a line drive from Ed Sprague that bounced off his right knee — a ball that deflected into Scott Brosius' glove for the start of an inning-ending double play. Pettitte limped off the mound but came back to pitch into the sixth.

In the sixth, though, he ran into trouble, giving up singles to the first two hitters before striking out Jose Canseco and Carlos Delgado with runners on first and third. Then, with Mike Stanley and his .435 average versus lefties at the plate, Torre brought in righty Jeff Nelson to strike Stanley out.

When Pettitte saw Torre, a pitching change "was the last thing I thought he'd do." But Torre was worried about Pettitte's knee getting stiff in the cold. "It hurt a little bit," Pettitte said. "But I've been through it, getting hit so much, your mind can overcome all that."

Regardless, Torre had already decided Pettitte wouldn't get another inning so he figured he'd make the move then, with Stanley at the plate. So Pettitte gave way to the impressive trio of Nelson, Stanton and Rivera, who pitched a perfect ninth for his second save.

Together, they gave up just two hits in 3 1/3 innings. "I felt in spring training that would be the strongest part of our staff," Torre said. "I don't hesitate at all to go to those guys."

"The bullpen was unbelievable," Pettitte added. "They just did an awesome job."

FINAL
TORONTO BLUE JAYS 0, AT NEW YORK YANKEES 1

TORONTO	ab	r	h	rbi	NEW YORK	ab	r	h	rbi
Stewart cf	4	0	2	0	Knoblauch 2b	3	1	0	0
Green rf	4	0	1	0	Jeter ss	4	0	1	0
Canseco lf	4	0	0	0	O'Neill rf	2	0	0	0
Delgado 1b	4	0	1	0	Martinez 1b	3	0	0	1
Stanley dh	4	0	0	0	B.Williams cf	3	0	1	0
Sprague 3b	4	0	1	0	Raines dh	3	0	1	0
Fernandez 2b	4	0	3	0	Curtis lf	2	0	0	0
Gonzalez ss	3	0	1	0	Brosius 3b	3	0	0	0
Fletcher c	2	0	0	0	Girardi c	2	0	0	0
a Samuel ph	1	0	0	0					
Totals	34	0	9	0	Totals	25	1	3	1

a reached on a fielder's choice for Fletcher in the 7th.

Toronto	000 000 000	—	0
NY Yankees	001 000 00x	—	1

Toronto	ip	h	r	er	bb	so
Clemens L	7	3	1	1	6	8
Plesac	1	0	0	0	0	1

NY Yankees	ip	h	r	er	bb	so
Pettitte W	5 2/3	7	0	0	0	7
Nelson	2/3	2	0	0	0	2
Stanton	1 2/3	0	0	0	0	1
Rivera S	1	0	0	0	0	0

Andrew Perry, a season ticket holder, wears a Yankee hardhat to the game.

REST OF THE WEEK

APR 26	SUN	Detroit Tigers	PPD	
APR 27	MON	Toronto Blue Jays	1-0	W
APR 28	TUES	Toronto Blue Jays	2-5	L
APR 29	WED	Seattle Mariners	8-5	W
APR 30	THU	Seattle Mariners	9-8	W
MAY 1	FRI	at Kansas City Royals	2-1	W
MAY 2	SAT	at Kansas City Royals	12-6	W

> "Just like they say about hitting and pitching and even fielding, stealing bases is contagious. Right now, a lot of guys have that fever."
>
> —Derek Jeter

OFF AND RUNNING

By Peter Botte, Daily News Sports Writer
April 27, 1998

You think of baseball's dominant offensive teams, particularly in the American League, and power generally is the common denominator. Speed — disruptive, demon speed — is supposed to be intended for the other league.

Then there are the Yankees, who have embarked on a transformation from reliance on the long ball to the point they are running up the so-called score on opposing catchers.

The run-and-gun Bombers surprisingly lead all of baseball in stolen bases despite playing fewer games than any other team. The latter condition is due to a combination of the recent crumbling of Yankee Stadium and the weather, as further evidenced by yesterday's home washout against the Tigers.

Paul O'Neill steals second base as shortstop Ozzie Guillen waits for the throw.

DAILY NEWS Linda Cataffo

"Just like they say about hitting and pitching and even fielding, stealing bases is contagious. Right now, a lot of guys have that fever," Derek Jeter said after yesterday's game, which never should have been started, was postponed after 3 1/2 innings were played in driving rain and the Yankees had built a 2-1 lead.

"I've always wanted to run but just never really had the speed to do it with," Joe Torre said. "Once we got (Chuck) Knoblauch, I knew we were going to be significantly better, because that stuff is catching. I've always liked to have a club that's able to be aggressive and able to move."

This club has been just that, right from the time Torre implored each Yankee early in spring training to take extra bases whenever the opportunities arose.

They are hardly the '85 Cardinals, and even Torre suggested such thievery eventually might "come to a screeching halt," when asked if his team should be expected to keep this up over a full season.

The Yankees, however, entered yesterday's action leading the majors with 35 steals in 43 attempts, a snappy 81% success rate. Darryl Strawberry had his fifth stolen base on his rehabbed knee — to go along with his team-best five homers — washed out by yesterday's postponement.

"It's just a matter of being smart on the bases. You don't have to have blazing speed to steal in this league," said Knoblauch, who led the AL last year with 62 for the Twins.

Interestingly enough, as much as Knoblauch's presence has been contagious, he has swiped only four bags while batting .231 through 19 games. The Yankees, instead, currently boast eight players with at least two steals, paced by Jeter's eight.

"Jeter, that's coming. He's going to be probably a consistent 30-guy down the line," Torre said. "But with this club, we don't swing and miss a whole lot, which makes you a little freer to move a runner."

While they have only belted 15 home runs through 19 games, the Yanks also are batting .284 and averaging 6.1 runs in their 14-5 start. Paul O'Neill and Bernie Williams have yet to go deep, which only emphasizes how scary this lineup can get.

Derek Jeter slides into second.

DAILY NEWS Linda Cataffo

STANDINGS AT THE END OF WEEK 5

American League East

	W.	L.	PCT.	G.B.
NEW YORK YANKEES	19	6	.760	-
Boston Red Sox	19	9	.679	1.5
Baltimore Orioles	15	14	.517	6
Tampa Bay Devil Rays	12	16	.429	8.5
Toronto Blue Jays	11	17	.393	9.5

GAME OF THE WEEK

APRIL 27, 1998 VS. TEXAS RANGERS

YANKEES OUTSLUG RANGERS

MAY 7, 1998

By Peter Botte, Daily News Sports Writer

WEEK 6 ● MAY 3 - 9

Games often are over before they even begin these days for the Yankees, but this was far from one of them.

Jorge Posada's two-out RBI single in the eighth snapped a wild football-score tie and propelled the Yanks to a 15-13 marathon victory over the Rangers late last night at The Ballpark. The only higher scoring game in baseball this season was the Yanks' similarly bizarre 17-13 victory over the A's in the home opener on April 10.

And so the Yankees' miraculous month-long run continues, even as they attempted to give away a game in which David Wells and the bullpen squandered leads of 9-0 and 13-7.

The Yanks already have posted winning streaks of eight, six, and seven games this season. They now have swept three consecutive series on the road—with eight straight road wins—without blinking an eye. They have lost just two games in one calendar month (21-2)

Mariano Rivera earned his fifth save against the Rangers.

DAILY NEWS Linda Cataffo

since standing at 1-4 on April 7, and have won 21-of-23 games for the first time since 1953.

The Yanks tied their season-high with 18 hits, including four triples, which was one shy of the team record set in 1934. The most important of those was Bernie Williams' second of the game leading off the eighth.

Tim Raines and Chad Curtis initially failed to deliver the tie-breaking run with less than two outs, but Posada, who to that point was the only Yankee without a hit, rapped a single off reliever Danny Patterson over shortstop Kevin Elster's outstretched glove for the winning run.

Derek Jeter (four hits, career-high five RBI) added a 429-foot solo homer, his fifth, in the ninth off ex-mate John Wetteland. Mariano Rivera, the Yanks' seventh pitcher, hurled the final 1 1/3 innings to seal the win for Mike Stanton (2-0) and record his fifth save.

The Yankees struck swiftly and chased Bobby Witt after 1 1/3 innings. They walked Wells to a 9-0 lead that ended up being entirely necessary since the free-spirited lefty frittered away nearly all of it by allowing Texas a seven-spot in the third, although only one of the runs was earned due to a Chuck Knoblauch error.

Knoblauch rifled Witt's 2-2 pitch into the left-field seats for his 14th career leadoff home run in the first.

One batter later, Paul O'Neill embarked on his suddenly daily jog around the bases, belting his third homer in as many games after not going deep this season until Sunday in Kansas City.

The Yanks sent 11 batters to the plate against Witt. Tino Martinez greeted Crabtree by rapping a double for his team-high 34th homer of the season for the final two runs, 409 feet to left-center.

DAILY NEWS Linda Cataffo

FINAL

NEW YORK YANKEES 15, AT TEXAS RANGERS 13

NEW YORK	ab	r	h	rbi
KnoblaucH 2b	5	2	1	1
Jeter ss	6	2	4	5
O'Neill rf	6	2	3	2
T Martinez 1b	5	1	1	1
B Williams cf	5	2	3	0
Raines dh	5	2	2	3
Curtis lf	4	1	1	0
J Posada c	3	2	1	1
Brosius 3b	4	1	2	2
Totals	**43**	**15**	**18**	**15**

TEXAS	ab	r	h	rbi
T Goodwin cf	6	1	1	0
Mclemore 2b	3	2	0	0
Greer lf	4	2	2	1
J Gonzalez rf	5	3	3	5
W Clark 1b	5	2	3	1
I Rodriguez c	5	1	2	4
Simms dh	3	1	1	2
a-Stevens dh	1	0	1	0
D Cedeno pr	0	0	0	0
Elster ss	5	0	0	0
F Tatis 3b	3	1	2	0
b-Alicea 3b	2	0	0	0
Totals	**42**	**13**	**15**	**13**

HR - Knoblauch, O'Neill, Raines, Jeter.   HR - Simms, Gonzalez.

a-intentionally walked for Simms in the 6th;
b-flied to right for Tatis in the 6th.

NY Yankees	270 400 011	— 15
Texas	007 303 000	— 13

NY Yankees	ip	h	r	er	bb	so	hr	era
Wells	2 2/3	7	7	7	1	2	1	5.77
Banks	1	2	3	3	2	2	1	12.00
Buddie	1 2/3	3	2	2	0	0	0	8.59
Mendoza BS	0	2	1	1	1	0	0	5.06
Holmes	2/3	0	0	0	0	0	0	2.70
Stanton W	1 2/3	1	0	0	1	2	0	3.93
Rivera S	1 1/3	0	0	0	0	0	0	0.00

Texas	ip	h	r	er	bb	so	hr	era
Witt	1 1/3	4	7	7	4	3	2	8.33
Crabtree	1 2/3	7	4	4	0	1	1	5.52
X Hernandez	2/3	2	2	2	1	0	0	9.00
Gunderson	3 1/3	2	0	0	0	1	0	0.56
D Patterson L	1	2	1	1	0	2	0	3.52
Wetteland	1	1	1	1	0	0	1	1.54

Crabtree pitched to 2 batters in the 4th.
Mendoza pitched to 3 batters in the 6th.

All that was left was for Wells to be able to handle a lead as bulky as his uniform and last at least five innings for his fourth win.

The hefty lefty seemed headed toward escaping a bases-loaded, one-out jam while allowing only one run in the third. At least, that is, until Knoblauch played Juan Gonzalez' two-out liner into an error for two more runs en route to the Rangers drawing within 9-7.

Following Knoblauch's error - after which Gonzalez motioned incredulously to the official scorer in the press box because he lost two RBIs - Wells become completely unglued in what would prove to be his shortest outing (2 2/3 IP) as a Yankee.

By early May, Tino Martinez led the Yankees with over 30 RBI.

REST OF THE WEEK

MAY 3	SUN	at Kansas City Royals	10-1	W
MAY 5	TUES	at Texas Rangers	7-2	W
MAY 6	WED	at Texas Rangers	15-13	W
MAY 8	FRI	at Minnesota Twins	5-1	W
MAY 9	SAT	at Minnesota Twins	1-8	L

" I hope we bore people to death all season. We're obviously very happy to date, but cautiously happy. We still have five months of road ahead of us. It's like scoring seven runs in the first inning. It's great, but you still have eight innings to go."

—GM Brian Cashman

BOMBERS ARE STILL CLIMBING

By Peter Botte, Daily News Sports Writer
May 5, 1998

You wait for someone to slug a cab driver or a marshmallow salesman, and it never comes. You wait for someone to get accused of some crime or for George Steinbrenner to rant, and it no longer seems even a mild threat.

You'd kill for someone to make up a good trade rumor, but who in baseball would want to help this team?

Pick up a newspaper every day for a month and read all about it. Read all about how good and talented and, well, boring this is starting to get with the Yankees, and it's still the first week of May.

"I hope we bore people to death all season," GM Brian Cashman said yesterday. "We're obviously very happy to date, but cautiously happy. We still have five months of road ahead of us. It's like scoring seven runs in the first inning. It's great, but you still have eight innings to go."

About the only saving grace has been that the

Chuck Knoblauch

DAILY NEWS   Mike Albans

Red Sox also have started strongly. But as one Yankee official said this weekend, "You almost hope we don't win 110 games this easily, because then the hardest thing to do will be to win that first five-game series in October."

These are the 1998 Yankees — professional, thorough, opportunistic and easily the best little 20-6 team in baseball that $72 million can buy.

And try this one on for size: They also just may be underachieving. How frightening must that be to the rest of the American League?

Chuck Knoblauch has scored 14 runs (a pace of 87), is batting .235 and, at times, has resembled Steve Sax making inexplicably wild throws around the infield.

Bernie Williams hasn't hit a home run and has

only 11 RBI (a pace of 69) to start his contract push, while batting exclusively fourth or fifth in a lineup that has averaged 6.1 runs per game.

Paul O'Neill didn't pop his first homer until Sunday. Catchers Jorge Posada and Joe Girardi have hit a combined .214 while each has started 13 games behind the plate. Mariano Rivera missed three weeks, Chili Davis has been out for all but two games and Graeme Lloyd is on the DL.

Since causing a citywide panic by going 1-4 on the West Coast to open the season, all the Yankees have done is posted winning streaks of eight, six and five games in winning 19 of 21 for the first time since 1977. The 1996 world champions never won more than five straight games. But that was storybook. And this is becoming the same old story. The manager, in his words, simply "writes down the names and stays out of the way."

"Oh, we're better than '96," Joe Torre said this weekend. "This team has more ability to score runs. The '96 team was sort of the no-name guys . . . a team effort. This is a team effort, too, but we have a lot more ammunition."

This team has more potential power, more team speed, more depth and better starting pitching than its '96 forebears.

And the question marks going in — Darryl Strawberry (.333, 7 HRs, 18 RBI), David Cone (3-1), Scott Brosius (.297, spectacular defense) and Hideki Irabu (22 Ks and a 1.47 ERA in 18.1 innings) — even have provided the biggest and brightest answers.

DAILY NEWS   Linda Cataffo

Yankees general manager Brian Cashman.

When the most compelling controversy with the Yankees is the team's latest multimillionaire international investment (Orlando Hernandez) arriving several weeks from now to possibly take the job of the fifth starter (Ramiro Mendoza), even we have to admit we're reaching for something to write about.

STANDINGS AT THE END OF WEEK 6

American League East

	W.	L.	PCT.	G.B.
NEW YORK YANKEES	23	7	.767	-
Boston Red Sox	23	11	.676	2
Baltimore Orioles	18	16	.529	7
Toronto Blue Jays	16	19	.457	9.5
Tampa Bay Devil Rays	13	20	.394	11.5

GAME OF THE WEEK

MAY 10, 1998 VS. MINNESOTA TWINS

RAMIRO'S TWIN PEAK

Shuts out Minny as Yanks finish 7-1 trip

May 11, 1998

By Peter Botte, Daily News Sports Writer

WEEK 7 ● MAY 10 - 16

MINNEAPOLIS—Joe Torre never had a problem with the Yankees parting with young pitching if it meant acquiring Chuck Knoblauch. The manager's only request was to limit the prized arms to one.

Torre's scouting skills were on display yesterday at the Metrodome, as the pitcher he adamantly requested the Yankees keep out of February's five-player deal, Ramiro Mendoza, easily outdueled the hurler the Yankees eventually surrendered.

Four early runs off former Yankee farmhand Eric Milton were more than enough for Mendoza to cruise to his first complete game and shutout, as the Yanks went on to a 7-0 thumping yesterday to end their ungodly one-game losing streak.

"Awesome. I think that was the best game he ever threw in his life," catcher Jorge Posada said after Mendoza's sinkerballed his way to a

Bernie Williams avoids a pickoff attempt.

DAILY NEWS Gerald Herbert

five-hitter for the Yanks' second shutout victory of the season. "He was easy to catch today. It was just sinker after sinker after sinker."

The 25-year-old righthander actually recorded only 11 groundball outs, but he induced the Twins (four double plays) into an out virtually every time he needed one.

The shutout marked the first time the Panamanian saw the ninth inning as a starter in his big-league career, even though Mendoza apparently misled teammate and acting interpreter Luis Sojo afterward that he had been there before.

"You lied to me, you said you threw like five (shutouts)," Sojo said jokingly to Mendoza.

"It just feels great," Mendoza said a few minutes later. "Hopefully, I'm going to keep doing it."

Just like the Yankees (24-7), who were

thumped here 8-1 Saturday night, but still haven't lost consecutive games since beginning the season 0-3 on the West Coast. Scott Brosius (first homer of the season) and Tino Martinez (sixth) went deep to lead the Yanks' 16-hit attack.

"To sum it up, it was a damn near-perfect trip," Torre said of the Yanks' 7-1 mark on this road swing. "The only thing that concerns you when you do lose is being able to bounce back, and we did that today."

As for Milton (2-4), the 21-year-old lefty showed early life on his mid-90's fastball but faded quickly, as the Yanks battered him for four runs on nine hits. They sprayed line drives off Milton throughout his five-inning stint, with Knoblauch fittingly leading off the game with a double down the left-field line.

The Yanks led 3-0 after two innings, before Brosius rifled his first homer as a Yankee with one out in the fourth, leaving Bernie Williams as the most notable regular without one this season.

One inning after the Yanks plated a single run in the sixth on Paul O'Neill's second sacrifice fly, Martinez extended Mendoza's lead to 6-0 with his sixth homer of the season and team-best 36th RBI.

"I think it was important to try to score early, so Mendoza (2-1, 3.95) could relax a little bit," said Jeter, whose triple in the fourth hit inches from the top of the wall in dead center. "He took it from there."

"He pitched really well," Torre said. "He was into it mentally. Especially in the last three innings; he was like a locomotive."

With the Twins threatening in the sixth and seventh, Mendoza said he noticed activity in the bullpen.

"I didn't want to come out," he said.

He didn't. It was his game all the way.

FINAL
NEW YORK YANKEES 7, AT MINNESOTA TWINS 0

NY YANKEES	ab	r	h	rbi	MINNESOTA	ab	r	h	rbi
Knoblauch 2b	4	1	2	1	T Walker 2b	4	0	1	0
Jeter ss	5	1	3	0	Gates 3b	4	0	0	0
O'Neill rf	3	0	0	2	Molitor dh	4	0	0	0
B Williams cf	4	0	2	0	Lawton cf	3	0	0	0
T Martinez 1b	4	1	2	2	Coomer 1b	3	0	1	0
a-Sveum ph-1b	1	0	0	0	Merced rf	3	0	1	0
Raines dh	4	1	2	0	Steinbach c	3	0	1	0
Curtis lf	5	0	1	0	Meares ss	2	0	1	0
J Posada c	5	1	2	0	Latham lf	3	0	0	0
Brosius 3b	3	2	2	1					
Totals	38	7	16	6	Totals	29	0	5	0

HR-Brosius, T Martinez.

a-struck out for T Martinez in the 8th.

NY Yankees	210 101 200	—7	
Minnesota	000 000 000	—0	

NY Yankees	ip	h	r	er	bb	so	hr	era
Mendoza W	9	5	0	0	0	2	0	3.95

Minnesota	ip	h	r	er	bb	so	hr	era
Milton L	5	9	4	4	2	2	1	4.50
Naulty	1/3	2	1	1	1	1	0	9.82
Guardado	2/3	2	2	1	0	0	1	3.00
Carrasco	2	1	0	0	2	3	0	4.63
Aguilera	1	2	0	0	0	2	0	4.50

Guardado pitched to 2 batters in the 7th.

Fans react to a game at Pips Comedy Club.

REST OF THE WEEK

MAY 10	SUN	at Minnesota Twins	0-7	W
MAY 11	MON	Kansas City Royals	PPD	
MAY 12	TUES	Kansas City Royals	3-2	W
MAY 13	WED	Texas Rangers	8-6	W
MAY 14	THU	Texas Rangers	5-7	L
MAY 15	FRI	Minnesota Twins	6-7	L
MAY 16	SAT	Minnesota Twins	5-2	W

> "Same as before, I'm not trying to hit home runs. But I'm gonna be like a surfer right now, just trying to ride the wave."
> —Bernie Williams

BERNIE'S SLAM TOASTS TEXAS

By Peter Botte, Daily News Sports Writer
May 14, 1998

Imagine the potency of the Yankees, you were forewarned, once Bernie Williams finally pops some home runs. Or once Chuck Knoblauch finally performs like the sparkplug so defined by his seven years in Minnesota. Or once David Cone finally trims his ERA below the touchdown mark.

As the Yankees steamrolled to their best start in 40 years, those were the what-if provisos that suggested this team actually might be better than even its gaudy early-season record indicated. And then there was last night's 8-6 victory over the Rangers at the Stadium.

"There's a real good feeling in the clubhouse for those guys to get going, too," Cone said after his fifth consecutive victory was fueled by Williams' grand slam (his second in as many days) and Knoblauch's four hits, including a huge insurance RBI single in the eighth.

Add it all up, and the 23,142 paying customers

Derek Jeter turns a double play.

DAILY NEWS Linda Cataffo

who showed up at George Steinbrenner's temporary Bronx address got to witness much more than simply Newman from "Seinfeld" throwing out the first pitch.

They saw the Yanks (26-7) win for the 25th time in 28 games for the first time since 1947. They saw the Yankees remain the only team in the majors to be unde-feated when scoring four or more runs (21-0). They saw the Yankees improve to 20-0 in games in which they have belted at least one home run, and 2-0 in games in which Williams goes deep.

"Same as before, I'm not trying to hit home runs. But I'm gonna be like a surfer right now, just trying to ride the wave," said Williams, who had belted his first homer of his all-important contract season in

36

his 120th at-bat Tuesday night. "Last night felt good, but tonight definitely felt better."

Cone (5-1, 6.46), of course, was forced to have this start pushed back from Sunday to last night by a mildly sprained left knee, but has maintained all week that his physical well-being has been the least of his concerns.

Cone's 63-year-old mother, Joan, is to undergo surgery to remove a mass on her lung this morning at Sloan Kettering Cancer Center in Manhattan. "There's only so much you can do," Cone said. "I know my mother would want me to perform, to continue to play well."

Aside from a trio of homers by Juan Gonzalez, Will Clark (back-to-back in second) and Ivan Rodriguez (seventh), Cone performed admirably. Before leaving with a 7-4 lead with one out in the seventh, he was reached for four runs and seven hits, while fanning seven.

Derek Jeter's three-run homer — his sixth — to left-center in the third had provided a 3-2 lead, although Cone quickly permitted the Rangers to draw even in the fourth, with Gonzalez (double) and Clark (RBI single) again doing the damage.

The Yankees quickly loaded the bases off Rick Helling (6-1) in the fifth, however, to set the stage for Williams. Batting left, the switch-hitter crushed Helling's chest-high 0-1 offering into the right-field bleachers.

A few moments later, Yankee fans who had been booing him earlier this season called Williams out of the dugout for his reluctant curtain call. "Any time you hit a grand slam," Williams said, "it definitely feels

good."

The celebration would be short-lived, however, as the Rangers scraped back for three runs in the seventh. Jeff Nelson replaced Cone one out after Rodriguez' homer made it 7-4, and promptly allowed a walk and double to the only two batters he faced. Mike Stanton then fanned pinch-hitter Mike Simms, before Mark McLemore shaved the lead to 7-6 with a two-out single to center.

Darren Holmes recorded two huge outs (Gonzalez and Clark) in the eighth, before Knoblauch's RBI-single plated the immense insurance run. Mariano Rivera pitched in and out of trouble (three hits) over the final 1 1/3 innings for his seventh straight save.

DAILY NEWS   Keith Torrie

Bernie Williams

STANDINGS AT THE END OF WEEK 7

American League East

	W.	L.	PCT.	G.B.
NEW YORK YANKEES	27	9	.750	-
Boston Red Sox	26	15	.634	3.5
Baltimore Orioles	20	21	.488	9.5
Toronto Blue Jays	19	22	.463	10.5
Tampa Bay Devil Rays	18	22	.450	11

GAME OF THE WEEK
MAY 17, 1998 YANKEES VS. MINNESOTA TWINS

WELLS IS NOW PERFECT GUY

Pitches Yanks' First in Regular Season

MAY 18, 1998

By Peter Botte, Daily News Sports Writer

WEEK 8 ● MAY 17-23

The last Yankee anyone ever expects to be perfect is David Wells. Leave it to him to provide the first regular-season display of perfection in this franchise's storied history.

Wells yesterday improbably joined Don Larsen—the other "Imperfect Man," whose perfect gem came in Game 5 of the 1956 World Series—as the only Yankees ever to record 27 consecutive outs from all 27 batters they faced in a single game.

And all those fun little "extras" that go along with the Yankees' hefty lefty—the free-spirit persona, the beer guzzling, the scale crunching, the head-banging—suddenly seem acceptable again. That is, as long as Wells understands he is capable of being this dominant a major-league pitcher when he wants to be.

"This is a dream come true for me," Wells said after becoming only the 13th pitcher in modern baseball history (Larsen included) to throw a perfect game in what was—almost as an afterthought—a 4-0 Yankees' victory at a rockin' and rollin' Stadium.

"You just go out and try to do the best you can every outing, but you never expect something like this. . . . You just have to cherish it," said Wells, who is three days shy of his 35th birthday. "There will always be a special place in my heart for what we accomplished today."

As usual Wells' day began with a little help from his friends. A little Smashmouth, some Guns 'N' Roses, his usual Metallica. And

Yankee pitcher David Wells pitches a perfect game and celebrates.

DAILY NEWS   Linda Cataffo

pitching coach Mel Stottlemyre immediately noticed that the ever-pumped lefty was on the verge of something special, even before the opening pitch left Wells' hand at 1:35 p.m.

"Mel came out of the bullpen and I asked him how it went. All he said was 'Wow,'" Joe Torre said. "That doesn't normally mean a perfect game or even a win. But it did today. . . . The Boomer was outstanding. That's something he can take with him wherever he goes."

Wells, of course, was lustily criticized by

Torre just last week for being "out of shape" after nearly blowing all of a nine-run lead without getting out of the third inning in an eventual 15-13 victory in Texas.

Following a heart-to-heart sitdown with his manager, however, Wells (5-1) emerged to hurl eight strong innings against Kansas City on Tuesday, retiring the final 10 batters he faced and 17 of 18. Thus, over the last two games, he has retired 37 straight batters (an AL record) and 44 of 45.

Staked to the four-run lead by the seventh, Wells struck out 11 and reached a three-ball count on only four batters. The only at-bat that came close to resulting in a base hit was Ron Coomer's hard one-hopper to Chuck Knoblauch in the eighth. But the ex-Twin knocked it down and threw out the runner in plenty of time to heighten the mounting anticipation.

As Pat Meares' routine fly ball nestled safely into Paul O'Neill's glove to conclude the 120-pitch masterpiece, Wells even let the other side of his emotionally charged personality shine through.

He let out a hearty bellow of relief as a crowd of 49,820—swelled by a Beanie Baby giveaway—roared in appreciation. He jumped around like a schoolkid and pumped his left fist before his teammates mobbed him.

And several minutes later, he fought back tears as he finally etched his place in the Yankees' baseball lore he

David Wells celebrates with his teammates.

DAILY NEWS Linda Cataffo

FINAL
NEW YORK YANKEES 4, MINNESOTA TWINS 0

MINNESOTA	ab	r	h	rbi	NEW YORK	ab	r	h	rbi
Lawton cf	3	0	0	0	Knoblauch 2b	4	0	0	0
Gates 2b	3	0	0	0	Jeter ss	3	0	1	0
Molitor dh	3	0	0	0	O'Neill rf	4	0	0	0
M Cordova lf	3	0	0	0	T Martinez 1b	4	0	0	0
Coomer 1b	3	0	0	0	B Williams cf	3	3	3	1
Ochoa rf	3	0	0	0	Strawberry dh	3	1	1	1
Shave 3b	3	0	0	0	Curtis lf	3	0	1	1
J Valentin c	3	0	0	0	J Posada c	3	0	0	0
Meares ss	3	0	0	0	Brosius 3b	3	0	0	0
Totals	27	0	0	0	Totals	30	4	6	3

HR - B Williams.

Minnesota	000	000	000— 0
NY Yankees	010	100	20x— 4

Minnesota	ip	h	r	er	bb	so	hr	era
Hawkins L	7	6	4	4	0	5	1	5.26
Naulty	1/3	0	0	0	1	0	0	5.14
Swindell	2/3	0	0	0	0	1	0	3.65

NY Yankees	ip	h	r	er	bb	so	hr	era
Wells W	9	0	0	0	0	11	0	4.45

so reveres, even if the most important people in his life were not present to witness the remarkable feat.

"Nobody can take this away from me. Ever. No matter what happens," Wells said. "I'm honored and couldn't be happier. I just wish a few other people were here to see it."

Those people are literally a part of Wells. His mother, Ann, died more than one year ago and he has a tattoo of her on one arm. His 6-year-old son, Brandon—who was in town this week but left yesterday morning with Wells' father—is on the other. He has several more family members depicted across his back.

"It's easy to dedicate a game when something goes good, but I dedicate every game to my mom," Wells said. "My family is always with me in heart, mind and soul."

As Bernie Williams and Darryl Strawberry hoisted Wells on their shoulders and carried him off the field to start the jubilation, no one was joking about his notable physical characteristics.

The man was a pitcher again. Not a sideshow, not a walking time bomb. For one glorious day, he was the greatest pitcher in the Yankees' regular-season history.

MAY 17	SUN	Minnesota Twins	4-0	W
MAY 19	TUES	Baltimore Orioles	9-5	W
MAY 20	WED	Baltimore Orioles	9-6	W
MAY 21	THU	Baltimore Orioles	3-1	W
MAY 22	FRI	at Boston Red Sox	4-5	L
MAY 23	SAT	at Boston Red Sox	12-3	W

"To be honest, I was wishing the crowd would shush. I was starting to get nervous about the seventh inning and the crowd was starting to get to me."
—David Wells

LIKE LARSEN, DAVID QUITE IMPERFECT

By Bill Madden
May 18, 1998

BILL MADDEN

The million-to-one odds of becoming the second imperfect man from Point Loma High School in San Diego to pitch a perfect game at Yankee Stadium was just beginning to sink in on David Wells when Yankees vice president Arthur Richman frantically summoned him into Joe Torre's office to take a phone call.

On the other end of the line was not President Clinton, but Don Larsen, the original imperfect man, as immortalized by Daily News baseball writer Joe Trimble in his account of the only perfect game in the World Series, Oct. 8, 1956. Like Wells, Larsen was quite a free spirit and bon vivant, having reportedly partied heavily with Richman on the eve of his perfecto. The two pitchers could only laugh at the incredible coincidence of baseball history.

"I'm honored to share this with you, Don," Wells said. "I mean two guys from the same high school doing this? What were the odds? Who would ever believe it?"

Torre, sitting behind his desk a few feet away, was one who could. The Yankees' manager was 16 years old that October afternoon in 1956 and he was sitting in the upper deck in left field while Larsen was making history.

"I was there as a Dodger fan," Torre said, "but by the time the ninth inning came around, I was rooting for Larsen like everybody else in the park. It is quite a coincidence, isn't it? Both guys free spirits. You don't check their rooms at night."

It is hard to imagine anyone among the 49,820 "Beanie Babies" crowd yesterday rooting for the Twins, but if they were, it wasn't for long. Even Twins manager Tom Kelly admitted getting caught up in Wells' bid for immortality.

"As much as we were fighting to win the game, deep down I was hoping to see something special," Kelly admitted. "I like the guy, I really do. He has the charisma for something like this and I guess his stars were in alignment today."

Actually, they started getting aligned in Wells' last start,

Congratulate David Wells on a Perfect Game

DAILY NEWS   Misha Erwitt

David Wells addressing the crowd at City Hall.

on Tuesday, when he retired the final 10 batters he faced against Kansas City. If you're counting that makes 37 consecutive batters Wells has retired, which is quite a reversal of form from his start before that—when he couldn't get out of the third inning against the Rangers after being staked to a 9-0 lead.

But then that's Wells. Like Forrest Gump's proverbial box of chocolates, you just never know what you're going to get.

Yesterday it was pure domination. About the only time you thought he might be losing his decided edge was in the seventh, when he ran the count full on both Brent Gates and Paul Molitor in succession. The crowd groaned when Wells

DAILY NEWS   Misha Erwitt

David Wells receives the key to the city from Mayor Rudolph Giuliani on the steps of City Hall after pitching a perfect game against the Minnesota Twins last Sunday.

went to 3-1 on Molitor and as Torre would say later, "The thing I'll take with me from this game was David coming back from that to strike him out. Getting Molitor, that's when I thought he was going to do it."

And when Wells came out for the ninth, they were all on their feet, imploring home plate umpire Tim McClelland to call everything a strike. By this time, though, Wells seemed almost numb to it all and threw almost nothing but strikes. Barely hittable strikes.

"The way he kept his composure was the most impressive part of the whole performance," marveled Twins pitcher Bob Tewksbury. "I mean just holding onto the ball in Yankee Stadium in front of 50,000 screaming fans and keeping that focus after two long (Yankees) innings (in the seventh and eighth) is incredible. I have to tell you, even from the other side it was pretty thrilling."

"To be honest," said Wells, "I was wishing the crowd would shush. I was starting to get nervous about the seventh inning and the crowd was starting to get to me."

The place really exploded when Paul O'Neill settled under Pat Meares' soft fly ball to right to end it and suddenly Wells was engulfed by his teammates and couldn't hear anything. The man who made them cringe by trading on-the-air profanities with talk radio shock jocks "Bubba The Love Sponge" in Tampa and Howard Stern was now being carried off the field by Darryl Strawberry and Bernie Williams, the toast of the team.

"I just hope the Yankees treat him better than they treated me," Larsen said. "I barely got a raise from (then Yankees GM George) Weiss. What David did was quite remarkable. It's tough enough today just to pitch a complete game with all these bullpens."

Was there anything in particular he told Wells, Larsen was asked.

"Oh yeah," he said. "I told David we have to have a few drinks this summer and raise a little hell."

What else would you expect from two imperfect kindred spirits?

STANDINGS AT THE END OF WEEK 8

American League East

	W.	L.	PCT.	G.B.
NEW YORK YANKEES	32	10	.762	-
Boston Red Sox	29	17	.630	5
Toronto Blue Jays	24	24	.500	11
Tampa Bay Devil Rays	22	25	.468	12.5
Baltimore Orioles	21	27	.438	14

TAKE ME OUT TO THE BRAWL GAME

Yanks, Orioles in Rumble

MAY 19, 1998 YANKEES VS. BALTIMORE ORIOLES

By mary Ann Giordano and Leo Standora, Daily News Staff Writers

MAY 20, 1998

A routine Yankees-Orioles game erupted into a 10-minute brawl in the Bronx last night, clearing both benches and spurring Bombers fans to stand and scream.

"It just goes to show the kind of team the Yanks have this year," Greg Clements, 25, said after the pinstripers came from behind in last night's contest, then became embroiled in the brawl. "They're not gonna let a team like the Orioles stand in their way."

The free-for-all was unleashed in the eighth inning, when Oriole hurler Armando Benitez drilled

Orioles manager Ray Miller argues with the umpires about B.J. Surhoff being tossed out of the game.

DAILY NEWS Linda Cataffo

> **"It just goes to show the kind of team the Yanks have this year," said Greg Clements, 25, "They're not gonna let a team like the Orioles stand in their way."**

Yankee first baseman Tino Martinez in the upper back with his first pitch.

One pitch earlier, Bernie Williams hit a three-run homer to put the Yanks ahead 7-5 in what was to that point a mostly dull game.

Plate umpire Drew Coble immediately

ejected Benitez. Darryl Strawberry and Chad Curtis led the Yankees' charge from the first-base dugout.

Benitez dropped his glove, motioning for Strawberry to fight, and then both teams went crazy.

"It was the worst brawl I've seen in 25 years," said Yankees owner George Steinbrenner, who spoke to his team after the game. In contrast to Yankee pitcher David Wells' historic outing Sunday, Steinbrenner called last night's contest "an imperfect game."

> **"It was exciting and upsetting, but it was the wrong thing to do. I think both teams should be suspended."**
> **—11-year-old fan, Joel Ballenilla**

In the stands, 11-year-old Joel Ballenilla agreed with the Boss.

"It was exciting and upsetting, but it was the wrong thing to do," he said. "I think both teams should be suspended."

Whoa there Joel, said attorney Bob Bing of Suffern:

"Something like this is never good for the game, but they're only human beings."

He blamed the O's rude behavior on "frustration." The Yanks, he noted, have the best record in baseball, while the Orioles are near the cellar in the American League East.

The Birds' struggle got harder with last night's 9-5 loss.

There was no immediate word on penalties.

Fans leaving the Stadium seemed festive, singing, "Tino, Tino . . . Bernie, Bernie . . . " into the night.

FINAL

BALTIMORE ORIOLES 5, AT NEW YORK YANKEES 9

BALTIMORE	ab	r	h	rbi	NEW YORK	ab	r	h	rbi
B Anderson cf	4	1	1	0	Knoblauch 2b	3	2	1	0
Hammonds rf	4	0	1	1	Jeter ss	5	2	3	2
R Alomar 2b	3	1	1	1	O'Neill rf	5	1	2	1
R Palmeiro 1b	5	1	1	1	B Williams cf	2	1	0	0
Baines dh	2	1	1	0	Raines dh	5	1	3	3
a-Carter ph-dh	2	1	1	0	Curtis lf	4	0	1	0
C Ripken 3b	4	0	2	0	J Posada c	5	0	2	2
Reboulet 3b	1	0	0	0	Brosius 3b	3	1	2	1
Surhoff lf	5	1	3	3	Sojo 1b	4	1	1	0
Hoiles c	5	0	0	0					
Bordick ss	3	0	1	0					
Totals	38	6	12	6	Totals	36	9	15	9

HR: R Alomar, R Palmeiro, Surhoff.   HR: Brosius.

a-flied to right for Baines in the 7th.

Baltimore	100 001 004 — 6	
NY Yankees	400 203 00x — 9	

Baltimore	ip	h	r	er	bb	so	hr	era
Key L	5 2/3	12	9	9	2	6	1	4.06
Charlton	2/3	2	0	0	3	1	0	7.41
Munoz	1 2/3	1	0	0	1	1	0	5.40

NY Yankees	ip	h	r	r	bb	so	hr	era
Irabu W	6 1/3	6	2	2	3	2	0	1.40
Lloyd	2/3	0	0	0	0	0	0	2.79
Nelson	1	2	0	0	0	0	0	3.57
Holmes	1	4	4	4	0	1	3	4.50

DAILY NEWS Linda Cataffo

Armando Benitez after being tossed by the home umpire.

GAME OF THE WEEK

MAY 25, 1998 YANKEES VS. CHICAGO WHITE SOX

PALE HOSING

Yanks bash White Sox

MAY 26, 1998

By Peter Botte, Daily News Sports Writer

WEEK 9 ● MAY 24-30

CHICAGO—The Yankees continue to make a mockery of the American League. Fueled by a six-run first inning and Hideki Irabu's continued mastery, they pasted the worst pitching staff in baseball last night with a 12-0 thrashing of the White Sox at Comiskey Park for their third straight blowout win.

"Wow," Joe Torre said. "I don't know what I can say."

That's a perfectly acceptable response, of course, because his team's ongoing actions and reactions have spoken much louder all season than any words could describe.

The incredible Irabu (4-0) didn't need anywhere near such run support, as he tossed a six-hitter — three in the ninth inning — and struck out five for the

Hideki Irabu

DAILY NEWS Linda Cataffo

first complete game and shutout of his Yankee tenure.

"Today I wanted to do my best to throw a complete game," the 29-year-old righthander said. "I'm very happy."

He's also very dominant. The $12.8 million import — who has not allowed more than two runs in any of his seven starts this year — lowered his ERA to a Gibsonesque 1.13. He also finally has compiled enough innings (47 2/3) to qualify for the major-league lead in that category.

"Consistent-wise, he's been our best pitcher," Paul O'Neill said. "Every fifth day I look forward to going out there behind him. And you can tell he's having a lot of fun out there."

As are the Yanks, whose 34-10 start, in what is fast becoming a season in which the only intrigue until October will be how many of them — Irabu included — will end up at Coors Field for the July 7 All-Star Game.

O'Neill had four hits and three RBI to boost his average to .318. Derek Jeter had three more hits, is batting .344 and combined with Chuck Knoblauch to score six runs. Scott Brosius had a two-run single and is hitting .338. Bernie Williams blasted his sixth home run in two weeks and had four RBI to push his average to .320.

With their leading run producer, Tino Martinez (.331, 38 RBI), sidelined nursing a shoulder injury, the Yankees have scored an incredible 38 runs over their last three games.

On the heels of a 26-run explosion in their previous two games in Boston, the first six Yankees batters against Jaime Navarro (one-third of an inning) reached safely en route to a six-run first on a two-run double by O'Neill and two-run

FINAL

NEW YORK YANKEES 12, AT CHICAGO WHITE SOX 0

NEW YORK	ab	r	h	rbi	CHICAGO	ab	r	h	rbi
Knoblauch 2b	2	3	1	0	Durham 2b	2	0	0	0
Bush 2b	1	0	0	0	J Abbott lf	1	0	0	0
Jeter ss	4	3	3	1	Cordero 1b	4	0	1	0
Sojo ss	1	0	0	0	F Thomas dh	2	0	0	0
O'Neill rf	5	2	4	3	Belle lf	2	0	0	0
B Williams cf	5	2	3	4	Norton 3b	1	0	0	0
Strawberry dh	3	1	1	0	Ventura 3b	3	0	0	0
J Posada c	5	1	1	2	Snopek 2b	1	0	0	0
Curtis lf	4	0	0	0	M Ordonez rf	4	0	1	0
Brosius 3b	5	0	1	2	Cameron cf	4	0	1	0
Sveum 1b	5	0	0	0	O'Brien c	4	0	2	0
					M Caruso ss	4	0	1	0
Totals	40	12	14	12	Totals	32	0	6	0

HR - B Williams.

NY Yankees	600 204 000	— 12
Chi White Sox	000 000 000	— 0

NY Yankees	ip	h	r	er	bb	so	hr	era
Irabu W	9	6	0	0	5	6	0	1.13

Chicago	ip	h	r	er	bb	so	hr	era
Navarro L	1/3	5	6	5	2	0	0	6.15
Fordham	3 1/3	4	2	2	2	0	0	9.47
T Castillo	2 1/3	4	4	4	0	0	1	7.23
C Castillo	1	0	0	0	0	3	0	5.35
Simas	2	1	0	0	1	2	0	2.25

Derek Jeter

singles by Jorge Posada and Brosius. And that was only half the night's damage.

All of which, of course, had to be a bit of a foreign concept for Irabu, who had entered the game accustomed to only 4.3 runs per game of support in his first six starts.

Irabu, perhaps not knowing what to do with the newfound offensive wealth, quickly loaded the bases on a single and two walks with one out in the first. The righty import, however, has been nothing short of spectacular with runners in scoring position all season, and escaped that jam.

By the time he retired Jeff Abbott for his final out with two runners on in the ninth, opposing batters had dropped to a 4-for-32 (.125) success rate this season against him in such situations.

MAY 24	SUN	at Boston Red Sox	4-14	W
MAY 25	MON	at Chicago White Sox	0-12	W
MAY 26	TUES	at Chicago White Sox	5-7	W
MAY 27	WED	at Chicago White Sox	12-9	L
MAY 28	THU	Boston Red Sox	8-3	W
MAY 29	FRI	Boston Red Sox	6-2	W
MAY 30	SAT	Boston Red Sox	2-3	L

> "We just sort of set a projection for (Hernandez) for later on. Plus, we were looking for a reliever at this point. And we're not sure what his role is going to be when the time comes."
>
> —Joe Torre

YANKS CUT BANKS; STILL NO EL DUQUE

By Ralph Vacchiano, Daily News Sports Writer
May 29,1998

A spot opened in the Yankees' bullpen yesterday when Jersey City's Willie Banks was designated for assignment. But when the Yanks dipped down to Triple-A Columbus to replace him, they didn't grab the pitcher most thought they would.

Banks was replaced by Todd Erdos, who was "dominating the International League," according to GM Brian Cashman. Meanwhile, just north in Ottawa, Orlando (El Duque) Hernandez was making another start in Triple A.

"We just sort of set a projection for (Hernandez) for later on," Yankees manager Joe Torre said. "Plus, we were looking for a reliever at this point. And we're not sure what his role is going to be when the time comes."

Hernandez has been exclusively a starter since signing a four-year, $6.6 million contract with the Yankees on March 7, and going into last night's game he was 5-0 with a 3.47 ERA, and ranked fourth in the IL with 50 strikeouts in 36 1/3 innings.

Cashman said, "There was no question in anybody's mind who would come up" since Erdos had struck out 11 and given up just one hit in his last nine innings. But he also hinted El Duque's arrival is

growing closer since the organization has already begun discussions about moving him from the rotation to the bullpen.

"We've discussed in the last day or two that maybe he could help us in the pen," Cashman said. "But we haven't made the decision to move El Duque to the pen."

Hernandez, however, could still fit into the rotation. Ramiro Mendoza, the only one in danger of losing his rotation spot to Hernandez, was terrible in Chicago Wednesday night, giving up five runs and nine hits in just three innings.

As bad as he was, though, Banks was worse. He relieved Mendoza in what was a 5-5 game and gave up three hits and three runs in two innings. Only a Yankees rally saved the 29-year-old from a loss.

But it couldn't save him from getting cut — not with a 10.05 ERA (14 1/3 innings, 16 runs), a far cry from the 3-0 record and 1.93 ERA he posted in five appearances last September.

"It's because he didn't get enough time out on the mound," Torre said. "In our situation you really can't afford to bring somebody along. It was very tough doing that. He was a favorite here, he was a manager's favorite. I just hope he gets to pitch somewhere."

Banks is confident he will, and Cashman said he will do what he can to get Banks another major league job. The GM said he's had some inquiries about the righty and figured with the state of pitching in baseball, someone somewhere will take a chance.

"Who? I don't know," Banks said. "But I have a good feeling that I'll get picked up. A lot of teams out there need pitching, and by all means I'm no slouch. I've got a lot of good years left in me. Right now I don't care if it's Little League. I just want to go out there, get stretched out and pitch."

> ## "I have a good feeling that I'll get picked up. A lot of teams out there need pitching, and by all means I'm no slouch. Right now I don't care if it's Little League. I just want to go out there, get stretched out and pitch."
> ### —Willie Banks

DAILY NEWS Linda Cataffo

Even in May, Yankee fans were awaiting the arrival of El Duque.

STANDINGS AT THE END OF WEEK 9

American League East

	W.	L.	PCT.	G.B.
NEW YORK YANKEES	37	12	.755	-
Boston Red Sox	30	22	.577	8.5
Toronto Blue Jays	28	26	.519	11.5
Baltimore Orioles	25	29	.463	14.5
Tampa Bay Devil Rays	24	29	.453	15

YANKEE PROFILE
DEREK JETER

TO GAL FANS, NO ONE'S NEATER THAN JETER

SEPTEMBER 13, 1998

By Tara George , Daily News Sports Writer

SS

Derek Jeter

High-pitched squeals ripple through Yankee Stadium as hyperventilating girls leap to their feet and screech.

The ballgame suddenly seems like a Leonardo DiCaprio appearance. And that can only mean one thing: Derek Jeter is on the field.

"De-Rek! De-Reeeeeeek!" the girls scream, their arms outstretched with autograph pads covered in colored spangles. "I love you De-Rek!"

To most Yankee fans, the 24-year-old shortstop from Kalamazoo, Mich., is one of the heroes of the best Yankee team in recent memory.

But to hordes of young girls, Jeter is the "sweet," "cute" pinstriped star of their intense teenage fantasies.

They send him piles of fan mail — letters, autograph requests and pictures of themselves surrounded with Jeter memorabilia, a Yankees

Yankees shortstop Derek Jeter is saluted by teenage girls.

DAILY NEWS Mike Albans

spokesman says.

His correspondence arrives at the rate of about 20 pieces a day — far outstripping the other players — and amasses in buckets at his locker, awaiting his personal reply.

The girls know his sports statistics, but they'd rather discuss his other assets, such as his "sweet face," "nice eyes" and "really, really cute butt."

"I've been here 42 years and I've never seen girls go fanatical about a ballplayer like this," says Kenneth Spinner, a Stadium vendor. "Every time his name is announced, they go berserk."

James Mitchell, an usher, confirms the madness.

"They go nuts. He's sexy . . . the girls love

him . . . from 16-year-olds to about 40," he says.

The young Jeterettes live him, breathe him and run Web sites devoted to him. They paint his number — 2 — on their faces, plaster their walls with his image and craft posters to hoist at games in the hopes they'll appear on the jumbo screen and Jeter will notice.

"Oh my God! Oh my God! We were really, really close," an excited Stefanie Dicrocce, 13, of Long Island, tells her family as she rushes back from the autograph pack above the dugout, her face flushed and sweating. "It was, like, the highlight of my life."

Her mother, Maria, hands her daughter a pickle to snack on and then takes it back, realizing the girl is too whipped up to eat.

"My daughter is insane about Derek Jeter," she laughs. "She has scrapbooks. She saves every single clipping. She knows all his stats. She knows his underwear size. She follows him better than his own mother."

The girls say they like Jeter because he likes kids — a fact not wasted on the makers of Skippy peanut butter, who've paid him to endorse their product.

"He respects kids, unlike other players," says Jillian Barra, 15, of Queens, who has her own Derek Jeter Web site and fan club with 49 members.

They like that he's single and relatively young. They've done the math. They figure he's young enough that one day they could possibly get married. Needless to say, they were thrilled when their idol ended his

DAILY NEWS Linda Cataffo

Early in the season, Jeter was dating pop star Mariah Carey.

much-hyped romance with singer Mariah Carey.

Jeter's dad, Charles, who runs the children's charity his son started, is unmoved by the fact that he's spawned a stud.

"I don't make anything of it," he laughs. "You'll have to ask my son."

But Jeter is characteristically shy about the adulation.

"I'm a big fan of kids," he says, ducking the question.

In an era of an adulterous President, parents say the polite young ballplayer is a role model they're happy with.

"He's clean-cut, he's responsible. I like the fact that he endorses not smoking," said Lauren Robertson, whose 11-year-old daughter, Lizzy Lee, is a fan. "I'd let her marry him."

Derek Jeter Stats

1998 REGULAR SEASON

AVG.	G	AB	R	H	TB	2B	3B	HR	RBI	BB	SO	SB	CS	SH	SF	HP	SLG%	OBP%
.325	148	622	126	202	300	25	8	19	84	57	118	30	6	3	3	5	.482	.384

GAME OF THE WEEK

MAY 31, 1998 YANKEES VS. BOSTON RED SOX

BOSOX BOMB BRONX

Score 11 in third, hold on to beat Yanks

JUNE 1, 1998

By Rafael Hermoso, Daily News Sports Writer

WEEK 10 ● MAY 31-JUNE 6

Their one-time ace got shelled. Their usually steady defense gave away three outs by hesitating. And they gave up 11 runs in the third inning, leaving the postgame clubhouse unusually quiet.

That's what allowing the biggest inning in 55 years can do to your mood. The Yankees lost their second straight game to the Red Sox yesterday, 13-7, in front of a sellout crowd of 55,711 at Yankee Stadium.

Not even a futile comeback could overcome Boston's 16-batter, 42-minute third inning. It was the most runs the Yankees have allowed in an inning since July 2, 1943.

"If you don't pitch well, they're going to kick your butt," Joe Torre concluded.

George Steinbrenner must have been happy he returned to Tampa after Saturday's game. After winning seven straight, the Yankees have lost two in a row for only the third time this season. They lost their first three games of the season in California and lost May 14 and 15 to

the Rangers and Twins, respectively, at the Stadium. Andy Pettitte also lost that second game. Yankees starters have lost two straight after going 13 games without losing.

A seven-run comeback by the Yankees fell short, but their lead over Boston is still 7 1/2 games.

Young fans watch the Yankees before the game.
DAILY NEWS Linda Cataffo

"The more frustrating part than how I'm struggling is these guys are battling," said Pettitte (6-5). "If I throw anywhere near a decent game, we'd have a chance."

"He'll be fine," Torre said. "I'm confident he'll be fine. His stomach has a lot of guts in it."

Joe Girardi's first home run of the season — his first in 419 at-bats since April 28, 1997 — brought the Yankees within 11-4 in the sixth and forced Pedro Martinez (6-1) from the game.

"I don't hit 'em very often so I think guys get a little more excited when I hit them," Girardi said.

The Yankees scored three runs off three

Boston relievers in the seventh to draw within 11-7 and had the tying run at the plate with the bases loaded. But Lou Merloni's diving play on pinch-hitter Jorge Posada's hard grounder turned into an inning-ending double play. Two Red Sox runs in the ninth sealed the win.

"Even when he dove for it, I thought it was going through," Torre said.

"I'm no psychic," Bernie Williams said, "but I'd say we had a very good chance because we had momentum."

Pettitte's wife, Laura, delivered the couple's second child on Thursday after induced labor. Pettitte had left the Yankees the morning after his last start Tuesday night in Chicago to join her in Texas.

Pettitte rejoined the team Saturday and, Torre hoped, returned without distractions. His head was spinning after yesterday's game.

After striking out four of the first eight batters he faced, Pettitte couldn't escape the third. He allowed eight runs in 2 2/3 innings, his shortest outing since a Cal Ripken line drive knocked him out in the second inning last Sept. 5.

Even more confusing, everyone agreed his stuff was good. Pettitte disagreed with Torre's assessment he was overthrowing.

Pettitte wasn't helped by his teammates' hesitation. The Yankees could've escaped the inning trailing 3-0 if not for the blunders. "We gave them six outs," Girardi said.

Chuck Knoblauch threw home wide instead of throwing to first to allow Boston to score its third run. Jim Leyritz followed with a grounder to Scott Brosius. The third baseman looked home but Girardi had gone up the first-base line to back up a double-play throw. Brosius only had time for one out at second and the Sox led, 4-0. "It's tough to fault either guy," Torre said.

"I assumed and you should never assume," Girardi said. "I felt kind of stupid."

Brosius said, "Looking back at it, we probably, with the runners we had, could've turned two."

After Troy O'Leary's RBI single, Merloni hit a catchable ball into short center field. But Williams started back on the ball and barely got a glove on it.

"I did go back and the ball just stopped," Williams said. "Then by the time I went back there, it was too late."

FINAL

BOSTON RED SOX 13, AT NEW YORK YANKEES 7

BOSTON	ab	r	h	rbi	NEW YORK	ab	r	h	rbi
D Lewis cf	4	2	2	2	Knoblauch 2b	5	0	2	0
J Valentin 3	4	2	3	0	Jeter ss	5	1	2	0
N Garciaparra ss	6	1	3	3	O'Neill rf	4	1	1	1
Vaughn 1b	5	0	1	3	Martinez 1b	4	1	0	0
Leyritz dh	5	1	0	1	Williams cf	5	1	4	0
Oleary lf	5	1	1	0	Strawberry dh	3	0	1	0
Merloni 2b	5	2	2	1	a-Raines ph-dh	1	0	0	1
Bragg rf	5	2	3	1	Curtis lf	4	1	2	1
Varitek c	5	2	2	2	Brosius 3b	5	1	1	1
					Girardi c	3	1	1	3
					b-J Posada ph-c	1	0	0	0
Totals	44	13	17	6	Totals	40	7	14	7

HR - Girardi.

a-walked for Strawberry in the 7th; b-grounded to shortstop for Girardi in the 7th.

Boston	0 0 1	1 000	002	—13
Ny Yankees	0 0 0	103	300	— 7

BOSTON	ip	h	r	er	bb	so	hr	era
P Martinez W	5 2/3	8	4	4	2	6	1	2.63
J Wasdin	1/3	2	2	0	1	0	0	6.28
R Mahay	0	1	1	1	1	0	0	5.73
Eckersley	2	2	0	0	1	1	0	6.75
R Garces	1	1	0	0	0	0	0	3.00

NY YANKEES	ip	h	r	er	bb	so	hr	era
Pettitte L	2 2/3	6	8	8	2	4	0	4.88
Holmes	4 1/3	4	3	3	2	0	0	4.57
Nelson	1/3	3	0	0	0	0	0	4.88
Lloyd	2/3	0	0	0	1	0	0	2.03
Erdos	1	4	2	2	1	0	0	9.00

J Wasdin pitched to 2 batters in the 7th.
R Mahay pitched to 2 batters in the 7th.

DAILY NEWS Linda Cataffo

Pedro Martinez

REST OF THE WEEK

MAY 31	SUN	Boston Red Sox	7-13	L
JUNE 1	MON	Chicago White Sox	5-4	W
JUNE 2	TUES	Chicago White Sox	6-3	W
JUNE 3	WED	Tampa Bay Devil Rays	7-1	W
JUNE 4	THU	Tampa Bay Devil Rays	6-1	W
JUNE 5	FRI	Florida Marlins	5-1	W
JUNE 6	SAT	Florida Marlins	4-2	W

"It's great to be here."
—14-year-old
Ray Smith, Yankee manager for a day

BOMBER FOR A DAY

Boy with ailment leads Yanks

By Bill Egbert, Daily News Staff Writer
June 1,1998

A 14-year-old who has spent much of his life in a hospital bed watching the Yankees on TV yesterday lived a dream as the Bombers' Manager for a Day.

Ray Smith, a heart patient from Mount Marion, N.Y., even got to make up the starting lineup.

"He makes up the lineup at home every game," said Assistant-Manager-for-a-Day Joe Torre, "And we've matched up for the past two days."

"It's great to be here," said Ray, standing behind the batting cage, watching his heroes warm up. Ray hung onto the netting just a few feet away from Darryl Strawberry whacking balls into the outfield.

Joe Torre

DAILY NEWS Linda Cataffo

Torre met Ray through the Starlight Foundation, which grants wishes to ill children. Torre serves on Starlight's board of directors.

Ray has had three open-heart surgeries for a heart that had only two chambers when he was born.

Confined to Boston Children's Hospital for much of his youth, Ray still developed a love for the American pastime.

"He used to play whiffle ball in the hospital hallway," recalled his father, Ray Sr. "The doctors would even stop by and pitch."

Starlight invited the younger Ray to meet Torre at a sports auction last

November, but a heart failure and emergency surgery postponed his dream. So he wrote to Torre and offered support to Torre's brother Frank, who also suffers from heart problems.

"Tell him that my prayers and concerns are with him," Ray wrote.

Ray finally met Torre at a holiday charity event held by watch retailer Tourneau, and the manager invited Ray to spend a day in the dugout.

Yesterday, Ray went with Torre into the clubhouse to meet his heroes, including his favorite, Strawberry.

"He's been through a lot of problems in his life, like me," said Ray, "so I kind of relate to him."

Said Strawberry: "It's a real blessing to have someone like him feel that way."

DAILY NEWS Linda Cataffo

Ray Smith 14, talks over the lineup with Yankees manager Joe Torre during batting practice.

STANDINGS AT THE END OF WEEK 10

American League East	W.	L.	PCT.	G.B.
NEW YORK YANKEES	46	14	.767	-
Boston Red Sox	38	26	.594	10
Toronto Blue Jays	33	34	.493	16.5
Baltimore Orioles	32	35	.478	17.5
Tampa Bay Devil Rays	27	38	.415	21.5

GAME OF THE WEEK

JUNE 9, 1998 YANKEES VS. NEW YORK METS

EL DUQUE OF LE NORTH

Earns Expo win and a go from Joe

JUNE 10, 1998

By Peter Botte, Daily News Sports Writer

WEEK 11 ● JUNE 7-13

Whether Joe Torre decides to remove Ramiro Mendoza from the rotation or simply affords David Wells extra time to recover from mild shoulder tendinitis, there is no arguing that Orlando Hernandez' arrival has made an already formidable starting staff that much more daunting.

There also is no arguing that El Duque is here to stay, after the $6.6 million Cuban defector tossed nine four-hit innings last night for his second impressive victory in as many starts.

With three home runs among their 17 hits, the Yankees continued to steamroll inferior opponents, christening their first-ever regular-season appearance in French-speaking Canada with an 11-1 interleague pasting of the Expos before 16,238 at Olympic Stadium.

"He definitely deserves to (start) again, no question," Torre said of Hernandez. "But we just have to figure out how it's going to happen.

Orlando Hernandez

DAILY NEWS Linda Cataffo

He'll get another start. It's just a matter of playing with this thing and using six guys for a turn or two or maybe send somebody to the bullpen."

Again mixing arm angles and painting corners with precision, Hernandez (2-0, 1.13) struck out nine and walked one in his first career complete game. He allowed just a pair of singles through eight innings before Vladimir Guerrero's RBI single spoiled the shutout bid with one out in the ninth.

"It's very important for me," Hernandez said, with Jorge Posada serving as his interpreter. "It's my first complete game in the big leagues, and it gives some rest to the staff and the relievers. . . . I'm just looking forward to pitching no matter what level it's at. I just want to help out the team. I'm 2-0 in two starts and I'm looking forward to the next one."

The rout marked the Yanks' eighth straight

victory — all against this noted fearsome foursome of the White Sox, Devil Rays, Marlins and Expos, who entered last night with a combined record of 93-153 (.378). The Yanks improved to 44-9 since starting the season 1-4, thereby tying the 1941 Yankees for the best 53-game stretch in AL history.

Scott Brosius blasted two home runs and Bernie Williams added a solo shot in support of their new Cuban teammate, who had to feel as if he faced stiffer competition during his seven-start stint at Columbus.

"A carbon copy of his first start," said Brosius. "He has great composure, an ability to throw all of his pitches for strikes in any count. Batters don't know what to look for.

"He's shown he knows how to pitch. It's two starts and maybe too early to say he's gonna win 18 starts in a row. But if he pitches like that, he's gonna give us a chance to win every time, no matter who he's facing."

Which is nothing new during the Yanks' eight-game winning streak, since their starters have gone 7-0 with one no-decision and a 1.57 ERA over their last 63 innings.

Torre has maintained for weeks that Mendoza (4-1, 4.00) has done nothing to deserve a demotion, but clearly someone has to be sacrificed.

"If Wells can pitch (by this weekend), we'll have to find a way to do this," Torre said. "But I'm sure as hell curious for another look. . . . It certainly gives us something to chew on."

All dog-bite jokes aside, Joe Girardi likened Hernandez' style to that of David Cone, with all of his arm angles to deceive hitters. Torre likened him more to Juan Marichal with the big leg kick and the uncanny control. And to a lesser degree, Torre invoked Greg Maddux, at least as far as his knowledge of pitching.

"He's thinking all the time out there. It's sort of like a sixth sense," Torre said.

"The great thing about him is he has an idea how to pitch," Girardi said. "He doesn't need to learn how to pitch. He knows. The greatest things about watching him pitch are his humility, his appreciation for being able to pitch, and his emotion. It's kind of neat to see. The guy just brings a glove and a pair of shoes, and you see how spoiled we all are."

And just how spoiled we soon might be.

FINAL

NEW YORK YANKEES 11, AT MONTREAL EXPOS 1

NY YANKEES	ab	r	h	rbi	MONTREAL	ab	r	h	rbi
Knoblauch 2b	1	3	1	0	Santangelo lf	3	0	0	0
Bush 2b	2	0	2	1	McGuire lf	1	0	0	0
Sojo ss	6	1	4	1	Vidro 2b	4	1	2	0
O'Neill rf	4	0	1	2	V Guerrero rf	4	0	1	1
Spencer pr-rf	2	1	0	0	Fullmer 1b	4	0	0	0
B Williams cf	4	1	2	2	R White cf	0	0	0	0
T Martinez 1b	4	0	0	1	Stovall cf	2	0	0	0
Sveum 1b	1	0	1	0	Grudzielanek ss	3	0	0	0
Curtis lf	5	1	2	0	Kline p	0	0	0	0
Brosius 3b	5	2	2	3	M Batista p	0	0	0	0
Girardi c	5	2	2	0	Widger c	3	0	0	0
O Hernandez p	4	0	0	0	Hubbard c	0	0	0	0
					Andrews 3b	2	0	0	0
					Telford p	0	0	0	0
					Livingstone 3b	1	0	0	0
					C Perez p	1	0	0	0
					Bennett p	0	0	0	0
					Mordecai 3b-ss	2	0	1	0
Totals	43	11	17	10	Totals	30	1	4	1

HR - B Williams, Brosius 2.

NY Yankees	031 204 100	— 11
Montreal	000 000 001	— 1

NY Yankees	ip	h	r	er	bb	so	hr	era
O Hernandez W	9	4	1	1	1	9	0	1.13

Montreal	ip	h	r	er	bb	so	hr	era
C Perez L	4	7	6	6	3	1	3	3.45
Bennett	1 1/3	5	4	3	1	0	0	6.09
Telford	1 2/3	2	1	1	0	2	0	4.62
Kline	1	1	0	0	0	0	0	2.22
M Batista	1	2	0	0	0	2	0	3.92

Yankee catcher Joe Girardi appreciates El Duque's humility and emotion.

DAILY NEWS Linda Cataffo

JUNE 7	SUN	Florida Marlins	4-1	W
JUNE 9	TUES	at Montreal Expos	11-1	W
JUNE 10	WED	at Montreal Expos	6-2	W
JUNE 11	THU	at Montreal Expos	5-7	L
JUNE 12	FRI	Cleveland Indians	PPD	
JUNE 13	SAT	Cleveland Indians	PPD	

> "You know what sign I liked the most? One that read, 'El Duque 1, Castro 0.'"
> —Orlando Hernandez

ROYAL TREATMENT

Fans flock to El Duque

By Rafael Hermoso, Daily News Sports Writer
June 9,1998

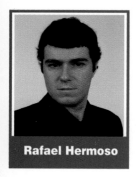

Rafael Hermoso

George Steinbrenner is not the only Yankee who has been stopped in Manhattan streets about Orlando Hernandez. El Duque himself admits he's seen plenty of Cuban flags, and fans have called his name and even confused him with his brother, Livan, of the Florida Marlins.

"They know. They identify me on the streets," Hernandez said Sunday before the Yankees completed a three-game sweep of the Marlins. "That calls my attention and fills me with pride. I'll try to keep identifying with them."

After an off-day yesterday — in which the Yankees learned Jorge Posada's sprained right ankle was fine — the El Duque show hits the road tonight in Montreal. For what it's worth, Hernandez maintained Sunday that he still had not been told he was making his second major-league start tonight, made necessary after David Wells was scratched from Sunday's game because of shoulder tendinitis.

After an emotional night at the Stadium in his debut last Wednesday — in which he allowed one run in seven innings — Hernandez said tonight won't be any different.

He will, however, be going from baseball's cathedral to its mausoleum. Olympic Stadium provides anything but a royal backdrop for El Duque.

The Expos, 13 games under .500 and 19 games behind the Braves in the National League East, are averaging a pathetic 10,363 fans at home this season. They expect 17,000-20,000 for tonight's game, largely because of the opponent, not the starting pitcher. The Montreal ticket office said yesterday that tickets were selling briskly for the past two days, but they would not provide figures.

Whatever the number, it should be a drop from the 27,291 fans who saw El Duque last week.

Since joining the Yankees a week ago today from Triple-A Columbus, the Cuban defector has experienced a whirlwind of emotion that could have overwhelmed his feelings.

"Just the opposite," El Duque said. "Those are things that made me feel good because that's why

I'm here, to pitch."

Hernandez said he has been most surprised by "the great reception that I've had here, that the fans have given me."

"You know what sign I liked the most?" he asked a visitor. "One that read, 'El Duque 1, Castro 0.'"

El Duque has preferred not to use his platform for a political message about Fidel Castro's Communist regime in Cuba. He would like to return to play in Cuba one day, though, when it's a free country.

After Wednesday's game, Hernandez said, "I'm a baseball player because if I mixed politics with baseball, I'd be part of the Cuban government."

Asked what he would tell Castro, Hernandez said, "I wouldn't say anything. I wouldn't waste my time standing in front of him."

Hernandez has tried calling his daughters, Yahumara, 7, and Steffi, 2, each day at their home in Havana, where they live with their mother. He defends his decision to leave them behind when he joined his girlfriend, Norris Bosch, and six others on a flimsy boat to freedom last December.

"It's been a while since I saw them," said Hernandez, who dedicated his first win to his daughters, among others. "I spent 10 years traveling with the national team and I left home a lot. I have my reasons, and they understand them."

DAILY NEWS Linda Cataffo

"El Duque" made an impressive major league debut.

STANDINGS AT THE END OF WEEK 11

American League East	W.	L.	PCT.	G.B.
NEW YORK YANKEES	50	17	.746	-
Boston Red Sox	43	28	.606	9
Toronto Blue Jays	36	38	.486	17.5
Baltimore Orioles	35	39	.473	18.5
Tampa Bay Devil Rays	31	41	.431	21.5

GAME OF THE WEEK

JUNE 14, 1998 VS. CLEVELAND INDIANS

CONE TAKES BITE OUT OF TRIBE

Fans 12 for 9th straight

JUNE 15, 1998

By Rafael Hermoso, Daily News Sports Writer

WEEK 12 ● JUNE 14-20

David Cone had his chance yesterday. He could distance himself from the infamous dog bite and erase any doubts about his previous start coming against less-than-major league hitters.

So what did Cone do? He credited his mother's 4-month-old Jack Russell terrier with turning around his season.

"Maybe the dog bite helped me," Cone said after striking out 12 Indians in a 4-2 win at the Stadium that was two days in the making following rain that continued through the fifth inning.

Someone even had a sense of humor or timing. The cast of the musical "Titanic" sang the national anthem.

"It gave me some rest. It made me throw my fastball and curveball more," Cone added. "Maybe the old dog has learned some new tricks. I've been stubborn to feature everything. I think it's nice to go back to the basics."

Cone helped the record-setting Yankees reach another milestone, tying the 1912 Red Sox and 1970 Reds by winning or tying 24 straight series.

Even after his complete-game win over the Marlins in his last start a week ago, Cone had to live with the thinly veiled jokes about his mother's puppy. And there was that asterisk next to the 14 Ks, the one that said the Marlins were anything but stiff competition.

Cone (9-1) agreed with that yesterday after winning his ninth straight decision. He threw 123 pitches in eight innings and allowed four hits, including a solo homer to nemesis Kenny Lofton in the eighth.

"That's true," Cone said. "This was a great barometer. Going against Cleveland you find out how good you really are."

"Last time he was on a roll," Joe Torre said. "Today he didn't have some pitches that he made adjustments for."

How good was Cone? Though he and

DAILY NEWS Linda Cataffo

David Cone struck out 12 batters while earning his ninth straight win.

catcher Joe Girardi admitted cutting down on Cone's trademark split-fingered fastball and throwing more fastballs since The Bite, Indians manager Mike Hargrove said, "I don't think he threw 10 fastballs all day."

Cone's fastball actually seemed too good early. He walked two of the first six batters. But he eventually found enough of the plate for umpire Drew Coble to call six strikeouts looking.

"That's as good as he's been," Girardi said.

"I feel like I know what I'm doing now," Cone said.

His teammates took the cue against Jaret Wright (5-4). Tino Martinez opened the scoring in the third with a sacrifice fly and then padded it with a two-run single off second baseman David Bell's glove into right field in the fifth. Tim Raines' RBI single in the seventh gave the Yankees a 4-0 lead.

Mariano Rivera, pitching for the first time in eight days, allowed Sandy Alomar's run-scoring double in the ninth before notching his 13th save.

FINAL

CLEVELAND INDIANS 2, AT NEW YORK YANKEES 4

CLEVELAND	ab	r	h	rbi	NEW YORK	ab	r	h	rbi
Lofton cf	3	1	3	1	Knoblauch 2b	4	1	1	0
Vizquel ss	4	0	0	0	Brosius 3b	3	2	1	0
M Ramirez rf	4	0	1	0	Oneill rf	4	1	2	0
Thome 1b	3	0	0	0	T Martinez 1b	3	0	1	3
Fryman 3b	4	0	0	0	Raines dh	4	0	2	1
Justice dh	3	1	1	0	Curtis cf	3	0	1	0
S Alomar c	4	0	1	0	Ledee lf	3	0	1	0
M Whiten lf	4	0	0	1	Girardi c	4	0	1	0
Da Bell 2b	3	0	0	0	Sojo ss	4	0	0	0
a-Luke ph	1	0	0	0					
Totals	33	2	6	2	Totals	32	4	10	4

HR - Lofton.

a-grounded to first for Da Bell in the 9th.

Cleveland	000 000 011	— 2
NY Yankees	001 020 10X	— 4

Cleveland	ip	h	r	er	bb	so	hr	era
Wright L	6	6	3	3	4	4	0	3.80
Villone	2/3	3	1	1	0	0	0	2.19
Assenmacher	1/3	0	0	0	0	0	0	3.32
Plunk	1	1	0	0	0	0	0	4.50

NY Yankees	ip	h	r	er	bb	so	hr	era
Cone W	8	4	1	1	2	12	1	4.56
Rivera S	1	2	1	1	0	1	0	0.83

DAILY NEWS Linda Cataffo

Mariano Rivera

REST OF THE WEEK

JUNE 14	SUN	Cleveland Indians	4-2	W
JUNE 15	MON	at Baltimore Orioles	4-7	L
JUNE 16	TUES	at Baltimore Orioles	0-2	L
JUNE 17	WED	at Baltimore Orioles	5-3	W
JUNE 18	THU	at Cleveland Indians	5-2	W
JUNE 19	FRI	at Cleveland Indians	4-7	L
JUNE 20	SAT	at Cleveland Indians	5-3	W

" I just know it's really starting to come together for me now. I feel like I know what I'm doing now. The dog bite gave me extra rest for my shoulder, too. Maybe this old dog is learning new tricks."
—David Cone

ENOUGH OF A GOOD THING

By Bill Madden, Daily News Sports Writer
June 15, 1998

Bill Madden

One of the many tales told about the '27 Yankees (with whom this Yankees team has been so prematurely compared) involves a conversation around the batting cage prior to the first game of that World Series.

A sportswriter from Pittsburgh was trying to convince the scribes from New York how the heavy underdog Pirates could actually win the Series because they had five quality starting pitchers. Standing a few feet away, Babe Ruth overheard this assessment and, as the story goes, retorted: "What good are five starting pitchers gonna do you in a four-game Series?"

The Babe had a point — which the Yankees emphatically proved by beating the Pirates in four games. But the story came to mind again this rain-slogged weekend as the '98 Yankees were trying to figure out what good six quality starting pitchers were to them in a no-game series. Happily for them, David Cone and the 42,949 fans who got "two-fer" tickets for another game for their perseverance, the rain subsided enough to allow a game to finally get played against the hated Indians.

And make no mistake, from the Yankees' standpoint everything about this game — from Cone's 12-strikeout dominance, to beating Jaret Wright, to Mariano Rivera's save — was a long time coming.

Most of all, though, the game itself was a long time coming as Cone, who hadn't pitched since his 14-strikeout gem against Florida a week ago Sunday,

DAILY NEWS Gerald Herbert

Ricky Ledee

readily testified. For a variety of reasons, starting with his recovery from off-season shoulder surgery, Cone has pitched on his normal four days' rest only three times in 12 starts. There was the early-season "baby-ing" he got because of his circulation problems, his mother's surgery, a sprained knee, a dog bite and finally all this rain.

But considering the results of his last two starts, Cone is beginning to think an extra day's rest might actually be a good thing for him.

"It's probably going to help me," he said. "Certainly my last two starts it did. I've had good stuff and it didn't affect my control. I'll pitch every Sunday if they want. I'm hell on Sundays!"

Did that mean, he was asked, he's a proponent of the six-man rotation?

Cone couldn't help but chuckle at the question.

"I don't know," he said. "I just know it's really starting to come for me now. I feel like I know what I'm doing now. The dog bite gave me extra rest for my shoulder, too. Maybe this old dog is learning new tricks."

Across the way in the visitors' clubhouse, Wright, whose victory over the Yankees in Game 2 of the division series swung the momentum to the Indians, was also discussing the effects of the unwanted extra idle days because of the rain. Unlike Cone, the 22-year-old Wright saw no advantage to the added rest.

"It was a seven-day layoff for me," he said. "I wouldn't say it hurt me, but it didn't help, either. You just have to get used to it. You're pitching every five days and then you get set back by the rain. You deal

DAILY NEWS   Mike Albans

Chuck Knoblauch scored 116 runs for the Yankees during the regular season.

with it."

When he was told the Yankees were especially anxious to get this series on and settle some scores, Wright shrugged. "It crossed my mind that this was the first time I'd pitched here since last October. But this is a new day and a new year."

The Yankees couldn't agree more.

STANDINGS AT THE END OF WEEK 12

American League East

	W.	L.	PCT.	G.B.
NEW YORK YANKEES	55	19	.743	-
Boston Red Sox	47	31	.603	10
Toronto Blue Jays	41	40	.506	17.5
Baltimore Orioles	37	44	.458	21.5
Tampa Bay Devil Rays	33	46	.418	24.5

GAME OF THE WEEK

JUNE 27, 1998 VS. NEW YORK METS

TINO TAKES YANK EXPRESS

Three-run HR railroads Mets

JUNE 28, 1998
By Thomas Hill, Daily News Sports Writer

WEEK 13 ● JUNE 21-27

Andy Pettitte was not perfect, but he was more than good enough. The team that played behind him had a few moments to savor, but not much else. The Yankees subtly reminded skeptics of their special position only because they won, again. The Mets were not impressed, just beaten.

The Yankees defeated the Mets, 7-2, yesterday at Shea before a second consecutive sellout crowd, this one numbering 53,587, clinching the much-anticipated showdown between the city's teams with one game left to play tonight. With Tino Martinez' fourth-inning, three-run home run supporting Pettitte, the Yankees turned the final act of this three-game set into nothing less than a moment of desperation for the Mets, who can only try to avoid a sweep.

"I hope no one feels this is a make-or-break series for our season," Mets catcher Mike Piazza said, "because it's not."

Strains of disappointment ran through the

Tino Martinez

DAILY NEWS   Linda Cataffo

ballpark all the same. With three-fourths of a once-energized stadium empty at the start of the ninth inning, remaining fans broke into a "Let's Go Yan-kees!" chant. They stood and cheered as Bernard Gilkey swung and missed at a full-count pitch from Mike Stanton for the final out. Those gathered around the visitors' dugout offered a final ovation as the Yankees left the field.

"Everyone was saying we were supposed to be good and we were supposed to win," Pettitte said. "We were the only ones that if we (lost), we were going to look bad."

By beating the Mets (42-34), the Yankees improved to 4-1 against them in the two years of interleague play. The Yankees (55-19) are eyeing their sixth sweep of a three-game series this season. The Mets lost for the seventh time in 11 games.

"We expect to win," Yankees manager Joe

Torre said. "We expect to win every game. There's a difference between expecting to and assuming to."

Pettitte, who endured a rocky start in the very first Mets-Yankees game last year, dominated this time. He allowed two runs on four hits and four walks over 6 1/3 innings. On a humid, overcast afternoon, Pettitte (9-5) took the air out of the Mets, totaling a season-high nine strikeouts.

What the Mets found most impressive about their Bronx counterparts was both their ability to succeed without great performances, and to overcome mistakes. The Yankees committed three errors, only one of them leading to a run. Butch Huskey scored in the second when Chuck Knoblauch made a wild relay throw to first on a double play attempt as Brian McRae took him out at second.

"I've seen two games where they're capitalized on mistakes, and capitalized very well," Mets manager Bobby Valentine said. "That's the sign of a great team. They're not intimidating. It's not like they're sending up Murderer's Row, but they got hits when they had to get hits . . . and they hit two three-run homers. I like both.

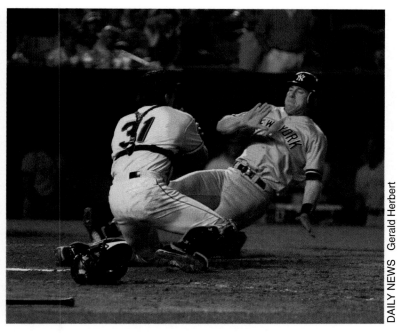

DAILY NEWS Gerald Herbert

The Yankees won the Subway Series against the Mets two games to one.

I'd like a lot more of those on my team."

Martinez took care of the three-run homer yesterday. He clubbed an 0-and-1 hanging curveball from Bobby Jones (6-5) into the Mets bullpen in the fourth to put the Yankees ahead for good. Jones, undermined by two errors, allowed seven runs, just three of them earned, on six hits and three walks.

FINAL

NEW YORK YANKEES 7, AT NEW YORK METS 2

NY YANKEES	ab	r	h	rbi	NY METS	ab	r	h	rbi
Knoblauch 2b	4	1	0	0	Alfonzo 3b	4	0	0	0
Jeter ss	5	0	1	2	B Gilkey lf	4	0	2	1
O'Neill rf	5	1	1	1	Piazza c	4	0	0	0
Strawberry lf	3	1	1	0	Olerud 1b	3	0	0	0
Ledee lf	0	0	0	0	Huskey rf	4	1	1	0
T Martinez 1b	3	2	2	3	Baerga 2b	3	0	0	0
J Posada c	4	1	2	0	Pulsipher p	0	0	0	0
Curtis cf	3	0	0	1	Wendell p	0	0	0	0
Brosius 3b	3	1	1	0	a-Pratt ph	1	0	0	0
Pettitte p	2	0	0	0	Hudek p	0	0	0	0
Buddie p	0	0	0	0	McRae cf	2	0	0	0
Stanton p	1	0	0	0	Ordonez ss	3	1	1	0
					B Jones p	2	0	1	0
					L Lopez 2b	2	0	0	0
Totals	33	7	8	7	Totals	32	2	5	1

HR - T Martinez.
a-fouled to catcher for Wendell in the 8th.

NY Yankees	000 300 400	— 7
NY Mets	010 000 100	— 2

NY Yankees	ip	h	r	er	bb	so	hr	era
Pettitte W	6 1/3	4	2	2	4	9	0	4.05
Buddie	1/3	0	0	0	0	0	0	8.22
Stanton	2 1/3	0	0	0	1	2	0	5.35

NY Mets	ip	h	r	er	bb	so	hr	era
B Jones L	6 2/3	6	7	3	3	1	1	3.94
Pulsipher	1/3	1	0	0	0	1	0	6.00
Wendell	1	1	0	0	1	1	0	4.44
Hudek	1	0	0	0	0	2	0	3.24

The Yankees' four-run seventh highlighted the difference between the clubs. Martinez led off with a double to right. Jorge Posada reached on a bunt single that sent Martinez to third. Chad Curtis hit a sacrifice fly to right. Brosius hit a grounder to Rey Ordonez, who tried to catch Posada at third, but hit him in the back. Jeter singled to center, driving home two runs and ending Jones' afternoon.

Bill Pulsipher came in to face O'Neill, but the lefty-lefty matchup did not work in the Mets' favor much better than Mel Rojas vs. O'Neill had worked Friday night. O'Neill singled to right, driving home Knoblauch for a 7-1 lead and putting the finishing touches on an understated expression of superiority.

"This is the first half of the season," Darryl Strawberry said. "We're just playing the type of baseball we're capable of playing."

From their prone vantage point, the Mets would tend to agree.

JUNE 21	SUN	at Cleveland Indians	0-11	L
JUNE 22	MON	Atlanta Braves	6-4	W
JUNE 23	TUES	Atlanta Braves	2-7	L
JUNE 24	WED	at Atlanta Braves	10-6	W
JUNE 25	THU	at Atlanta Braves	6-0	W
JUNE 26	FRI	at New York Mets	8-4	W
JUNE 27	SAT	at New York Mets	7-2	W

Believe the hype. Believe these are the teams you'll be seeing in October. And believe the Braves still have something to prove, a vendetta pickling in the juices of resentment for two seasons now.

SUBWAY SERIES INTERNATIONAL HIT

By Mark Kriegel, Daily News Sports Writer
June 23,1998

The Yankee-Mets subway series is a world series in its own right.

In the city known for being a melting pot, one-third of the two teams' rosters are made up of ballplayers born in foreign lands or Puerto Rico.

The teams, which meet in interleague play for three games at Shea Stadium starting Friday, have cornered the market on Japanese pitchers — Hideo Nomo and Masato Yoshii on the Mets, Hideki Irabu on the Yanks.

Australia, Cuba, Venezuela, Panama and the Dominican Republic, in addition to Japan and Puerto Rico, are represented on the rosters. The Yankees have nine players born outside the mainland U.S., the Mets, eight.

On Tuesday, the Mets sent to the minors Benny Agbayani, who had become the team's first Hawaiian ballplayer. The Yankees' pitching staff has been sparked by the presence of El Duque — Cuban emigre Orlando Hernandez. The Mets' star shortstop, Rey Ordonez, is also of Cuban background.

The Mets and Yankees also each have a representative from Venezuela — Edgardo Alfonzo and Luis Sojo. And the Yankees even have a player from Australia — left-handed relief specialist Graeme Lloyd.

DAILY NEWS **Gerald Herbert**

Yogi Berra

Robert Liebowitz and Joanne Johnstone, of Greenwich, Connecticut, with subway car hat he made, outside Shea Stadium prior to game.

DAILY NEWS Linda Cataffo

STANDINGS AT THE END OF WEEK 13

American League East	W.	L.	PCT.	G.B.
NEW YORK YANKEES	46	14	.766	--
Boston Red Sox	38	26	.593	10
Toronto Blue Jays	33	34	.493	16.5
Baltimore Orioles	32	35	.478	17.5
Tampa Bay Devil Rays	27	38	.435	21. 5

GAME OF THE WEEK

JULY 2, 1998 YANKEES VS. PHILADELPHIA PHILLIES

TINO POWERS YANKEE RALLY

Upper-decker in 9th paves way for Ledee

JULY 3, 1998

By Peter Botte, Daily News Sports Writer

All night they refused to quit, because these Yankees don't have the vaguest concept what that word means.

The feeling came long before Tino Martinez strode to the plate representing the tying run in a three-run game with two outs in the ninth. It came long before rookie Ricky Ledee became the latest improbable contributor to the runaway first-place cause with the game-winning RBI-single in the 11th inning.

There was just this feeling somewhere in the middle of the Yankees' miraculous 9-8 series-sweeping, multiple-comeback victory over the Phillies last night at The Stadium that somehow, in some way, some member of this incredible 25-man roster was going to find a way.

"That's really a great feeling for a manager," Joe Torre said, "to know your players don't ever phone it in, even when they get behind."

And make no mistake, the Yanks (58-20)

Yankees pitcher Hideki Irabu gave up three homers and five runs in four innings and was taken out by manager Joe Torre.

fell behind early in the latest disturbing performance by Hideki Irabu. Irabu was tagged for three more homers — including two by ex-Met Rico Brogna — and five runs last night in three-plus shoddy innings.

"I'm concerned, yeah. He's been inconsistent with his location and his stuff," Torre said. "If there's something physically wrong with him, we don't know about it."

Said Irabu, whose ERA has ballooned from a major league-leading 1.48 to its current 2.91 since June 20: "It's three games I haven't done well, and I realize I'm hurting the team," Irabu said. "I have no physical problems at all, but I just haven't been able to get out of trouble."

Instead, Irabu's teammates bailed him — and soon-to-be-suspended reliever Mike Stanton (2.1 IP, 3 R, 2 ER) — out of all sorts of trouble.

Darren Holmes hurled three scoreless innings of relief in his first appearance in 10 days. Chuck Knoblauch made a diving stab of Doug Glanville's smash to end the fourth. Tim Raines made a sweet running catch of Brogna's

DAILY NEWS Linda Cataffo

blast to the warning track in left and doubled off Scott Rolen at first to end the fifth.

Derek Jeter made a nifty scoop of a liner off Holmes' leg to start a double play in the sixth. Scott Brosius made a diving stop in the eighth.

But while Martinez (first of two), Jeter (career-high-tying 10th) and Paul O'Neill (11th) all had homered in the middle innings, the Yanks still trailed 8-5 heading into the ninth.

With two outs, Jeter rapped his third hit, a double to left-center. O'Neill then worked out a walk before Martinez crushed Mark Leiter's 2-1 pitch into the vacant seats in a closed-off section of the upper deck.

"He's like a pitcher throwing 95 miles per hour right now," Torre said. "His bat is flying through the strike zone."

Martinez' second homer of the game, 14th of the season and third in two nights might very well have been the biggest hit by a Yankee in a half-season chocked full of them.

"As soon as Tino got to the plate, guys knew something special was going to happen," said David Cone.

"To come through there, I was just glad it was my turn for once," said Martinez, who has slumped since the Armando Benitez beanbrawl in May, but still leads the team with 65 RBI after totaling eight in his last two games. "It just seems that every time those situations arise for us, the hot man is up."

Two innings later, it was Ledee's RBI single with the bases loaded in the 11th that enabled the Yanks to sweep the stunned Phillies.

Rookie Mike Buddie (3-0) hurled a scoreless 10th and 11th, and earned the win as the Yanks loaded the bases with no outs against reliever Jerry Spradlin on singles by O'Neill and Martinez and a walk to Darryl Strawberry.

Ledee, the heralded rookie who most likely will return to Columbus when Bernie Williams is activated from the DL, slapped a single up the middle past a drawn-in infield.

"Whatever happens, it made me feel like I contributed to the team, to another win," said Ledee, who entered the game as a pinch-runner for Tim Raines in the tenth.

"Just incredible," Cone said.

Sometimes they even surprise themselves.

FINAL

PHILADELPHIA PHILLIES 8, AT NEW YORK YANKEES 9

PHILADELPHIA	ab	r	h	rbi	NEW YORK	ab	r	h	rbi
Glanville-cf	5	1	1	0	Knoblauch-2b	5	1	1	0
Jefferies-lf	3	0	0	1	Jeter ss	6	2	3	1
Amaro-lf	2	0	0	0	O'Neill rf	5	3	2	2
Rolen-3b	5	0	1	0	T Martinez-1b	5	3	3	4
Brogna-1b	5	2	2	2	Strawberry-dh	3	0	0	0
K Jordan-dh	5	1	3	1	Raines-lf	3	0	0	0
Abreu-rf	3	0	0	0	Ledee pr-lf	1	0	1	1
Lieberthal-c	4	2	2	2	J Posada-c	5	0	2	1
M Lewis-2b	5	2	3	2	Curtis-cf	5	0	0	0
Relaford-ss	4	0	1	0	Brosius-3b	5	0	2	0
Totals	41	8	13	8	Totals	43	9	14	9

HR - Brogna 2 , M Lewis.   HR - T Martinez 2, Jeter , O'Neill.

Philadelphia	030 200 111 00	— 8
NY Yankees	000 101 033 01	— 9

Philadelphia	ip	h	r	er	bb	so	hr	era
Ty Green	6	5	2	2	1	7	2	4.60
Gomes	1 1/3	1	1	1	0	2	0	3.73
Y Perez	1/3	1	2	2	2	1	1	3.27
M Leiter BS	2 1/3	4	3	3	2	1	1	3.28
Spradlin L	0	3	1	1	1	0	0	3.92
NY Yankees	ip	h	r	er	bb	so	hr	era
Irabu	3	5	5	5	3	0	3	2.91
Holmes	3	2	0	0	0	2	0	4.50
Stanton	2 1/3	4	3	2	1	1	1	5.45
Buddie W	2 2/3	2	0	0	1	1	0	6.10

Irabu pitched to 4 batters in the 4th.
Spradlin pitched to 4 batters in the 11th.

Tino Martinez celebrates after hitting a three-run homer in the bottom of the 9th inning to tie the game and send it into extra innings.

JUNE 28	SUN	at New York Mets	1-2	L
JUNE 30	TUES	Philadelphia Phillies	9-2	W
JULY 1	WED	Philadelphia Phillies	5-2	W
JULY 2	THU	Philadelphia Phillies	9-8	W
JULY 3	FRI	Baltimore Orioles	3-2	W
JULY 4	SAT	Baltimore Orioles	4-3	W

"Everything they do they do as a team. They are like some great Yankee team out of the '50s, except that there is no Mantle here. There are names everybody knows. But the real star here is the whole band."

—Mike Lupica

FEW EGOS HERE, JUST REGULAR JOES

By Mike Lupica, Daily News Sports Writer
July 1, 1998

MIKE LUPICA

David Wells

DAILY NEWS Linda Cataffo

The fans who vote for the All-Star Game inadvertently pay the Yankees a huge compliment now, the best possible compliment to the best team in baseball, and don't elect a single starter to the American League team. It tells you everything about who these Yankees are, how they are doing this.

Everything they do they do as a team. They are like some great Yankee team out of the '50s, except that there is no Mantle here. There are names everybody knows. But the real star here is the whole band. Somebody new seems to step up every day and blow some big horn solo. Sometimes this looks like a baseball team with more of the old Knicks in them than the old Yankees.

"Or the old Celtics," Joe Torre said yesterday. "Everybody in double figures. That's the kind of ball we play."

In 1996, when the Yankees won it all, there was no position player in the top 10 of the MVP voting. Now no starter on the All-Star team, even if Tino Martinez came close to beating out Jim Thome. No Yankee is the star of the season because the whole room is the star.

"We'll be represented mightily on the All-Star team," Joe Torre said. "But no one around here is consumed with it. That's not our style."

So it becomes the height of style. No one appreciates it more than the manager, who looks around and sees ballplayers as professional as he is, no matter which way he looks.

"There's only one thing that really seems to aggravate these guys," Torre said. "And that is losing the game."

I would have Paul O'Neill in the AL starting lineup, on principle: He is the best player on the best team and he is having a better season than Kenny Lofton, who got elected. Derek Jeter could go start for the other league, but in his league he is up against Alex Rodriguez. Maybe Bernie Williams could have made a big move if he had stayed healthy.

And they had won 55 out of 75 games before last night. Only three teams in history — the '02 Pirates, '07 Cubs, Giants of 1912 — ever won 60 games out of their first 81. The Yankees still had a chance to get there going into the Phillies series. They beat you with clean, hardnosed baseball. The Mets saw that. "They capitalized on every single mistake," John Olerud said after the first two games of the Subway Series. You give them an opening, you pay.

And only one player on the field, Scott Brosius, is having a career year so far. Think about that. Martinez took a bullet to the back from Armando Benitez. Williams got hurt, Jeter got hurt. You know O'Neill has had better numbers in the books on July 1. Chuck Knoblauch hasn't even come close to showing us all the game he has.

The pitching staff is splendid, of course. David Wells and Hideki Irabu have been the two best guys for the Yankees from the first week of April until now. David Cone starts slow, comes on. Andy Pettitte starts slow, now look at him come on. And it was Orlando Hernandez, El Duque, who threw the best stuff at the

Scott Brosius

DAILY NEWS   Linda Cataffo

Mets. Ramiro Mendoza, who can't crack the first team, would be the ace of some staffs.

It is not all pitching. Sometimes it is the kind of three-run homer Paul O'Neill hits on Friday night against the Mets. The next day, Tino gets a three-run homer of his own off Bobby Jones. An inning looks like nothing and suddenly Knoblauch is on base and before you know it, you are gone. But they only kill you with the long ball occasionally. Nine teams in the league have more home runs. The '61 Yankees they are not.

They do it by using the whole park, moving the runner, getting the two-out hit, stealing bases. They keep putting people on base, and then they just wait for somebody new to come through.

"When they need a hit they get a hit," is the way Bobby Valentine put it after the Yankees-Mets series. "That's how it goes for you in a special season, and so far they are having a special season."

It is a special season. Special team. The manager knows better than anyone. He has the best seat in the most famous baseball house.

"I would love to tell you I'm surprised," Joe Torre said. "But I sensed something about these guys in the spring. I just didn't know we'd pitch this good."

Maybe there has been another team this good without a starter in an All-Star Game. No one could remember one yesterday. The season belongs to all of them. In the sports age of I and me, Torre's team only thinks in the first person plural.

STANDINGS AT THE END OF WEEK 14

American League East	W.	L.	PCT.	G.B.
NEW YORK YANKEES	64	20	.762	-
Boston Red Sox	52	36	.591	14
Toronto Blue Jays	46	45	.505	21.5
Baltimore Orioles	41	50	.451	26.5
Tampa Bay Devil Rays	34	55	.382	32.5

GAME OF THE WEEK

JULY 5, 1998 YANKEES VS. BALTIMORE ORIOLES

CURTIS TAKES ONE FOR TEAM

JULY 6, 1998

By Peter Botte, Daily News Sports Writer

WEEK 15 ● JULY 5-11

They are halfway there. Either halfway to a run at history that could eclipse their storied franchise's past, or halfway to a cataclysmic disappointment.

Now, there is no in-between for the 1998 Yankees; that much has been clear almost from the beginning of this dream first half, which concluded yesterday with what is now a familiar result.

But that doesn't mean the best team in baseball shouldn't take pride in the mind-boggling numbers it has compiled before the three-day All-Star respite begins today.

David Cone shut out the Orioles for eight

Chad Curtis

innings yesterday at the Stadium, and Chad Curtis was hit by a pitch with the bases loaded in the third to give the Yankees a 1-0 victory — the Yanks' sixth consecutive win and 61st in 81 games.

"We definitely should be proud about that," said Cone.

"We know it's a long season, and everyone is conditioned to downplay the start and downplay everything. . . . But in essence, we should be proud. It's a great start and a great accomplishment to be mentioned with the best teams of all-time."

To most, though, it's still not the primary goal, nor the primary focus. Their ho-hum

DAILY NEWS   Linda Cataffo

blanking of the listing Orioles before 52,506 on Cap Day at the Stadium tied the Yankees with the 1902 Pirates and the 1907 Cubs for the best 81-game starts in major league history.

Ahead are runs at both the American League mark for victories in a season by the 1954 Indians (111) and the major league mark of 116 by the 1906 Cubs.

"It's nice, but it only means something if we win our last game of the year," said Joe Girardi, who clearly was not speaking about the regular-season finale on Sept. 27 against Tampa Bay.

"Those kinds of records are always nice to look back on later, but you don't get a ring for what you do in the first half of a season," said All-Star shortstop Derek Jeter, who left with three teammates for Denver following the game. "We don't look at what records we can set. If we don't win the World Series, it doesn't make a difference."

Joe Torre warned about the 1954 season, when "the Yankees won 103 games and lost the pennant by eight games to a team (Cleveland) that won 111 games in a 154-game schedule and then lost four straight to the Giants (in the World Series).

"The record means something to me. It means you had a dominant first half. But you need to play both halves," Torre said.

"You have to be very cautious and not get too overconfident, or thinking that we don't have to work hard. That's what we basically need to do the rest of the way. We have to work hard and get to what our goal is."

Yesterday, Cone (12-2) — who may not have had his ticket punched for Denver — was magnificent in tying Texas' Aaron Sele for the AL lead with 12 victories, one more than All-Star teammate David Wells.

Cone scattered seven hits, struck out four and didn't walk a batter for the third straight game, the first time

in his career he has pulled off that feat. In 14 starts since allowing 16 earned runs in his first two starts this season, the 35-year-old righty has gone 11-1 with a 2.95 ERA.

The Yankees' lone run off hard-luck loser Scott Erickson scored when Curtis was hit by a pitch on the left shoulder with the bases loaded and one out in the third. Mariano Rivera hurled a perfect ninth for his 22d save.

Torre simply shook his head. "One-nothing and a hit batter?" he said. "That's nuts. Nuts."

No crazier, however, than a half-season already defined by such moments. One that either has placed the Yankees on the brink of history or has set them up for a great pitfall.

FINAL

BALTIMORE ORIOLES 0, AT NEW YORK YANKEES 1

BALTIMORE	ab	r	h	rbi	NEW YORK	ab	r	h	rbi
R Alomar-2b	4	0	0	0	Jeter ss	3	0	1	0
B Anderson-cf	3	0	2	0	Sojo 2b	4	1	1	0
Reboulet ss	0	0	0	0	O'Neill rf	4	0	2	0
E Davis dh	4	0	1	0	T Martinez 1b	3	0	1	0
R Palmeiro 1b	4	0	1	0	Raines dh	2	0	0	0
Surhoff lf	4	0	0	0	Curtis cf	3	0	0	1
C Ripken 3b	4	0	1	0	Ledee lf	4	0	0	0
Carter rf	3	0	1	0	Sveum 3b	4	0	1	0
Webster c	3	0	1	0	Girardi c	3	0	1	0
Bordick ss	2	0	0	0					
a-Becker ph-cf	1	0	0	0					
Totals	32	0	7	0	Totals	30	1	7	1

a-grounded to second for Bordick in the 8th.

Baltimore	000 000 000	—	0
NY Yankees	001 000 00X	—	1

Baltimore	ip	h	r	er	bb	so	hr	era
Erickson L	8	7	1	1	4	7	0	4.24

NY Yankees	ip	h	r	er	bb	so	hr	era
Cone W	8	7	0	0	0	4	0	4.05
Rivera S	1	0	0	0	0	1	0	1.14

"We know it's a long season, and everyone is conditioned to downplay the start and downplay everything. . . . But in essence, we should be proud. It's a great start and a great accomplishment to be mentioned with the best teams of all-time."

—David Cone

REST OF THE WEEK

JULY 5	SUN	Baltimore Orioles	1-0	W
JULY 9	THU	at Tampa Bay Devil Rays	2-0	W
JULY 10	FRI	at Tampa Bay Devil Rays	8-4	W
JULY 11	SAT	at Tampa Bay Devil Rays	2-0	W

"I've seen better line-ups in this place. I'm not sure I've ever seen a better team."
—Jerry Antonucci, Yankee Stadium worker for 42 years.

THE '61' YANKS OF '98

Win total is magical digit heading into All-Star break

By Mike Lupica, Daily News Sports Writer
July 6, 1998

MIKE LUPICA

The Yankees got to 61 wins yesterday and once again that was a magic number at Yankee Stadium. Back in 1961, Roger Maris hit 61 home runs and beat Babe Ruth's record, which was 60 and looked as if it would stand forever. Now, all this time later, the Yankees' record goes to 61-20 at the All-Star break, and no baseball team in this century has ever done better than that. It is only one of the great seasons, at least so far, the city has ever seen, in baseball or anything else.

These Yankees, the Yankees of Joe Torre and Paul O'Neill and David Cone and Derek Jeter and the rest, got to 61 by beating the Orioles 1-0 yesterday. Cone got his 12th win.

Mariano Rivera got the save. There were 50,000 people at Yankee Stadium to watch. Once again, it

Derek Jeter fans.

DAILY NEWS Linda Cataffo

is the best stage for the best team in baseball, maybe one of the best Yankee teams anyone has ever seen.

To here, all the Yankees have done is beat the rest of the American League, and the record books. To be remembered with the '27 Yankees or the '61 Yankees or even the Yankees who turned the city upside down in October of '96, they must close the deal and win it all. But the October season is something for down the road. For now there is this summer at the Stadium. This amazing record.

This amazing baseball team.

"They can't do nuthin' wrong," Jerry Antonucci said yesterday morning.

He is with Local 176, Licensed Ushers and Ticket Takers, and he has been working at Yankee Stadium for 42 years. So he has seen plenty, sneaking his looks since the summer of 1956 from behind Gate 2 or 4 or 6. Yesterday he came walking past the ticket windows, past the red calliope set up for Fourth of July weekend, toward the crowd of people already lined up near the players' entrance at 9:30, waiting for the Yankees to show up and win again.

"I've seen better lineups in this place," Jerry Antonucci said. "I'm not sure I've ever seen a better team."

A couple of years ago, the Chicago Bulls finished with a regular-season record of 72-10 in the NBA. That is the kind of summer the Yankees are now having. A Michael Jordan summer at the Stadium. You might never see another summer like it in this world.

They started off 1-4 and we worried about the safety of Torre. Since then, they are 60-16. Ridiculous numbers. Only the Cubs of '07 and the Pirates of '02 ever got to 61-20 at this point in the season. The Yankees of 1928 and 1939 were 58-23 after 81 games. These Yankees blow past them now, the way they blow past the league.

They do nothin' wrong, all the way into the All-Star break.

More than 140,000 fans paid to watch the Yankee-Orioles series this weekend. Rudy Giuliani, the official Yankee team mascot, and George Steinbrenner keep panhandling for a new Yankee

Fans turned out in droves to see the Yankees.

Stadium, even as this Yankee team is on its way to breaking the team's all-time home attendance record.

At 9:45 a.m., Yankee first baseman Tino Martinez is already out of the parking lot, down the stairs, making his way to the Yankee clubhouse. The game doesn't start for four hours. There are plenty of players already in the clubhouse ahead of Martinez. It is as if they race each other to the ballpark every day.

"Oh, don't worry, we appreciate what we're doing," Martinez said on the day when he and his teammates hit 61. "And we appreciate where we're doing it."

The Yankees smack the rest of baseball around the way Mark McGwire smacks home runs. They do it with 9-8 wins like they had against the Phillies the other night. They do it nice and neat and clean, the way Cone and Rivera did it to the Orioles yesterday.

Some of the Yankees go to the All-Star Game in Denver now. The rest get a vacation. It will probably make them crazy. They don't get to beat somebody until the Devil Rays on Thursday night.

"You read those standings every day," Jerry Antonucci of Local 176 said, "and you can't believe your eyes."

Sixty-one wins today. Another magic 61 at the Stadium. Read that today in the standings. Believe that.

STANDINGS AT THE END OF WEEK 15

American League East

	W.	L.	PCT.	G.B.
NEW YORK YANKEES	68	23	.747	-
Boston Red Sox	56	39	.589	14
Toronto Blue Jays	49	50	.495	23
Baltimore Orioles	47	50	.485	24
Tampa Bay Devil Rays	36	60	.375	34.5

YANKEE PROFILE
SCOTT BROSIUS

SCOTT SUITED FOR PINSTRIPES
Brosius is perfect fit

AUGUST 10,1998
By Lisa Olson, Daily News Sports Writer

3B

Scott Brosius

He was sitting in a restaurant in White Plains, a place called City Diner, about to tuck into a steak dinner, his wife and three kids by his side. This is when Scott Brosius realized life as a Bronx Bomber can get quite insane.

He had heard about the Yankee mystique, of course. Even though he grew up in a place called Milwaukie, Oregon— "Yes, the people there know how to spell. I guess they just wanted to be different than Wisconsin," Brosius says with a laugh — the Yankees were Oregon's team. If the kids at Rex Putnam High School weren't wearing Trailblazers hats, they were wearing caps with the intertwined NY. Maury Brosius, Scott's father, memorized everything he could about Mickey Mantle, including his shoe size.

Later, when Brosius was wearing Mantle's No. 7 as a relatively anonymous infielder for the Oakland A's, he would visit Yankee Stadium twice a year. He would listen incredulously to the catcalls and the boos and the constant chatter that flowed like a fire hose from the stands, and still he'd wonder: What would it be like to play here all the time? How fun would it be to dress in Mantle's pinstripes?

"I had no idea it would be like this," says Brosius, the Yankees first-year third baseman. "I played for the A's for six years and could still go to a restaurant and not get recognized. It took me all of two days in New York for people to notice me. I knew but I didn't know quite how much the fans were into the team and how heavily they follow them. The attention the Yankees get is just incredible. I understand the fans are die-hard, but I didn't know to what extreme."

It is a good extreme, says Brosius, even for a guy who never saw a big league game until 1987, his first year of A ball. There weren't a lot of famous baseball players roaming the streets of Milwaukie, unless you count Brosius' grandfather and great-grandfather, both of whom were decent semi-pro players. Maury played a mean game of fast-pitch softball. Raised in Oregon's lush wine country, Scott was equal parts genes

Gov. Pataki gives Scott Brosius a special MVP license plate.

DAILY NEWS Bill Turnbull

and talent — blond, buff, tan, his high school jacket covered in letters from three different sports.

"Aw, don't make it sound like I was the All-American kid," he says. "I wasn't top dog or anything. I didn't do much in football because I was always afraid of getting bashed."

Defensive back and kicker were more his style. These days, he's still Mr. Everyman, the Jimmy Stewart of baseball. This season he has 67 RBI — including a home run in yesterday's win over Kansas City — from the 7th, 8th and 9th spots in the batting order, the most in the majors from those positions. When he's not at the hot corner, he looks like he should be doing your taxes or fixing your air conditioning.

"To come to New York can be a tough thing to do but Scott's fit in so well," says right fielder Paul O'Neill. "He's had a great year defensively. What more can we ask for? He's a good person, and when you bring that to the table it makes it easier for everyone."

DAILY NEWS   Keith Torrie

One of Scott Brosius' many fans.

re-energized swing that has him hitting .289.

The same day he found out he was an All-Star, Brosius learned his father's colon cancer was in remission. There is nothing that will ever match the joy that came with learning Maury could live long enough to see his son finish his career in pinstripes, with Mantle's team, especially since Scott's mother died of cancer nine years ago. But a ticker tape parade would still be something. It might even be more insane than all of Oregon was back in 1977, when the Trailblazers won the NBA championship.

"I remember our neighborhood after that, it was like the Fourth of July," says Brosius. "Everybody went out banging pans and all this stuff, making a lot of noise."

He leans back and smiles again. It's supposed to be bad luck for baseball players to think beyond the here and now. Brosius allows his mind to wander

Especially when you bring All-Star credentials, something Brosius, 31, did for the first time this year when he was named to the AL team. Traded for the much-maligned Kenny Rogers during the off-season, Brosius went from batting .203 last year at Oakland to representing the Yankees in Colorado in July thanks to a

nonetheless.

" I can only imagine what it's going to be like," he says of what many in baseball think is inevitable.

"You see how the people are who follow the team now. I can imagine the parades and things like if we won the World Series. It would just be mind-boggling."

Scott Brosius Stats

1998 REGULAR SEASON

AVG.	G	AB	R	H	TB	2B	3B	HR	RBI	BB	SO	SB	CS	SH	SF	HP	SLG%	OBP%
.302	151	527	86	159	250	34	0	19	98	52	97	11	8	8	3	10	.474	.373

GAME OF THE WEEK

JULY 12, 1998 YANKEES VS. TAMPA BAY DEVIL RAYS

ODYSSEY WITH HOMER

Bush keys Yanks' win

JULY 3, 1998

By Peter Botte, Daily News Sports Writer

There are so few chances to open eyes, so few chances to contribute to the runaway train that this Yankees' season has become. But Homer Bush always remains prepared for when those opportunities arise.

In the seventh inning — and again in the eighth — of a tie game between two polar opposite clubs, that predictably would end up just another 9-2 score in the blink of an eye — this was a game that was just begging for one member or another of the Yankees' passel of stars to keep them on track toward history.

Only, there was Homer Bush — the little-used rookie and 25th man on baseball's deepest team — ardently stretching and doing wind sprints inside the Yankees clubhouse just in case this would be one of his few opportunities to chip in to the cause.

As it turned out, Bush pinch-ran for Darryl Strawberry with no outs in the ninth inning

Darryl Strawberry

DAILY NEWS Mike Albans

and twice legged out sacrifice bunts to fuel a seven-run outburst. And just like that, the Devil Rays were swept away with a 9-2 beating yesterday before 43,373 at Tropicana Field.

"It's a luxury that we have with our record (65-20), that we can have a guy like Homer here," Joe Torre said after his team's 10th consecutive win. "He is such an aggressive kid. We send him out there to do what he does."

And so, the best team in baseball continues to do what it does, which is force statisticians to scramble for the record books time and again.

The Yankees are 45 games over .500 for the first time since the end of the 1963 season. Their now-15-game lead over Boston in the AL East is their largest since August 12, 1958 — and thus, their largest since divisional play began.

And with one more victory tonight in

Cleveland, they will own the best start in modern baseball history. The '02 Pirates got to 65-20, but were unable to secure win No. 66 one game later.

"This team is just incredible, that's all you can say," said Mike Stanton (4-0), who earned the victory in relief in his first appearance since returning from a five-game suspension. "Win or lose, we battle until the final out. And it seems somebody different plays the hero every night."

With David Wells (day-to-day) leaving after five innings with a bruised big toe on his right foot, Ramiro Mendoza was charged with a single run over 2 2/3 inning to give the Devil Rays false hope of salvaging one game of the opening four-game set of the second half.

And never before has a pitcher so personally dominated every play in one inning — especially in such a negative manner — as Tampa closer Roberto Hernandez did in what began as a 2-2 tie in the ninth.

The first five batters Hernandez faced resulted in one walk, two defensive miscues by him on sacrifice attempts, one strikeout and a hit batsman with the bases loaded to plate the go-ahead run.

Hernandez, the Rays' $22.5 million free-agent investment, walked Strawberry leading off the inning.

Bush came on to pinch-run, took what he called his "4 1/2 step stealing lead" and was ruled safe on a close play at second as Hernandez was indecisive on a bunt by Chad Curtis (3-for-4).

David Wells pitched five innings against the Devil Rays.

FINAL

NEW YORK YANKEES 9, AT TAMPA BAY DEVIL RAYS 2

BALTIMORE	ab	r	h	rbi	NEW YORK	ab	r	h	rbi
R Alomar-2b	4	0	0	0	Jeter ss	3	0	1	0
B Anderson-cf	3	0	2	0	Sojo 2b	4	1	1	0
Reboulet ss	0	0	0	0	O'Neill rf	4	0	2	0
E Davis dh	4	0	1	0	T Martinez 1b	3	0	1	0
R Palmeiro 1b	4	0	1	0	Raines dh	2	0	0	0
Surhoff lf	4	0	0	0	Curtis cf	3	0	0	1
C Ripken 3b	4	0	1	0	Ledee lf	4	0	0	0
Carter rf	3	0	1	0	Sveum 3b	4	0	1	0
Webster c	3	0	1	0	Girardi c	3	0	1	0
Bordick ss	2	0	0	0					
a-Becker ph-cf	1	0	0	0					
Totals	32	0	7	0	Totals	30	1	7	1

a-grounded to second for Bordick in the 8th.

Baltimore	000 000 000	—	0
NY Yankees	001 000 00X	—	1

Baltimore	ip	h	r	er	bb	so	hr	era
Erickson L	8	7	1	1	4	7	0	4.24

NY Yankees	ip	h	r	er	bb	so	hr	era
Cone W	8	7	0	0	0	4	0	4.05
Rivera S	1	0	0	0	0	1	0	1.14

Bush next beat Hernandez' bounced throw to third on another sac attempt by Scott Brosius to load the bases with no outs.

"Even in blowout games, I always feel like I have to get a hit, just to make an impression on Joe . . . to tell him I'm still around if he needs me," said the 25-year-old Bush, who has just 22 at-bats all season.

"He won us a ballgame in Cleveland one night (earlier this season) going first to third just like (yesterday)," Torre said.

"He's a luxury; you just don't know how much longer we can afford to have someone out there just to pinch-run in close games. But I'm glad we have him."

After Ricky Ledee struck out, Chuck Knoblauch — in his second consecutive feisty offensive game despite officially going just 1-for-4 — was plunked on the back of the left shoulder by Hernandez's 1-2 forkball to force in the go-ahead run.

Derek Jeter's two-run single chased Hernandez, before Tampa native Tino Martinez (four RBI) ripped a three-run double to blow off the teflon roof on yet another positive result.

"We haven't been hitting . . . and (Tampa was) in every game," Torre said.

"But it all fell out for us at one time. Hopefully the ninth is the start of something for us."

REST OF THE WEEK

JULY 12	SUN	at Tampa Bay Devil Rays	9-2	W
JULY 13	MON	at Cleveland Indians	1-4	L
JULY 14	TUES	at Cleveland Indians	7-1	W
JULY 15	WED	at Detroit Tigers	11-0	W
JULY 16	THU	at Detroit Tigers	1-3	L
JULY 17	FRI	at Toronto Blue Jays	6-9	L
JULY 18	SAT	at Toronto Blue Jays	10-3	W

"He said the kind of injury I had is not going to be a problem in the long run," said Williams, still the AL's leading hitter at .353. "I should be able to do whatever I feel I can do, using common sense."

BERNIE GETS GOOD NEWS

By Peter Botte, Daily News Sports Writer
July 13, 1998

Bernie Williams finally was told what he wanted to hear. And the steamrolling Yankees might be getting back their leading hitter and Gold Glove center fielder as early as this weekend in Toronto.

With the Yankees medical staff wavering on how much Williams should be allowed to do — and how soon — Williams boarded George Steinbrenner's private jet in Tampa before Saturday night's game. A puddle-jump flight to Fort Lauderdale later, he consulted with Marlins team physician Dr. Dan Kanell for a second opinion on his improving right knee.

"There was just a slight disparity in opinion (among Yankees personnel), but his was a different opinion," said Williams. "(Dr. Kanell) was more favorable in terms of being more aggressive in the rehab process."

Dr. Kanell, father of Giants QB Danny Kanell,

Bernie Williams

DAILY NEWS Linda Cataffo

told Williams that as long as he is able to withstand whatever residual pain will linger in the knee he strained on June 10, there is little chance of him aggravating the injury.

The 29-year-old Williams, of course, suffered a minor setback last Monday in the first-game of a minor-league rehab assignment.

"He said the kind of injury I had is not going to be a problem in the long run," said Williams, still the AL's leading hitter at .353. "I should be able to do whatever I feel I can do, using common sense, of course."

Wearing a protective brace, Williams participated in a batting-practice session thrown by disabled reliever Jeff Nelson before yesterday's 9-2 victory. He will remain at the team's Tampa training complex today, and hopes to embark on his second try at a minor-league rehab stint by the middle of the week.

"Hopefully, I'll start playing in a couple of days," Williams said.

Asked if he had concerns about possibly returning on SkyDome's artificial surface — when he could just as easily wait for the Yanks to return home Monday — Williams could not be deterred. "I've tested the last few days on the turf here and I've had no problems," he said. "I'll have to play on it eventually. I'm ready to play. I'll be an all-surface kind of guy."

Yankee brass didn't attempt to discourage his optimism. "I think towards the end of the weekend (in Toronto), or back in New York, we'll see him again," GM Brian Cashman confirmed.

"I've tested the last few days on the turf here and I've had no problems. I'll have to play on it eventually. I'm ready to play. I'll be an all-surface kind of guy."
—Bernie Williams

DAILY NEWS Linda Cataffo

Bernie Williams (center) during a Yankee workout.

STANDINGS AT THE END OF WEEK 16

American League East

	W.	L.	PCT.	G.B.
NEW YORK YANKEES	72	26	.735	-
Boston Red Sox	59	43	.578	15
Toronto Blue Jays	52	52	.500	23
Baltimore Orioles	52	53	.495	23.5
Tampa Bay Devil Rays	39	62	.386	34.5

TIGERS 4, YANKEES 3 (17 INN.)
YANKEES 4, TIGERS 3

GAME OF THE WEEK

JULY 20, 1998 YANKEES VS. DETROIT TIGERS

YANKS' FIRST IS THE WORST

But after loss in 17, Hideki gains split

JULY 21, 1998

By Rafael Hermoso, Daily News Sports Writer

Joe Torre spent part of yesterday afternoon basking in his Yankee Stadium surroundings and telling us why the Yankees won't rest on their big cushion.

Oops.

The Yankees lost for only the 25th time this season in the first game of last night's doubleheader, but it was easily their most frustrating defeat. With the game nearly six hours in the making, they were unable to dent the fourth-worst pitching staff in the AL.

Ten innings after he tied the game, Joe Randa hit a two-out single to center field off Darren Holmes in the top of the 17th to lead the Tigers to a 4-3 win. It was the longest game for both teams since they played 18 innings on Sept. 11, 1988. The Yankees' record for most innings is also against the Tigers: 22 at Detroit in 1962.

In the second game, Hideki Irabu pitched seven-plus innings in leading the Yankees to a 4-3 win and a morale-boosting split that lasted

nine hours and 11 minutes, was witnessed at one point by 36,285, and ended at 1:17 a.m. Detroit's Brian Hunter ended the marathon by grounding out, setting a major league record by going 0-for-13 in the twin bill.

The Yankees left 22 runners on base in game 1 of the doubleheader.

DAILY NEWS Mike Albans

"It was real important," Derek Jeter said. "We don't like to lose. We felt we blew the first game. We had a lot of opportunities to score."

The AL's 1 a.m. curfew was waived because it was the Tigers' last trip to New York. The first game began at 4:06 p.m. and ended five hours and 50 minutes later. Game 2 began at 10:32 p.m. and lasted 2:45.

"I told everybody if this game goes until midnight, they're all eligible," joked Torre, whose team lost for the fourth time in five games. "A couple of guys bit on it."

In retrospect, Torre won't find much humor in this pre-game quote: "The thing I'm glad about is normally when you come home from a trip like we had and have a doubleheader, you're dragging. These guys are animated. The only reason I say that is whatever happens today, it's not because we're dragging."

The Yankees, who had been on the road since the All-Star break, left the bases loaded in the eighth, 10th,

> ## "It was real important," Derek Jeter said. "We don't like to lose. We felt we blew the first game. We had a lot of opportunities to score."

12th and 15th innings. They left 22 runners on base, nearly breaking the 71-year-old franchise record. The 1927 Yankees stranded 23 in a 12-11, 18-inning loss in the first game of a doubleheader at Boston. The major league record is 25.

Helped by five Yankees double plays, the Tigers left nine men on base.

"It's not a concern," Torre said. "It's a little frustrating. Guys can only do what they can do."

The Yankees went 1-for-19 with runners in scoring position, including 0-for-their-last-16. Heck, when Jeter singled home Joe Girardi in the third inning of Game 2, it snapped a 16-inning scoreless streak by the Yankees.

Torre went through all six of his relievers in Game 1, including Holmes (0-3), who pitched the final 2 2/3 innings. How much more did Holmes' arm have left? "Who knows?" Torre said, "but we were going to drain it."

With another game to play, Torre was anything but conservative. He said catcher Joe Girardi or infielder Luis Sojo would've pitched next.

"You have to think of the first game," Torre said. "That's all you can think about. We had the game in hand."

After building a 3-0 lead in the first three innings, the Yankees plodded through the next 14.

In the seventh inning, Jorge Posada approached David Wells on the mound in an obvious attempt to buy Ramiro Mendoza more time to warm up. Wells soon was replaced by Torre and stalked off, and Randa hit Mendoza's third pitch for a single to right, scoring Gabe Alvarez to tie the game at 3-3.

FINAL
DETROIT TIGERS 4, AT NEW YORK YANKEES 3

DETROIT	ab	r	h	rbi	NEW YORK	ab	r	h	rbi
Bl Hunter cf	8	0	0	0	Knoblauch 2b	8	0	0	0
Easley ss 2b	7	0	3	1	Jeter ss	8	2	4	0
Higginson rf	6	0	1	0	O'Neill rf	7	1	3	1
To Clark 1b	7	0	1	0	B Williams cf	8	0	3	2
Berroa dh	3	1	2	0	T Martinez 1b	6	0	0	0
K Bartee pr dh	3	0	0	0	Strawberry dh	3	0	0	0
L Gonzalez lf	6	1	1	0	Raines ph dh	2	0	0	0
G Alvarez 3b	6	1	1	0	Bush pr dh	1	0	0	0
D Cruz ss	0	0	0	0	Sveum ph	0	0	0	0
Casanova c	2	0	0	0	J Posada c	6	0	0	0
Bako c	4	0	2	1	Curtis lf	6	0	0	0
Randa 2b 3b	7	1	3	2	Brosius 3b	6	0	0	0
Totals	59	4	14	4	Totals	32	4	10	3

Detroit	000 001 200 000 000 01	—	4
NY Yankees	102 000 000 000 000 00	—	3

Detroit	ip	h	r	er	bb	so	hr	era
Greisinger	6	4	3	3	4	3	0	5.30
M Anderson	1	0	0	0	1	1	0	.82
Runyan	1/3	1	0	0	2	1	0	3.27
Brocail	1 2/3	1	0	0	1	1	0	3.55
T Jones	1	0	0	0	2	0	0	5.06
Bochtler	2	2	0	0	2	0	0	4.78
Crow	3	3	0	0	3	1	0	2.15
Sager W	2	1	0	0	0	0	0	7.18

NY Yankees	ip	h	r	er	bb	so	hr	era
Wells	6 2/3	8	3	3	0	2	0	3.69
Mendoza Bs	2/3	2	0	0	0	0	0	3.62
Stanton	1 1/3	0	0	0	3	0	0	6.09
Rivera	1 1/3	0	0	0	1	0	0	1.50
Buddie	2 1/3	1	0	0	1	0	0	5.17
Llyod	2	0	0	0	0	2	0	2.01
Holmes L	2 2/3	3	1	1	0	1	0	4.76

Losing pitcher Darren Holmes of the Yankees walks back to the mound after giving up the winning run in the 17th inning of the first game.

REST OF THE WEEK

JULY 19	SUN	at Toronto Blue Jays	9-3	L
JULY 20	MON	Detroit Tigers	4-3	W
JULY 20	MON	Detroit Tigers	4-3	W
JULY 21	TUES	Detroit Tigers	5-1	W
JULY 22	WED	Detroit Tigers	13-2	W
JULY 24	FRI	Chicago White Sox	5-4	W
JULY 25	SAT	Chicago White Sox	2-6	L

> "They always think they are supposed to win the game, even when they are in a stretch like they are right now where they play the kind of scratchy baseball they played the first week of the season . . ."
> —Mike Lupica

FINALLY, THERE'S ONE BOMBERS CAN'T WIN

By Mike Lupica
July 21, 1998

MIKE LUPICA

The long day and night seemed to begin when Paul O'Neill made a wonderful running catch in the outfield, stopped himself short of the right-field wall, wheeled and made a perfect throw to Tino Martinez. The throw doubled Geronimo Berroa off first base and it was the kind of play the Yankees have made all season, as they have found a way to make all the plays and win the game. Now O'Neill had doubled in a run in the bottom of the first and started this double play in the top of the second and the Yankees were on their way again. The start of this one only looked like the whole summer.

And no one knew at the time, with the sun high in the sky and the Yankees and Tigers ready to play a doubleheader, that the Yankees were on their way to an amazing loss in what has been an amazing season of winning. They would blow a 3-0 lead to the Tigers. They eventually would blow one bases-loaded opportunity after another and leave 22 men on base and hit 1-for-19 with runners in scoring position and lose 4-3 to the Tigers in 17 innings.

"We were trying to keep the game going until we were supposed to win it," Joe Torre said afterward.

They always think they are supposed to win the game, even when they are in a stretch like they are right now, when they play the kind of scratchy baseball they played the first week of the season and actually had us worrying about Torre's job. Since then they have done some job on the American League and anybody the National League has sent their way. They have won games around big brawls. They came back and tied the Phillies one night with a three-run homer from Tino Martinez in the bottom of the ninth, beat them in extra innings, of course.

One day they got behind 11-0 to the Red Sox with Pedro Martinez pitching and even that day, the Yankees tried to come back. If the Red Sox second baseman hadn't made a tremendous play on Jorge Posada, the Yankees would have come back to 11-9, with the tying run at the plate. The Red Sox would win 13-7 finally, but only after this Yankee team, one that will play you all the way to the front door of the bus, had scared them half to death.

So they would keep playing yesterday, for nearly six hours in the first game of a doubleheader, until they were supposed to win. Because that is what they do. They are the '98 Yanks. They are supposed to win today's game, and then the league and finally the

World Series. They are supposed to give themselves a chance to win more regular-season games than any Yankee team has ever won. They have set the bar as high as any Yankee team ever has. And built a season where anything less than winning it all will turn 110 or 115 victories into one of the great disappointments in Yankee history.

"We always feel that second place is not an option," Joe Torre said before the 17 innings of Game 1.

In the clubhouse, Darryl Strawberry was talking about the Mets of 1986. They won 108 games in the regular season. Another team that was supposed to win.

"It wasn't easy, as good as we were," Darryl Strawberry said. "All eyes were on us, all season. Everybody wanted to beat us, every day."

Strawberry paused in front of his locker, a huge box of mail at his feet, smiled.

"Seasons like this look easy," he said. "And they're real hard."

It all looked hard enough for the Yankees in Game 1 yesterday, the way it looked hard against Toronto over the weekend. All those bases-loaded chances, even after the Tigers came back to 3-3. Jorge Posada took a called third strike one time and flied out to the wall another time. Chuck Knoblauch tried to win the game

DAILY NEWS Linda Cataffo

Paul O'Neill doubled in a run in the Yankees' 4-3 loss to the Tigers.

himself with the bases loaded, and hit a bullet to right field. Caught. The way the Tigers caught the Yankees yesterday, then passed them a few minutes before 10 o'clock.

All across the six hours the Yankees made splendid plays in the field, the way they have across the summer. O'Neill's double play. A diving play by Chad Curtis, going toward the left-field wall. Knoblauch slashing in front of second base, gunning a throw across his body. Bernie Williams, back where he belongs in the outfield, running one down in left-center, running all the way until his glove was at the top of the blue wall.

All it got any of them was a fourth loss in five games. Derek Jeter led off the bottom of the 17th with a single. But O'Neill hit into a 6-4-3 double play. Williams flied out, it was finally over. O'Neill had thrown a fist into the air after he started that double play early. Now he stood in a corner of the dugout, staring out at the field, watching the Tigers celebrate as though they had won a title.

Everybody wants to beat the Yankees. Every day. Tough loss. Long game. The Yankees hope the rest of the summer doesn't feel this way.

STANDINGS AT THE END OF WEEK 17

American League East	W.	L.	PCT.	G.B.
NEW YORK YANKEES	77	27	.740	-
Boston Red Sox	64	44	.593	15
Toronto Blue Jays	55	55	.500	25
Baltimore Orioles	55	56	.495	25.5
Tampa Bay Devil Rays	43	64	.402	35.5

BERNIE PLAYS IT HIS WAY — WITH CLASS

SEPTEMBER 27, 1998

By Jim Dwyer, Daily News Sports Writer

Bernie Williams ● OF

DiMaggio moved across center field, the old-timers always said, as if he were on skates that could cover acres of grass with one mere glide. But DiMaggio is nearly 50 years out of the game. And the sprawling center field in Yankee Stadium has shrunk since then, with shorter fences and less room to gallop.

Too bad.

Because in all professional sports, no one moves like the man who has played center field in Yankee Stadium for the last five years: Bernabé Figueroa Williams of Bayamón, Puerto Rico. Sometimes, all that stops him from chasing flyballs clear to the Grand Concourse is the center field fence.

This afternoon, Bernie Williams could win his first league batting championship and play his last regular season game for this team. "This is where I became a man," he was saying the other night. "I do like it here, but I have an open mind."

He has been around so long that people forget how far he has come. All the familiar pictures of Williams are true, but not true enough. He plays classical guitar, speaks softly and thoughtfully. He arrives in the clubhouse at a dead run, with about two minutes to jump into his uniform. And he naps after batting

Bernie Williams acknowledges the crowd's cheers after he clinched the American League batting title.

DAILY NEWS Linda Cataffo

practice — "That's no joke," says his friend, left fielder Tim Raines. "He wakes up at 7:15 for a 7:30 game."

Then he gets on base, and rockets from first to third, the speed coiled around strength. The sleepy manner turns out to be just the mask of a very determined man.

"Who were my most important teachers?" said Williams. "The Cap — Don Mattingly. Cecil Fielder showed me you can have a lot of fun in this game, all year round."

Then he drops an all but forgotten name.

"Mel Hall," he said.

How so?

"He had a real commitment to make my life miserable in every way he knew how. Good-natured? I wouldn't say that."

Hall would jab Williams over every rookie blunder, riding him to the point of tears. Finally, the management decided to dump Hall and protect Williams' psyche. "Whether he meant it or not, he taught me how to be mentally tough," says Williams.

He became the center fielder in 1993. Since then, his hitting has improved each year. At bat, he spreads the powerful legs that made him a 440 champion in high school, and crouches slightly at the knees. This drops him from a height of 6-feet-2 down to about 5-feet-9. His body explodes through the ball. Someone has scrambled a pile of statistics that supposedly prove Williams is the best center fielder in the sport.

There is no number for grace, but when he sprints across the outfield grass, you begin to see what they meant about DiMaggio. The only criticism of his game is that he does not steal many bases.

"He is tall and wiry, so he runs high," explains Raines, a master base-thief who is 6 inches shorter than Williams. "To steal, you need to have full speed almost from the first step. As big as he is, it takes a few steps to make it to full speed."

This month, he turned 30. His wife Waleska and their three children returned to Bayamon for school after spending the summer with him in Bergen County.

He recently ran a children's baseball clinic at Columbia's Baker Field for a corporate patron. Williams patiently fed the batting tee for each kid, adjusted their stances and gracefully praised them all. By the time he had to pose for pictures, he had worked up a sweat. Someone brought him a fresh T-shirt. With every move watched by scores of children and their parents, he looked around for a private place to change. As he trotted into a hallway, a general groan rose from the women in the stands. "Come on, Bernie," shouted one mother. "Show us your chest." He looked deeply embarrassed.

Bernie Williams at City Hall after the ticker tape parade.

DAILY NEWS   Pat Carroll

He regrets that the Puerto Rican ballplayers have not been more heavily marketed. "With the young guys coming along — Ricky Ledee, Jorge Posada — and with so many Latino people around the Stadium," said Williams, "I think we can find the fine line, to stand with the community, and still stay focused on our main job."

In the dizzy world of sports salaries, Williams has never been signed to a long-term contract, although he is being paid $8.25 million. So after the season, at the peak of his game, Williams will become a free agent for the first time. A change of venue, he observes, has helped some people.

"Paul O'Neill and Tino Martinez probably assumed they were going to stay with the teams they started with for their whole careers," said Williams. "Probably the best thing that happened to them was coming here. That's just my opinion. Who is to say the same thing couldn't happen to me?"

After batting practice, he retreats to a net with Chris Chambliss, the hitting coach. Chambliss softly tosses 30 or 40 balls from a bucket to Williams, who lines them into a net, the balls coming so quickly that he is nearly panting.

To make it look easy, you have to work like crazy.

When he comes to bat in the game, he strokes the first pitch to left field, as if it were just another toss from the coach.

Bernie Williams Stats
NEW YORK YANKEES

AVG.	G	AB	R	H	TB	2B	3B	HR	RBI	BB	SO	SB	CS	SH	SF	HP	SLG%	OBP%
.336	127	497	100	167	285	30	5	26	96	54	81	15	9	0	3	1	.573	.421

GAME OF THE WEEK

July 28, 1998 VS. ANGELS AT ANAHEIM

FLYING START

Cone gets 15th on 3 Yank HRs

JULY 29, 1998

By Peter Botte, Daily News Sports Writer

ANAHEIM —They find themselves at the turn of the century now, and not only in direct comparison with the greatest baseball outfits of all time.

The 1998 Yankees played their 100th game last night, returning to the scene of their 0-2 start — en route to 1-4. Nine innings later, they had opened a three-game showdown of first-place teams with a 9-3 thrashing of the West-leading Angels at Edison Field.

Derek Jeter, Darryl Strawberry and Bernie Williams each homered in support of David Cone, who became the majors' first 15-game winner with seven innings of three-run ball.

Cone (15-3, 3.33), who struck out six and walked two, was charged with just one earned

Paul O'Neill

DAILY NEWS Linda Cataffo

run on six hits in his bid to rebound from offseason surgery all the way to his second Cy Young Award.

"It's been an incredible run," said Cone, who reported he had a little trouble getting loose before the sixth in the wake of the Yankees' three runs in the top half, but said he was fine. "This team has been relentless, and hasn't allowed any complacency to set in, or allowed anything to distract us."

The only bright spot for Anaheim was Garret Anderson extending his hitting streak to a current major-league best 25 games with a single in the ninth.

With 62 games to play, the Yanks trail only

the 1902 Pirates — by a single game — for the best record at the century mark in modern big-league history. They are on pace to win a major-league record 120 games.

"I think they use whatever will help them get motivated," Joe Torre said. "We started out here 0-2, and it was 1-4 before we knew it. Then we started playing well, and we've been playing well ever since."

This nine-day, 10-game excursion westward began slowly for the Yanks, who boarded their charter at Newark Airport late Monday afternoon as planned, but didn't take off until more than four hours later due to mechanical difficulties.

Jeter had been just 1-for-8 in the first two losses to Anaheim, but he ignited last night's early outburst against Jason Dickson.

With one out in the first, Jeter rocketed the young righty's 1-0 pitch 424 feet over the wall just to the right of dead center for his career-high 12th HR.

Tino Martinez opened the second with a squib single down the third-base line. Strawberry may still be hobbled on his possibly arthritic left knee, but he clubbed his team-high 16th of the season—in just 202 at-bats—to extend the lead to 3-0.

"I feel better every day," Strawberry said. "All the extra work I'm doing is starting to pay off."

Chad Curtis and Scott Brosius laced consecutive singles, before Dickson threw late to third on Joe Girardi's sacrifice attempt to load the bases.

One out after Chuck Knoblauch walked to force in a run, Paul O'Neill lifted a sacrifice fly to deep center to boost Cone's early cushion to 5-0.

The Angels cut it to 5-2 with an unearned run in the third when Bernie Williams booted Darin Erstad's single to center with two outs.

For Williams, a defending Gold Glove winner, it was his first error since Aug. 26 of last season vs. Oakland, a span of 94 games in center.

Williams quickly atoned, however, tagging Dickson for an opposite-field solo homer, his 13th, with one out in the fifth. It was the second homer in as many games for the switch-hitting Williams.

FINAL

NEW YORK YANKEES 9, AT ANAHEIM ANGELS 3

NEW YORK	ab	r	h	rbi	ANAHEIM	ab	r	h	rbi
Knoblauch, 2b	4	0	0	1	Edmonds cf	5	1	1	0
Jeter ss	5	2	2	2	D Hollins 3b	4	0	1	0
O'Neill rf	4	0	2	2	Shipley 3b	0	0	0	0
B Williams cf	5	1	2	2	Erstad lf	3	1	2	0
T Martinez 1b	5	1	2	0	Fielder 1b	4	0	0	0
Strawberry dh	3	1	1	2	Salmon dh	3	1	1	1
a-Spencer ph	1	0	1	0	G Anderson rf	4	0	1	0
Curtis lf	5	2	1	0	Walbeck c	3	0	1	0
Brosius 3b	4	1	2	0	Baughman 2b	4	0	0	0
Girardi c	3	1	1	0	Disarcina ss	4	0	1	0
Totals	39	9	14	9	Totals	34	3	8	1

HR - Jeter, Strawberry, B Williams.   HR - Salmon.

a-singled for Strawberry in the 9th.

NY Yankees	140 013 000	—	9
Anaheim	011 001 000	—	3

NY Yankees	ip	h	r	er	bb	so	hr	era
Cone W	7	6	3	1	2	6	1	3.33
Stanton	2	2	0	0	0	1	0	5.70

Anaheim	ip	h	r	er	bb	so	hr	era
Dickson L	5 1/3	11	8	6	1	3	3	6.00
P Harris	1/3	0	1	0	0	0	0	4.18
Cadaret	3 1/3	3	0	0	1	3	0	4.15

DAILY NEWS Keith Torrie

Derek Jeter

JULY 26	SUN	Chicago White Sox	6-3	W
JULY 28	TUES	at Anaheim Angels	3-9	W
JULY 29	WED	at Anaheim Angels	10-5	L
JULY 30	THU	at Anaheim Angels	0-3	W
JULY 31	FRI	at Seattle Mariners	3-5	W
AUG 1	SAT	at Seattle Mariners	2-5	W

> "First, the goals is to get to .500 and then to five (games) over and 10 over. Increments of five. I remember last year how excited I was to finish 30 games over. I thought that was pretty damn good. But this is rarefied air here, pretty impressive. And obviously we're not satisfied with that."
>
> —Joe Torre

YANKS GO 50 OVER .500

By Peter Botte, Daily News Sports Writer
August 2, 1998

Star players go down, Yankees win. Chunks of steel crash, Yankees win. Deadlines pass, Big Units go elsewhere, The Boss speaks, and the Yankees still win.

Virtually every day, someone comes up with some statistic or another to try to place the Yankees' march toward immortality in perspective. And then there are those numbers that simply blow everyone away.

Yesterday was the first day of August. Yesterday ended with the Yankees at 50 games over .500.

Fifty.

"I always base what we do on .500," Joe Torre said yesterday after his juggernaut team celebrated the stand-pat passing of the trade deadline with a 5-2 victory over the Mariners at the Kingdome.

"First, the goal is to get to .500, and then to five (games) over and 10 over," Torre said. "Increments of five. I remember last year how excited I was to finish 30 games over. I thought that was pretty damn good. But this is rarefied air here, pretty impressive. And

Gerald Herbert

DAILY NEWS

George Steinbrenner

obviously we're not satisfied with that."

David Wells is not satisfied as he zeroes in on 20 wins for the first time in his career. But who really knows?

Wells might not be considered the most topical lefthand pitcher currently in the public's consciousness, either here or in New York. But he certainly has pitched better than ex-Mariner Randy Johnson throughout most of 1998. And he still can cause a post-game stir whether he opens his mouth or not, just like the Big Unit.

Wells was reached for a two-run homer by Alex Rodriguez in the first inning, but hurled eight shutout frames thereafter to improve to 13-2 with his third complete game of the season.

Following the game, however, Wells sent Yankees PR man Rick Cerrone out to inform reporters he couldn't share his thoughts about his day because he had "to go somewhere."

The media stuck around, nevertheless, and

when Wells returned to his locker to fetch his clothes, he said tersely, "I'll get you guys tomorrow." He said he had "someplace he had to be," even though he was seen talking with friends inside the Kingdome more than 30 minutes later.

Still, Wells told at least one person associated with the team that he was "ticked off at those guys" because an overflowing media contingent crowding around David Cone's neighboring locker late last week in Anaheim prevented Wells from getting dressed. Hence, the pre-planned blow-off.

"That's what makes the Boomer, the Boomer. Right there," Cone said. "But he was really outstanding today."

He was especially outstanding in an eighth-inning sequence Cone called "the litmus test for all pitchers." Wells allowed a pair of singles to Rich Amaral and Joey Cora with nobody out, but responded by striking out Rodriguez, getting Ken Griffey Jr. to tap to second and retiring Edgar Martinez on a fly ball.

"Boomer," Cone said, "did his best pitching right there."

And the Yankees, to no one's surprise, continued to play their best ball. They even picked up their fourth straight win at their former shop of

Ken Griffey Jr.

DAILY NEWS   Linda Cataffo

horrors, the Kingdome, where they were 4-18 over four seasons before the April 7 team meeting widely credited with turning around a 1-4 season.

Tino Martinez (16th) and Derek Jeter (14th) belted solo shots for the Yanks, who have ripped 11 homers in the first five games of this road trip. Martinez also added an incredible reaction play for an unassisted double play on a wicked shot by Griffey with a 3-2 lead in the sixth.

"That play could've turned the whole game around," Torre said.

"That ball was smoked. It was one of the hardest hit balls I've ever had hit to me," Martinez said.

"Tino was plain lucky, man. You can ask him," Jeter said. "Tino didn't even see the ball. But that was a big play for us. . . . We didn't want to lose this game."

Fifty games over .500, and the Yankees are not satisfied that, at 77-27, they remain tied with the 1902 Pirates for the best start in the 20th century.

Fifty games over .500, and not satisfied that the Red Sox could go unbeaten over the final two months and still not catch the Yanks for the AL East crown should the Bombers maintain their current pace.

"It's a significant achievement and one we're well aware of," Cone said. "This team has tremendous perspective. We understand anything can happen, but that said, we're very proud of our accomplishments."

STANDINGS AT THE END OF WEEK 18

American League East

	W.	L.	PCT.	G.B.
NEW YORK YANKEES	83	29	.741	-
Boston Red Sox	67	47	.588	17
Baltimore Orioles	60	55	.522	24.5
Toronto Blue Jays	57	59	.491	28
Tampa Bay Devil Rays	44	69	.389	39.5

GAME OF THE WEEK

August 8, 1998 VS. KANSAS CITY ROYALS

YANKS HOME SWEEP HOME

Darryl's 21st powers Cone's 16th

AUGUST 8, 1998

By Bill Madden, Daily News Sports Writer

NEW YORK—The late, great Yankees owner Jacob Ruppert was fond of saying "my idea of an entertaining day at the ballpark is for the Yankees to score 10 runs in the first inning and gradually pull away."

It wasn't quite that kind of a Yankees runaway in the matinee portion of the rare day-night doubleheader at Ruppert's old ball yard yesterday, but the Colonel would have been entertained. Joe Torre sure was and so were the 14,425 who got to soak up the sun and bask in the glow of David Cone's 16th victory and Darryl Strawberry's 21st home run.

It was business as usual for the Yankees, who are on pace to break the record of 116 wins in a season set by the 1906 Chicago Cubs.

After spotting the Royals a run in the top of the first inning, they batted around and scored four of their own, added another run in the second and, as Ruppert would have approved, gradually pulled away. The final was 8-2, but as Torre and Cone both conceded, this one was pretty much

David Cone

DAILY NEWS Linda Cataffo

tucked away with the 80 other Yankees victories after that 5-1 lead was forged by the second inning.

"Coming back for the four in the first inning was big," said Torre, "but getting that next one in the second was even bigger. A manager's nightmare is seeing your team score a bunch of runs early and never being able to add to it. We just kept tacking them on."

Cone was grateful.

"I struggled in the first inning trying to get my rhythm," he said, "but once we came back with those four runs I felt real comfortable. Any pitcher will tell you it's a lot easier pitching with a bunch of runs early."

In upping his perfect record at Yankee Stadium to 10-0, Cone (16-4) spaced four Royals hits after the shaky first and walked none before leaving with two outs in the seventh. In all, he gave up two runs and six hits, and struck out five, in 6 2/3 innings. His effort, like the hitters', was methodical. If there is anything more remarkable about him becoming the majors' first 16-game winner, it is the scant 37 walks he has issued in 149 innings.

"That's been one of my goals, to be more efficient," Cone said. "Pitching from the right side of the rubber has helped me get my breaking stuff over more."

By contrast, it was Royals starter Pat Rapp's inability to get the ball over the plate that led to his undoing. Successive one-out walks to Derek Jeter and Paul O'Neill in the first set up Bernie Williams' RBI single to center and Tino Martinez' RBI double. That prompted Royals manager Tony Muser to have Strawberry walked intentionally. Rapp (9-11) then walked Tim Raines unintentionally to force home the third run of the inning, and Scott Brosius' sac fly made it 4-1.

In the third, Strawberry hit a 405-foot shot into the upper deck in right for his 21st homer, and his ninth in the last 30 at-bats. Strawberry's last six hits all have been home runs.

"Walking Darryl intentionally was the ultimate show of respect," Torre said.

Strawberry, however, wasn't so sure. "I don't know," he said. "I was thinking maybe they were just trying to set up the double play. The count was 2-0 and maybe they just didn't want to make a mistake."

When you think of all the glorious elements that have gone into this Yankees season, which is more unlikely: Cone becoming the majors' first 16-game winner or Strawberry leading the Yanks in homers?

"How could I not be surprised?" Strawberry said. "I suppose it's just one of those things. I don't go home thinking about leading the team in homers. All I know is I feel confident up there right now. I would like to get a couple of base hits (instead of just homers). I want to run. I'm healthy enough now to run."

If old Jake Ruppert were around, he'd tell him not to bother. It's Strawberry's homers that entertain. And Cone's precision pitching. And the methodical Yankees machine.

FINAL

KANSAS CITY ROYALS 2, AT NEW YORK YANKEES 8

KANSAS CITY	ab	r	h	rbi	NEW YORK	ab	r	h	rbi
Damon cf	4	2	2	1	Knoblauch 2b	5	1	2	0
H Morris lf	4	0	0	0	Jeter ss	3	2	1	0
Offerman 2b	4	0	3	1	O'Neill rf	4	1	1	0
Palmer dh	4	0	1	0	B Williams cf	4	2	2	2
Pendleton 3b	4	0	0	0	T Martinez	4	1	2	3
J King 1b	4	0	0	0	Strawberry dh	3	1	1	1
Sutton rf	3	0	1	0	Raines lf	3	0	0	1
Sweeney c	4	0	1	0	Curtis lf	1	0	0	0
M Lopez ss	4	0	0	0	Brosius 3b	2	0	1	1
					Girardi c	4	0	2	0
Totals	35	2	8	2	Totals	33	8	12	8

HR - Damon.   HR - Strawberry.

Kansas City	101 000 000	—	2
NY Yankees	411 002 00X	—	8

Kansas City	ip	h	r	er	bb	so	hr	era
Rapp L	5 1/3	10	8	8	7	5	1	5.35
Byrdak	2/3	1	0	0	0	0	0	0.00
Pittsley	2	1	0	0	2	1	0	6.95

NY Yankees	ip	h	r	er	bb	so	hr	era
Cone W	6 2/3	6	2	2	0	5	1	3.50
Stanton	1 1/3	2	0	0	0	2	0	5.16
Borowski	1	0	0	0	0	1	0	0.00

Darryl Strawberry

REST OF THE WEEK

AUG 2	SUN	at Seattle Mariners	6-3	W
AUG 3	MON	at Oakland Athletics	1-14	W
AUG 4	TUES	at Oakland Athletics	5-10	W
AUG 5	WED	at Oakland Athletics	3-1	L
AUG 7	FRI	Kansas City Royals	8-2	W
AUG 7	FRI	Kansas City Royals	14-2	W
AUG 8	SAT	Kansas City Royals	14-1	W

> "You just enjoy watching it and hope to be a part of it. I want to feel I'm part of it. They've been doing it all year. I'm just trying to enjoy myself."
> —Shane Spencer

SPENCER LEADS SUBS' ASSAULT

By Rafael L. Hermoso, Daily News Sports Writer
August 8, 1998

Rafael Hermoso

It certainly didn't have the impact of Derek Jeter's home run in Game 2 of the 1996 ALCS against the Orioles, when Jeffrey Maier reached over the railing in right field and plucked the ball away from a stunned Tony Tarasco.

But Shane Spencer's first career home run last night appeared every bit as tainted.

His second, however, was clean.

Spencer capped a 5-for-5, three-RBI night by homering in his final two at-bats of the Yankees' 14-2 win over the Royals. The win capped a long day for the Yankees, who hammered Kansas City, 22-4, in the sweep and improved to 82-29.

"I say wow a lot, either out loud or to myself," Joe

Shane Spencer went 5-for-5 with two home runs and three RBI against the Royals.

Linda Cataffo

DAILY NEWS

Torre said, "They keep coming at you. It's a good mix of people. After the game, (Paul) O'Neill came up to me and said, 'I heard Spencer can play left field, too.'"

"You just enjoy watching it and hope to be a part of it," said Spencer, who started in right field to give O'Neill the night off. "I want to feel I'm part of it. They've been doing it all year. I'm just trying to enjoy myself."

Spencer already had three hits, including a pair of doubles, when he batted in the seventh last night. He hit a drive to left off rookie Tim Byrdak, but wasn't sure it was gone until he was halfway to second base.

Hal Morris appeared to have a bead on the ball as he backed to the left-field wall. But as

Morris went up for the catch, a fan in the first row leaned over and deflected the ball into the seats. As Morris held out his glove in protest, third-base umpire Eric Cooper signaled home run from his spot in left field.

"The second one put the doubt out of everyone's mind anyway," Torre said.

Spencer knew his second homer—a two-run drive in the Yankees' five-run eighth—was gone well before it landed in the second deck in left field. He began his home run trot right out of the batter's box.

"They were ragging on me because the first one was close," Spencer said.

The best was yet to come. The rookie got a Stadium curtain call from the 37,988 in attendance.

"I never expected anything like that in my life," said Spencer, who became the first Yankee with five hits in a game since Cecil Fielder on April 26, 1997.

Spencer capped a big night for the Yankees' subs. Luis Sojo replaced Tino Martinez at first and had three hits and three RBI. And Homer Bush, playing third to give Scott Brosius a rest, drove in a run.

DAILY NEWS   Linda Cataffo

Teammates celebrate another Yankee run.

Regulars Chuck Knoblauch and Bernie Williams both homered; Knoblauch a leadoff homer in the third and Williams a two-run job in the fifth, to help David Wells (14-2) win his sixth straight decision. Wells, who gave up six hits and struck out four, pitched his second complete game in a row. He is 9-0 at the Stadium.

Sojo lined reliever Ricky Bones' first pitch into the right-field corner to score two runs in the fifth. As the ball caromed past Johnny Damon, Sojo sprinted into third base. His head-first slide beat the throw and left the 32-year-old Sojo gasping for air, his tongue hanging out.

Derek Jeter laughed from the top step of the dugout.

"He had a truck on his back," Jeter said.

Wells couldn't prevent Jose Offerman from extending his hitting streak to 27 games. Offerman tripled off Bernie Williams' glove in the ninth after going hitless in his first three at-bats. ... Williams provided the only scare in the eighth when he was hit in the back of his helmet by third baseman Scott Leius' throw as he was running down the first base line. He remained in the game and scored from first on Jorge Posada's double. ... Yankees did not issue a walk in the doubleheader. "That eliminates runs most of the time," David Wells said.

STANDINGS AT THE END OF WEEK 19

American League East	W.	L.	PCT.	G.B.
NEW YORK YANKEES	89	30	.748	-
Boston Red Sox	71	49	.592	18.5
Baltimore Orioles	65	57	.537	25.5
Toronto Blue Jays	61	61	.500	29.5
Tampa Bay Devil Rays	47	73	.392	42.5

YANKEE PROFILE
Mariano Rivera

WHERE RIVERA GOES FOR RELIEF

Takes hat off to Panama

AUGUST 31, 1998

By Rafael Hermoso , Daily News Sports Writer

Mariano Rivera RHP

Broadway, the Met, MOMA and SoHo. You can keep them all. Mariano Rivera will gladly take a small fishing village any day.

"I won't trade Panama for New York," Rivera said last week at Yankee Stadium. "I'll take Panama."

Not that he has anything against the city. The Yankees' closer, his wife, Clara and their sons Mariano, 4, and Jafet, 1, are very happy renting movies and relaxing at their home in New Rochelle. But each year around this time he starts to yearn for his homeland.

"Come September and the end of the season, I miss it more," said Rivera, the son of a fisherman. "It's my land. You form a part of that land."

Perhaps it's the promise he made to his mother Delia years ago when he told her, "Mama, don't worry because I'll never leave."

So each offseason, the later the better, Rivera, 28, moves his family back to his house in Puerto Caimito, Panama, the same town where he grew up. He loves the tranquility of the Gulf of Panama on the Pacific and such simplicities as a plate of meat, rice and beans.

Delia and his father Mariano still live nearby in the same house Rivera grew up in, just slightly updated with help from Rivera after he signed with the Yankees.

With a salary of $750,000, Rivera joins teammate Derek Jeter as one of baseball's best bargains. Despite the team's many lopsided wins, Rivera has still converted 33 of 38 save chances. But he and Jeter are sure to multiply their earnings in arbitration this winter if they don't sign long-term contracts with the Yankees. Still, Rivera won't leave the town for the glamour of even Panama City.

"I like a calm life where nobody bothers me," he said.

"I don't know how he is here but Panama, that's his land and he feels better there," said Ramiro Mendoza, a fellow Panamanian and Rivera's closest friend on the team.

Mariano Rivera hugs Joe Girardi after winning the ALCS against the Indians.

DAILY NEWS Linda Cataffo

Delia Rivera knows how her son feels. She was skeptical when he signed with Yankees scout Herb Raybourn as a 20-year-old. Rivera would leave the fishing boats behind to play baseball in small towns scattered around the U.S.

"His father was convinced because it was his dream and Mariano's but as a mother, imagine, I was worried," Delia said Saturday from Panama. "At that time, we didn't have phones in this town so he wrote us and told us how he was. I think it was hard on both of us.

"Once he wrote a letter saying he was crying as he was writing because he was very lonely because it was strange there," she continued. "We both suffered. From here, he won't go. For work he will, but he'll always return because this is his home."

The Riveras will leave home for a while when they travel to New York today. Hopefully, their trip will last deep into October. Then they can all return.

"When he comes home, it's a joy for the whole town," Delia said. "He's very popular. We go find him at the airport and it's a caravan to here. When he comes here, they don't leave him alone. They love him because he lets them love him. He's very sensitive."

If the season ends the same as it did in 1996, Rivera could get a repeat reception.

"I was surprised," Rivera said. "I expected something but not so large."

In the past, Rivera has bought gifts such as gloves for the schoolchildren. He knows what a luxury they

DAILY NEWS Pat Carroll

Mariano Rivera celebrates after the Yankees win the World Series.

are. When he was 12, his father bought him his first leather glove so he could put away the home-made cardboard model he had used since he was 7.

Rivera has come a long way. Two years ago, some writers argued that he should have won the Cy Young award when he revolutionized the position of setup man. He took over closing duties last season when John Wetteland bolted for Texas and has oddly slipped into the background.

"The job I was doing at that time, nobody was doing it before," Rivera said. "That's why people were expecting it."

The greater responsibility has not changed Rivera. He's still a calming influence in the pen, serving a big-brother role to Mendoza as he did to his cousin Ruben Rivera two years ago. Rivera and Mendoza met in 1992 working out together as Yankee farmhands in Panama City. Their bullpen chats range from Panama to baseball. Their families socialize in the offseason.

"He talks a lot," Mendoza said. "He's helped me a lot, how to pitch to hitters, how to deal with the pressure of relief."

Mendoza felt "disillusioned" early this season when he was sent to the bullpen to make room in the rotation for Orlando Hernandez.

"The first thing he has to know is he can't control all things," Rivera said. "The only thing he can control is what he does. Once he relaxes, he's much better. I told him as a friend when you go out there you can't control that. Just go there and do your job."

Mariano Rivera Stats

1998 REGULAR SEASON

W	L	S	ERA	G	GS	CG	SHO	IP	H	R	ER	HR	BB	SO	HB	WP	BK
3	0	36	1.91	54	0	0	0	61.1	48	13	13	3	17	36	1	0	0

GAME OF THE WEEK

August 14, 1998 VS. TEXAS RANGERS

TINO SECONDS ANDY'S MOTION

AUGUST 15, 1998

By Rafael Hermoso, Daily News Sports Writer

Tonight after Orlando Hernandez mowed the Rangers down with strikeouts, the Yankees had to call for backup to beat Texas again, 6-4, last night at the Stadium. The signature play was an unconventional 8-3 forceout at second base recorded by first baseman Tino Martinez, who was backing up the play.

Yes, Johnny Oates, the Yankees may not be dominant. But they sure find ways to win.

The Yankees improved to 9-0 on this home stand and haven't lost at the Stadium since July 25. They are 60 games over .500 (89-29) for the first time since 1939.

And they scored four runs with two outs, including three in the seventh on two-out hits by Chuck Knoblauch and Derek Jeter.

"It's so important that what we do is think small," Joe Torre said. "Think of one bite at a time, one run at a time and if you do the little things all of a sudden you look

up and they turn it into a big thing. A couple of two-out base hits gave us a comfortable lead for a short period of time."

Clutch defense also helps. With the Yankees ahead, 3-1, Juan Gonzalez walked to lead off the seventh. Will Clark followed with a flare to short center that Jeter tracked down. But with his back to the plate, the ball popped out of Jeter's glove.

No problem. Bernie Williams, who earlier homered, grabbed the ball on one bounce and threw to Martinez, who wisely was covering second after Knoblauch had chased the ball.

"Usually when both middle infielders go out for a popup, I go to second base," Martinez said. "With nobody on, if the hitter hits a ball like that and both Jeter and Knoblauch are out there, the guy can get a double. I usually go out there to hold the guy to a single."

"It's heads-up," Torre said. "The good part about that play is people looked around and

Bernie Williams

DAILY NEWS   Linda Cataffo

knew common sense."

The Rangers didn't score, and three two-out runs in the bottom of the inning gave the Yankees a 6-1 lead. The Rangers scored twice after Andy Pettitte was replaced by Ramiro Mendoza in the eighth. Mariano Rivera got the third out and allowed Mike Simms' solo homer in the ninth before finishing for his 32nd save and second in as many nights.

Pettitte (14-6) allowed three runs in seven-plus innings to give Yankees starters a 1.86 ERA on this home stand.

"Our pitching's stayed really strong the whole season," Pettitte said. "I didn't realize guys would be on the roll they are. When I'm sitting on the bench when I'm not pitching, it's amazing to watch the stretch these guys are in."

Though the Yankees had won three of his previous four starts, Pettitte posted a 4.44 ERA in that span. He pitched only 5 2/3 innings in his last start, after a nine-day layoff because of a strained left shoulder.

"I thought he expected too much from himself after he missed the start," Torre said. "We tried to do more

counseling between this start and the last one."

"I was just real upset the last start," Pettitte said.

Joe Girardi's hit-and-run double in the second, Williams' homer in the fourth and Knoblauch's homer in the fifth produced a 3-0 lead.

Oates, Texas' manager, said Thursday that even if the Yankees win the most games ever, they still don't rank with the top 10 teams all-time. He's learning they are crafty if not dominant.

Williams tried a drag bunt leading off the fourth but fouled it off himself. Oates argued that Williams was out of the batter's box when the ball hit him, which would be an out, but plate umpire Ed Hickox ignored the complaint. Two pitches later, Williams hit a line drive into the right-field stands for a solo homer and a 2-0 Yankees lead.

DAILY NEWS Keith Torrie

Andy Pettitte

REST OF THE WEEK

AUG 9	SUN	Kansas City Royals	5-4	W
AUG 10	MON	Minnesota Twins	7-3	W
AUG 11	TUES	Minnesota Twins	7-0	W
AUG 12	WED	Minnesota Twins	11-2	W
AUG 13	THU	Texas Rangers	2-0	W
AUG 14	FRI	Texas Rangers	6-4	W
AUG 15	SAT	Texas Rangers	5-16	L

Torre admits the job is different these days. Players make more money and wield more power. The toughest part, he said isn't the strategy. Anyone who watches as many games as he has can learn the do's and don'ts.

HE'S JUST AN AVERAGE JOE

By Rafael Hermoso, Daily News Sports Writer
August 12, 1998

Rafael Hermoso

Joe Torre sat in the Yankees' dugout last night at the Stadium with a seven-run lead in the eighth inning when Derek Jeter came over.

"Are you nervous?" Jeter asked. "Are you going to bring in Mo?"

Torre didn't need Mariano Rivera to secure his .500 record. He just told Jeter, "Don't leave me there."

The Yankees' 7-0 win over the Twins made their manager the proud owner of a 1,168-1,168 career record. A .500 record may not be much, but consider that in less than three years, his Yankees are 109 games (274-165) over .500.

Torre, who endured 420 defeats with 286 wins as the Mets' manager from 1977-81, didn't have to sweat this

Joe Torre and his brother Frank.

one out. After Paul Molitor grounded out for the final out, Torre was congratulated by Jeter, Tim Raines and Tino Martinez.

"The way we're playing, he has the opportunity to go over that, way over that," David Wells said after the Yanks (86-29) won their sixth straight game and improved to 57 games over .500 for the first time since Sept. 10, 1939.

Wells (15-2), in his first start against the Twins since his May 17 perfect game, pitched a four-hitter to win his seventh straight game. Paul O'Neill's two-run homer in the bottom of the first gave the Yankees the lead for the 40th straight game, tying the major league record set by the '32 Yankees.

DAILY NEWS Gerald Herbert

When Torre was hired on Nov. 2, 1995, he was 109 games under .500 and was welcomed to New York with a back-page headline screaming: "Clueless Joe!" He corrected that by winning the World Series in 1996.

"I hope we got over that a long time ago," Torre laughed. "I hope I didn't have to get to .500 to do that. I can understand it. People look at your record and it's understandable. That's why I really didn't address it. I just said let's wait and see what happens and see if I am clueless or not."

"He's done a great job, man," Jeter said. "It really makes no difference what you did in the past. It's how you do in the present. Regardless of whether he just reached .500 in his career, he's been great here."

Yet long before this year's Yankees started winning games on a daily basis, Torre doubted his desire. Last summer, he expressed concern to his wife, Alice, that winning the World Series had zapped his enjoyment.

"I didn't want people to think that's all I really

Fans celebrate another Yankee victory.

DAILY NEWS Gerald Herbert

wanted," he recalled. "She said, 'You're not that way. What do you care what people think?' Ever since then, I started enjoying myself."

"Joe has just been a perfect man for this situation," said batting coach Chris Chambliss, who coached under Torre in St. Louis. "He's very competitive and you see that through his players."

Jose Cardenal recalls the early days. The first-base coach played for Torre with the Mets in 1979 and '80.

"He was a good manager with the Mets," Cardenal said. "We didn't win much, but we won because he made the right moves at the right time."

Torre admits the job is different these days. Players make more money and wield more power. The toughest part, he said, isn't the strategy. Anyone who watches as many games as he has can learn the do's and don'ts. He's changed as the players have. He's more open, he said, and tries to be honest with his team.

There's only one thing he doesn't want to repeat.

"I don't want to have to get to .500 any more times in my career," Torre said.

STANDINGS AT THE END OF WEEK 20

American League East	W.	L.	PCT.	G.B.
NEW YORK YANKEES	94	32	.746	-
Boston Red Sox	75	52	.591	19.5
Baltimore Orioles	69	60	.535	26.5
Toronto Blue Jays	66	63	.512	29.5
Tampa Bay Devil Rays	49	78	.386	45.5

GAME OF THE WEEK
August 22, 1998 VS. TEXAS RANGERS

BROSIUS HOMER HAS TEXAS ALL WETTE

AUGUST 23, 1998

By Rafael Hermoso, Daily News Sports Writer

WEEK 21 ● AUGUST 16-22

ARLINGTON—The Yankees and Rangers kept trying to give each other last night's game. Scott Brosius seized it for good.

Brosius hit a three-run homer off former Yankees closer John Wetteland in the eighth inning to cap a see-saw night. The Yankees won for the second straight night, 12-9, in front of 46,483 fans at The Ballpark, the second straight sellout to watch the Yankees.

They endured three hours and 57 minutes of American League baseball.

"I'm glad we were able to win the bad-pitched game," Joe Torre said. "To win a game like that is pretty impressive. We base all of our success on pitching. If we don't get pitching, it's basically flipping a coin."

With the Yanks trailing 9-8, Tino Martinez' one-out single and Chad Curtis' two-out single off Xavier Hernandez put runners on the corners and prompted Texas manager Johnny Oates to call

Scott Brosius

DAILY NEWS   Keith Torrie

on Wetteland, who had converted 33 of 37 save chances. But Brosius hit Wetteland's third pitch just over the right field wall to put the Yankees back on top.

"Obviously when he's on the mound it's no secret he's going to be aggressive and come after you," said Brosius, who was facing Wetteland for the first time. "I certainly didn't have home run on my mind."

The Yankees added a run in the ninth on Bernie Williams' run-scoring double. Williams went 4-for-5 to raise his AL-leading average to .353.

They blew three leads despite the Rangers doing their best to give the game away with five errors, one by each member of the infield.

In a game with five lead changes, Mariano Rivera, who earned his 33rd save, finally ended it. He allowed Rusty Greer's single in the eighth to put runners on the corners but got Juan Gonzalez, who had homered twice, to ground out to first base to end the inning.

Rookie Ryan Bradley, who was pitching for Single-A Tampa last month, won in his major-league debut. He threw 1 2/3 scoreless innings and hit a batter.

Bradley replaced Mike Stanton, who surrendered Gonzalez' second homer of the game in the seventh inning, a two-run shot that tied that game at 8-8. Gonzalez had barely caught his breath in the Rangers dugout when he watched Will Clark send Stanton's next pitch into the first five rows of the right field stands for a 9-8 Texas lead.

Stanton's ERA rose to 5.70.

"They won in spite of me and Stanton," said starter David Cone said. "And we were both joking about it in the clubhouse."

Cone spent his night being generous. He twice blew leads and left in the sixth inning before he could do it again. Tom Goodwin's two-run double chased Cone and forced Joe Torre to insert Stanton. The lefty got Mark McLemore looking at a 2-2 outside strike to end the inning and preserve the Yankees' 7-6 lead.

Cone walked Rusty Greer in the first inning before striking out Gonzalez swinging. Greer walked again with two outs in the third and Cone fell behind Gonzalez 3-0 before Gonzalez pulled a 3-1 pitch into the first row in the second deck in left for a three-run homer and a 3-2 Texas lead.

Gonzalez's homer was estimated at 449 feet, the third- longest at The Ballpark, which opened in 1994, and the longest of Gonzalez' career. Gonzalez has four of the six homers to land in the left field club level.

FINAL

NEW YORK YANKEES 12, AT TEXAS RANGERS 9

NEW YORK	ab	r	h	rbi	TEXAS	ab	r	h	rbi
Knoblauch 2b	5	2	1	0	T Goodwin cf	5	0	1	2
Jeter ss	5	3	3	2	Mclemore 2b	4	0	1	0
O'Neill rf	5	0	0	1	Greer lf	3	2	3	0
B Williams cf	5	0	4	4	J Gonzalez rf	4	2	2	5
T Martinez 1b	6	1	1	0	W Clark 1b	5	1	2	1
C Davis dh	5	1	2	0	I Rodriguez c	5	1	1	1
Strawberry lf	2	0	0	0	Zeile 3b	5	0	1	0
Curtis lf	2	1	1	0	Newson dh	5	1	1	0
Brosius 3b	5	3	3	3	Clayton ss	3	2	1	0
Girardi c	5	1	2	1					
Totals	45	12	17	11	Totals	39	9	13	9

HR - Brosius.

HR - J Gonzalez 2, I Rodriguez, W Clark.

NY Yankees	020 203 131	— 12	
Texas	003 102 300	— 9	

NY Yankees	ip	h	r	er	bb	so	hr	era
Cone	5 2/3	7	6	6	4	5	2	3.58
Stanton BS	1/3	3	3	3	0	1	2	5.70
Bradley W	1 2/3	0	0	0	0	1	0	0.00
M Rivera S	1 1/3	3	0	0	0	0	0	1.47

Texas	ip	h	r	er	bb	so	hr	era
Burkett	5	10	5	3	2	3	0	5.92
Crabtree	1 2/3	3	3	2	1	1	0	4.08
Gunderson	1/3	0	0	0	0	0	0	4.12
X Hernandez L	6 2/3	2	2	2	0	0	0	2.85
Wetteland BS	1 1/3	2	2	2	1	0	1	1.85

Burkett pitched to 1 batter in the 6th.
Stanton pitched to 3 batters in the 7th.

DAILY NEWS Linda Cataffo

Rookie Shane Spencer hits a home run to bring home Tim Raines and Tino Martinez.

REST OF THE WEEK

AUG 16	SUN	Texas Rangers	6-5	W
AUG 17	MON	at Kansas City Royals	7-1	W
AUG 18	TUES	at Kansas City Royals	3-2	W
AUG 19	WED	at Minnesota Twins	3-5	L
AUG 20	THU	at Minnesota Twins	4-9	L
AUG 21	FRI	at Texas Rangers	5-0	W
AUG 22	SAT	at Texas Rangers	12-9	W

After hitting an opposite-field home run into the upper deck in right in the first, Derek Jeter said, "Babe Ruth must've been blowing it."

BABE'S DAY IS A SMASH

By Rafael L. Hermoso, Daily News Sports Writer
August 17, 1998

Rafael Hermoso

The game was preceded by a moment of silence and followed by a burst of cheers. In between, home runs flew like rockets.

Babe Ruth would've been proud.

Bernie Williams' line drive into the upper deck in right field with one out in the bottom of the ninth inning broke a tie and gave the Yankees a 6-5 win over the Rangers yesterday on the 50th anniversary of Babe Ruth's death.

"It's a great way to win a game and I guess a great tribute to his memory," Williams said after giving 50,304 fans a curtain call.

Six home runs were the proper way to honor the unofficial architect of the Stadium and home run. Ruth could have had a hand in yesterday's game. The wind was blowing out to right field and at least one Yankee thought the Babe's ghost was responsible.

After hitting an opposite-field home run into the upper deck in right in the first, Derek Jeter said, "Babe Ruth must've been blowing it."

The Yankees avenged their 16-5 loss to the Rangers Saturday and took three of four from their possible first-round opponents in the playoffs. But the one player who

dressed to the nines for Ruth was the victim of the weapon the Babe invented.

David Wells, who wore Ruth's actual cap on the mound last June, instead scribbled No. 3 on the back of his cap yesterday. The number proved unlucky as Wells allowed three home runs. He left after giving up five runs on 10 hits in six innings.

"I think the world should honor him today because he's the Babe," Wells said. "It was haunting me."

Homers flew out in every direction. Jeter began the barrage with his shot for a 2-0 lead. He said he had never hit a ball there, even in batting practice, and Joe Torre couldn't find anyone who had seen a right-handed hitter hit one there, either. Darryl Strawberry's shot to the right-field bleachers made it 3-0 in the second.

But ex-Yankee Roberto Kelly pulled the Rangers within one, 3-2, in the third on a routine homer into the right-field stands. Royce Clayton sliced a homer inside the right-field foul pole, mirroring Rusty Greer's grand slam Saturday, tying it at 4 in the fourth.

"That's a Yankee Stadium homer," Wells

said.

Kelly's second homer, to left-center, gave Texas a 5-4 lead in the fifth before the Yankees tied it in the bottom of the inning when Tino Martinez grounded into a double play.

Ramiro Mendoza threw two shutout innings and Mariano Rivera (2-0) worked out of a self-created bases-loaded jam in the ninth to set up Williams' heroics.

The Yankees had left the bases loaded in the eighth, and Xavier Hernandez struck out leadoff hitter Paul O'Neill in the ninth. Williams swung over a split-fingered fastball for strike one, but Hernandez followed with a fastball that Williams belted six rows into the upper deck.

"You half expect him to hit a home run when he gets up there in that situation," Torre said. "It kind of reminded me of the home run he hit off (Baltimore's) Randy Myers in Game 1 of the 1996 (ALCS)."

For Williams, yesterday's moment vanished too quickly, just as all the great memories of this season have disappeared.

"It doesn't matter how slow it's going, it's always going so fast, way fast," Williams said. "Maybe some time after the season we'll look back but right now we're so focused. We don't have time to think back at memories."

File this memory under B for the Babe.

Babe Ruth would've been proud.
Bernie Williams' line drive into the upper deck in right field with one out in the bottom of the ninth inning broke a tie and gave the Yankees a 6-5 win over the Rangers yesterday on the 50th anniversary of Babe Ruth's death.
"It's a great way to win a game and I guess a great tribute to his memory,"
Williams said after giving 50,304 fans a curtain call.

STANDINGS AT THE END OF WEEK 21

American League East	W.	L.	PCT.	G.B.
NEW YORK YANKEES	98	36	.731	-
Boston Red Sox	79	54	.594	18.5
Toronto Blue Jays	70	66	.515	29
Baltimore Orioles	69	66	.511	29.5
Tampa Bay Devil Rays	52	82	.385	46

GAME OF THE WEEK
August 27, 1998 VS. ANAHEIM ANGELS

SPLIT IS LIKE NIGHT AND DAY

Jeter's single puts Yanks on Cloud 9

AUGUST 27, 1998

By Peter Botte, Daily News Sports Writer

WEEK 22 ● AUGUST 23-29

Call off the panic. But not all the way. The Yankees blew another lead to the Angels last night before Derek Jeter's RBI single in the ninth inning turned what could have been the most disastrous of a season's worth of giveaway losses in the last week into a wild 7-6 victory at the Stadium.

The Yanks halted their season-high losing streak at four in the nightcap of a day-night doubleheader.

In reaching that fourth loss in a row, 6-4 to the Angels, a possible playoff opponent, in the day game, the Yankees reached uncharted territory this year.

Panic? The Yankees?

"We knew we were capable of beating them," Jeter said.

"You never want anything to spiral," Joe Torre said. "Anytime you start losing games — two, three, four in a row — a little piece is chopped off as far as your confidence. Even though you know you're a good team, and win enough games and bounce back enough times, it gets frustrating. You lose a little spark. It was a big win for us, no question."

Homer Bush belted his first major-league home run — a three-run shot to kick off a five-run fifth inning — to initially ignite the Yanks from their week-long slumber.

After Mariano Rivera became the latest member of the bullpen to fail to hold a lead, Jeter drove home Jorge Posada from third with a single to right on a 3-2 count off reliever Shigetoshi Hasegawa to send waves of relief throughout the Bronx.

"It was more of a big hit for the team," Jeter said of his 70th RBI. "I like those situations. (Tuesday) I had the same opportunity against (Troy) Percival and didn't come through. We've been making a lot of mistakes lately, which is not like us. We (had) pretty much been dominating.

"But sometimes I think (a losing streak) can be good. It's sort of a wakeup call."

David Wells allowed two home runs to Jim Edmonds and was charged with five runs in seven-plus innings, but still left a 6-4 lead in Rivera's capable hands in the eighth.

Mariano Rivera

DAILY NEWS Linda Cataffo

"Where we've been and the trouble we've been in, he was the only one I was going to," Torre said of his team's bullpen woes. "We've called on Mo to do a little more than he normally would."

Called upon to record six outs, however, the star closer allowed the runner he inherited from Wells to score in the eighth. The Angels then forged a 6-6 tie in the ninth when Norberto Martin scored from first on a long single to right by Darin Erstad, who fouled off no less than seven pitches.

Regardless of what happened in the nightcap, however, the door of possibility that just one week ago seemed implausible already had opened with a thrust. And come October, that is precisely all it will take. One week.

One week of poor situational hitting, bullpen unreliability and substandard starting pitching to render any historic regular-season accomplishments meaningless.

"We'd like to bury everybody, but that still doesn't mean we're going to win in postseason," Torre warned between games. "Now all of a sudden, the questions aren't who we're going to play in the World Series. Now we're concerned about getting there. It's funny what a week does. W-E-A-K, weak."

The Angels boast a 6-4 mark against the Yanks — the only team in baseball with a winning record against them.

"Nothing means anything until you get to the postseason. In 1988, we beat (the Dodgers) 11 out of 12 and lost to them in the playoffs," David Cone said of the Mets' regular-season domination before losing in six games in the NLCS. "The regular season is irrelevant. All it does is set you up for the playoffs."

Still, this has been a season that has held so much daily relevance as the Yanks chase history. The Elias Sports Bureau has been mentioned in as many stories about the team as George Steinbrenner.

"We've been losing lately and giving you guys something to write about," Jeter said. "But I just don't think it makes a difference what happens this week. We may see them in the postseason, and we may not. Either way, both teams have reasons to feel capable of beating the other team."

FINAL

ANAHEIM ANGELS 6, AT NEW YORK YANKEES 7

ANAHEIM	ab	r	h	rbi	NEW YORK	ab	r	h	rbi
Edmonds cf	5	2	3	3	Bush 2b	4	1	2	3
N Martin 2b	5	1	3	0	Jeter ss	5	1	1	1
Erstad 1b	5	1	2	1	O'Neill rf	4	1	1	1
Salmon dh	5	1	2	1	B Williams cf	4	0	0	0
T Greene lf	4	0	1	0	T Martinez 1b	3	0	0	0
R Williams pr-lf	0	0	0	0	C Davis dh	2	0	0	0
G Anderson rf	4	0	0	1	b-Raines ph	1	0	0	0
Glaus 3b	4	0	1	0	Strawberry lf	3	0	0	0
Nevin c	3	0	0	0	Curtis lf	1	0	0	0
a-O Palmeiro ph	1	0	0	0	J Posada c	3	2	1	0
Walbeck c	0	0	0	0	Brosius 3b	2	2	2	0
Disarcina ss	4	1	1	0					
Totals	40	6	13	6	Totals	32	7	8	5

HR - Edmonds 2.   HR - Bush.

a-flied to center for Nevin in the 8th.
b-grounded to second for C Davis in the 8th.

Anaheim	001 000 221	—	6
NY Yankees	000 050 101	—	7

Two out when winning run scored.

Anaheim	ip	h	r	er	bb	so	hr	era
Sparks	6	6	5	4	3	5	1	4.31
Fetters L	2	2	1	2	2	2	0	4.22
Hasegawa	2/3	1	0	0	0	0	0	3.05

NY Yankees	ip	h	r	er	bb	so	hr	era
Wells	7	10	5	5	0	5	2	3.38
M Rivera W BS	2	3	1	1	0	2	0	1.56

Wells pitched to 2 batters in the 8th.
Fetters pitched to 1 batter in the 9th.

Derek Jeter

REST OF THE WEEK

AUG 23	SUN	at Texas Rangers	10-12	L
AUG 24	MON	Anaheim Angels	3-7	L
AUG 25	TUES	Anaheim Angels	6-7	L
AUG 26	WED	Anaheim Angels	4-6	L
AUG 26	WED	Anaheim Angels	7-6	W
AUG 27	THU	Anaheim Angels	6-5	W
AUG 28	FRI	Seattle Mariners	10-3	W
AUG 29	SAT	Seattle Mariners	11-6	W

> "All of a sudden the questions are not who we're going to be playing in the World Series, but how we're going to get there. Funny how a week is."
>
> —Joe Torre

FOR YANKS, HOMER A BLAST

By Bill Madden, Daily News Sports Writer
August 27, 1998

Such is the very fine line between potential greatness and potential calamity that when Derek Jeter's game-winning base hit saw its way through the right side of the infield last night, the collective "whew" heard 'round the Bronx said more about where this Yankee season is right now than their 16 1/2-game lead.

It is amazing what a mere four or five games can do to a city's psyche. A week ago, we were wondering whether the Yankees would break the Cubs' all-time record of 116 wins in a season and, after that, who would be their opponent in the World Series. That was before the Anaheim Angels came to town for what now seems like an eternity and began wreaking the same sort of relentless damage to the Yankees' egos as Hurricane Bonnie has been doing to North Carolinians in her prolonged stay on their coastline.

When the Angels — who themselves had been

Scott Brosius hit a three-run homer in the third.

DAILY NEWS   Howard Simmons

dismissed as Anaheim Afterthoughts in many baseball quarters as recently as a week ago — rallied from an early 2-0 deficit to extend the Yankees' losing streak to four games in the first game of yesterday's day-night twinbill, there was a distinct air of gloom and doom both going and coming at Yankee Stadium.

Even the unflappable Joe Torre conceded: "All of a sudden the questions are not who we're going to be playing in the World Series, but how we're going to get there. Funny how a week is."

Funny indeed. For awhile, it looked like Torre might be able to cut the Yankees' losses and restore everyone's confidence with the unlikeliest of sources — 22-year old rookie righthander Ryan Bradley, who got tapped for the game-one starting assignment when Ramiro Mendoza underwent emergency surgery for a cyst on his behind. The kid gave it a game effort, striking out eight in six innings, but ultimately the dogged Angels were able to solve him with three-run salvos in the fifth and sixth innings.

But baseball, as we know, is a funny game and, as it turned out, a rookie given an unexpected start did provide the spark Torre was hoping for to get the Yankees out of their funk. In this case it was Homer Bush, the so-called "25th man" who took advantage of his surprise, last-minute start for Chuck Knoblauch in the night-cap by clouting a three-run homer in the fifth and beating out an attempted sacrifice bunt to fuel another run in the seventh.

"Sometimes," said Darryl Strawberry, "it's the guys you least expect who come through when you most need it. Homer hasn't played much, but he's made some big contributions to this team when he has. None of them bigger than that, though."

DAILY NEWS Gerald Herbert

Chuck Knoblauch tries to turn the double play.

"When I was coming around first toward second (after the homer), I was just trying to remain composed," Bush said. "But then I saw the crowd and how excited they were and I pumped my fist. I wasn't trying to show anyone up. I was just excited.

"I don't look at myself as the 25th man here, but I know that's what it is. If it comes down to someone having to go, I'll be the one who's got to go."

He needn't worry, even though these last few days of not-nearly-so-great Yankee play has brought home the realization that, for all the best-laid plans of George Steinbrenner and his baseball people, they still may be one relief pitcher short of the great postseason expectations being held for them.

Certainly, had Jeter's two-out hit not made it through the Angels infield in the ninth inning last night, they were again about out of relief. It had to be unsettling, too, that Mariano Rivera couldn't preserve their one-run lead in the top of the inning. As it was, the biggest relief came in the clubhouse afterward, and in the middle of it all was Homer Bush, talking about the negotiations with the fan who caught his first major-league home run.

"He wants a bat," Bush said, "but I'm going to get him a Derek Jeter or Bernie Williams model to make it worth his while."

STANDINGS AT THE END OF WEEK 22

American League East	W.	L.	PCT.	G.B.
NEW YORK YANKEES	100	39	.719	-
Boston Red Sox	81	59	.579	19.5
Toronto Blue Jays	76	66	.535	25.5
Baltimore Orioles	70	71	.496	31
Tampa Bay Devil Rays	55	86	.390	46

GAME OF THE WEEK

September 1, 1998 VS. OAKLAND A's

NOT PERFECT, BUT NOT 2 BAD

Wells' bid ends in 7th; wins 17th

SEPTEMBER 2, 1998

By Peter Botte, Daily News Sports Writer

David Wells has said repeatedly that what happened back on May 17 against the Twins will never happen again. But the good people of New York lovingly asked him to be perfect a second time anyway.

The fortunate 29,632 at the Stadium last night weren't getting Beanie Babies, but why not ask the lefty Cy Young candidate for a repeat performance of his career-defining game?

"In like the third inning, I turned to (David Cone) and said, 'This can't be happening,'" Wells said. "Just the way it was going. . . . I couldn't help but think it. You try to start talking about it just to jinx yourself."

Wells retired the first 20 Athletics batters, but Jason Giambi's clean, two-out single to center in the seventh ended his bid for the impossible. Still, the imperfect lefty finished with a two-hit shutout to propel the Yanks to a 7-0 victory, their 99th in this increasingly remarkable season in the Bronx.

"Perfect. That explains it all," Joe Torre said. "Perfect means you're not allowed to breathe or do anything wrong. He was terrific. . . . He sort of dangled a carrot in front of himself (with the perfect game) and since that time, he's been a terrific pitcher."

For Torre, Wells' 13-strikeout gem couldn't have been more timely, considering the relative recent woes of his once-dominant starting staff. Yankees starters had been 15-9 in August with an ERA of 4.53.

Yanks' batting helmets wait in dugout.

DAILY NEWS   Gerlad Herbert

Leave it to Wells (17-2, 3.22), who has not lost since June 15 and has been a different pitcher since his bout with perfection, to stop the insanity.

In 218 career starts prior to his perfect game, Wells had tossed three shutouts. In the 18 starts since — including his perfecto — Wells has hurled five shutouts, including two in his last three starts.

"The season isn't over with yet. I've been more consistent in this second half than I have ever been in my life, but a better pitcher, I don't know," said Wells, whose win total establishes a career high. "Give me the ball and I do what I do. I don't really care for stardom or anything else. I just want to help our ballclub."

By the end of the fourth, the fans were clamoring for history to repeat itself, rising to their feet and stretching their vocal cords on nearly every pitch.

Wells said he knew early that his stuff had the makings of dominance; 90 of the 114 pitches he threw overall were for strikes. Unlike before his masterpiece against the Twins in May, however, this time Wells endured a shaky pre-game bullpen session.

"Aw, it was pitiful. I didn't think I was gonna last three innings out there," Wells said.

"And all of a sudden he comes in and is almost perfect," Torre marveled.

Wells' bid to add a second perfecto ended on a mistake pitch in the seventh. After retiring Rickey Henderson on a fly ball and fanning Ryan Christenson, Wells quickly got ahead of Giambi. Still, he hung an 0-2 curveball to the A's first baseman, who deposited it over the outstretched glove of Chuck Knoblauch to set off an appreciative minute-long standing ovation.

Following the inning, in which Torre had tempted fate and inserted Chad Curtis into left field in place of Tim Raines, Wells sought out his manager in the dugout.

"It's a jinx. It happened before. Davey Johnson did it. And Joe did it," said Wells, who told of the time he head-butted Johnson after similarly losing a no-hit bid with the Reds in '95 after a defensive switch.

"I told Joe, 'Davey's not gonna be the only one to get the satisfaction of a head butt,'" Wells said. "So I smoked him."

The Yanks, of course, had a similar effect on veteran knuckleballer Tom Candiotti (10-15), whom they battered for six runs in the first two innings

Still, from the start it was evident that Wells wasn't going to need anywhere near that much support on what was nearly another perfect night at the Stadium.

FINAL

OAKLAND ATHLETICS 0, AT NEW YORK YANKEES 7

OAKLAND	ab	r	h	rbi	NEW YORK	ab	r	h	rbi
Henderson lf	4	0	0	0	Knoblauch 2b	4	1	1	0
Christenson cf	4	0	0	0	Jeter ss	4	1	1	0
Giambi 1b	3	0	1	0	O'Neill rf	4	2	3	2
Stairs dh	3	0	0	0	B Williams cf	4	1	1	2
Blowers 3b	3	0	1	0	T Martinez 1b	4	2	2	2
Grieve rf	3	0	0	0	Strawberry dh	4	0	1	0
Spiezio 2b	3	0	0	0	Raines lf	3	0	2	0
Tejada ss	3	0	0	0	Curtis lf	1	0	0	0
Hinch c	2	0	0	0	J Posada c	4	0	1	1
MacFarlane c	1	0	0	0	Sojo 3b	4	0	0	0
Totals	29	0	2	0	Totals	36	7	12	7

HR - B Williams, T Martinez.

Oakland	000 000 000			— 0				
NY Yankees	420 000 10X			— 7				

Oakland	ip	h	r	er	bb	so	hr	era
Candiotti L	7	12	7	7	0	3	2	4.69
Holzemer	1	0	0	0	0	1	0	1.50

NY Yankees	ip	h	r	er	bb	so	hr	era
Wells W	9	2	0	0	0	13	0	3.22

DAILY NEWS   Gerald Herbert

In September, David Wells took an attempt at a second perfect game into the seventh inning.

AUG 30	SUN	Seattle Mariners	3-13	L
SEPT 1	TUES	Oakland Athletics	7-0	W
SEPT 2	WED	Oakland Athletics	0-2	L
SEPT 4	FRI	at Chicago White Sox	11-6	W
SEPT 5	SAT	at Chicago White Sox	5-9	L

> "If there is one thing that stands out about this record-setting Yankee team, it is that it has little or no regard for records. Or, for that matter, its place in history."
>
> **—Bill Madden**

WINNING 100 GAMES NOT THE BEST OMEN

By Bill Madden, Daily News Sports Writer
September 3, 1998

Bill Madden

If there is one thing that stands out about this record-setting Yankee team, it is that it has little or no regard for records. Or, for that matter, its place in history.

But before the Yanks were deprived by journeyman Gil Heredia from becoming the fastest American League team to reach 100 wins in a season, you were hard pressed to find anyone in the clubhouse even remotely aware of this achievement. Which brings to mind what Red Smith, the great New York sports columnist, once said about dying. "Dying," Smith observed, "is no big deal. People do it every day."

To some degree, winning 100 games in a season is no big deal either. In the last 25 years, 18 teams have done it. But as history has shown us, all too painfully, two-thirds of them died with their 100 wins. Only the '73 A's, '75 and '76 Reds,

Paul O'Neill

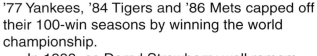
DAILY NEWS Linda Cataffo

'77 Yankees, '84 Tigers and '86 Mets capped off their 100-win seasons by winning the world championship.

In 1988, as Darryl Strawberry well remembers, Tommy Lasorda's upstart ragamuffin Dodgers upset two 100-win teams, the Mets and A's, en route to one of the most improbable world championships ever.

"That's why," Strawberry said last night, "we can't get too excited about (100 wins). It's a great accomplishment, don't make any mistake about it. You're winning 70% of well over 100 games, you're doing something. But I can tell you, I thought that '88 Mets team was the best team I ever played on and I still can't believe we lost to the Dodgers in the playoffs — especially after the way we had handled them all year."

As a matter of fact, the team that has held

this nebulous AL record for "fewest games to 100 wins — 140," the 1954 Cleveland Indians, got swept by the Giants in the World Series, which ought to be the most sobering aspect of this otherwise giddy achievement. Chances are, these Yankees aren't any more aware of that than they were of clinching a playoff berth last Saturday, which is just as well. They don't need to concern themselves with history.

"Hopefully," said Derek Jeter when apprised of the fact that only six of the last 18 100-win teams won the World Series, "we'll be No. 7. Otherwise, it means absolutely nothing. You don't get a ring for winning the regular season."

"Winning 100 games this time of year is kinda neat," echoed Paul O'Neill, "but it isn't a goal we set out to achieve in spring training."

The problem, of course, with finishing first and winning 100 or more games in the process is the great expectations that go with it. Until or unless you win it all, it is hard to take much satisfaction out of it.

Fans cheer the Yankees on to their 100th win.

"Look at Cleveland last year," said Tino Martinez. "They won, what? Eighty-six games? And yet they came within one out of winning the World Series. We could wind up winning 110 games, but that would also mean we went something like 10-25 in the last month of the season. That would mean we weren't playing very well. It's how many games you win in October that matters."

All of this is not to say, however, these Yankees shouldn't take some measure of pride in what they've accomplished this season. World Series ring or not, it has a chance of being every bit as remarkable as Mark McGwire and Sammy Sosa breaking Roger Maris' home run record.

"I don't buy this business about it meaning nothing if we don't win it all," said Don Zimmer. "This has been one special season. You mean to tell me what this team has done don't mean nothing? That's bull."

Then again, Zimmer, above all, can attest to how 100 wins can mean more than almost anything.

"In 1978," he said, a painful look coming across his face, "my Red Sox won 99 ballgames and so did the Yankees. I'd give anything to have that 100th win."

STANDINGS AT THE END OF WEEK 23

American League East	W.	L.	PCT.	G.B.
NEW YORK YANKEES	103	43	.705	-
Boston Red Sox	83	63	.568	20
Toronto Blue Jays	80	68	.540	24
Baltimore Orioles	75	72	.510	28.5
Tampa Bay Devil Rays	57	89	.390	46

GAME OF THE WEEK

September 9, 1998 VS. BOSTON RED SOX

YANKS CLINCH DIVISION TITLE

Second in Three Years for Bombers

SEPTEMBER 10, 1998

By Peter Botte, Daily News Sports Writer

WEEK 24 ● SEPTEMBER 6 - 12

BOSTON —There is only one champagne wish and caviar dream that ever really mattered to the Yankees. But that didn't stop the bubbly and various other items from flowing all over the visiting clubhouse of Fenway Park late last night, as the best team in baseball celebrated, rather vociferously, what long had been a foregone conclusion in clinching their second AL East title in three seasons.

"I think we needed something like this," Paul O'Neill said amid the champagne shower after both he and Derek Jeter blasted two home runs in the Yanks' 7-5 edging of the Red Sox. "All year, from the All-Star break into August, people have been telling us, 'You guys are doing so well.' But this is an actual accomplishment, something we've been pointing to since spring training.

"We don't take any of this for granted. We

The Yankees clinched the American League East title against the Boston Red Sox and Nomar Garciaparra.

DAILY NEWS Linda Cataffo

believe we have to enjoy this while we can, and we deserve to enjoy it." Perhaps reveling in clinching the division title on the home turf of a bitter rival, George Steinbrenner has been with the team for each of these three games, of which the Yankees won twice to even the season's next-to-last road trip at 3-3.

First-year GM Brian Cashman also joined The Boss here last night to share in the accomplishment.

"It's not over yet, and we still haven't won a damn thing yet except for a division," Steinbrenner said in all too familiar refrain as he stepped out of the elevator on his way to the clubhouse. "But it feels all right, right now."

Not much of a concession by The Boss, of course, but while his charges have always understood that ultimate directive, they still believe they were entitled to pat themselves on the back for the first step in accomplishing their mission.

"People all say that if we don't win a World Series, then our season is a failure," said Jeter, whose two solo homers off knuckleballer Tim Wakefield represented his second career two-homer game. "I don't see it being a failure, but it would be a huge disappointment. . . . But just because we have a big lead doesn't mean we shouldn't be able to enjoy this tonight and then come back tomorrow ready to keep going."

With the clinching, the Yanks established their largest lead of the season and largest in team history since 1941, in which the team secured the AL title by its earliest calendar date (Sept. 4). It also marked the earliest date the Yanks have clinched the AL East since divisional play began in 1969. The 1975 Reds clinched the NL Western Division title on Sept. 8.

"We're obviously going to be disappointed if we don't go any further than winning a division, but what we've accomplished in winning it is in and of itself an accomplishment and achievement and somthing to look back on and be happy about," Joe Torre said.

"Let's admit it, everybody wants to go to a Super Bowl, the Final Four, the World Series. When you start in February, that's your goal. If you don't get there, you're very disappointed. . . . If we don't get there, this is still going to be special, but it will lose a little luster. . . . But this is still a worthy accomplishment."

Orlando Hernandez, who has won just one of his last five starts, certainly is starting to lose some of the luster from his star. El Duque was staked to an early 5-0 lead, but was knocked out four batters after allowing a grand slam to Scott Hatteberg in the fourth.

Ramiro Mendoza (9-2) pitched Hernandez out of another bases-loaded jam to end the fourth, however, and hurled two frames of one-run ball before Mike Stanton (1 1/3 perfect innings) and Mariano Rivera (35th save) sealed the anti-climactic clinching.

It was a clinching which was celebrated on the field without fanfare, aside from a group hug and high-five session behind the mound. At least until the clubhouse doors were opened.

"This wasn't planned until late," David Cone said of the wet-bar clubhouse. "We didn't want to downplay it or be nonchalant, and we didn't want to overdo it either. It's a cause for celebration. I thought this was just the right balance."

FINAL

NEW YORK YANKEES 7, AT BOSTON RED SOX 5

NEW YORK	ab	r	h	rbi	BOSTON	ab	r	h	rbi
Knoblauch 2b	4	0	0	0	Bragg cf	5	0	0	0
Jeter ss	4	2	2	2	Valentin 3b	2	0	0	0
O'Neill rf	4	2	2	2	Vaughn 1b	3	1	1	0
B Williams cf	3	1	0	0	Garciaparra ss	4	2	3	0
T Martinez 1b	4	1	1	1	O'Leary lf	4	0	1	0
Raines lf	2	0	0	0	Stanley dh	2	1	0	0
Ledee lf	1	0	0	0	b-Snopek dh	1	0	0	0
Strawberry dh	3	0	0	0	Hatteberg c	3	1	1	4
a-C Davis ph-dh	1	0	0	0	c-K Mitchell rf	1	0	0	0
J Posada c	4	1	1	1	T Nixon rf	3	0	1	0
Brosius 3b	4	0	1	1	d-Varitek c	1	0	0	0
					Sadler 2b	3	0	1	0
					e-M Benjamin	1	0	0	0
Totals	34	7	7	7	Totals	33	5	8	4

HR - Jeter 2, O'Neill 2 . HR - Hatteberg.

a-grounded to third for Strawberry in the 9th; b-grounded to shortstop for Stanley in the 8th; c-flied to center for Hatteberg in the 8th; d-flied to left for T Nixon in the 8th; e-grounded to pitcher for Sadler in the 9th.

NY Yankees	101 310 010	— 7
Boston	000 410 000	— 5

NY Yankees	ip	h	r	er	bb	so	hr	era
O Hernandez	3 2/3	5	4	4	4	5	1	3.50
Mendoza W	3	3	1	1	0	1	0	3.18
Stanton	1 1/3	0	0	0	0	1	0	5.87
M Rivera S	1	0	0	0	0	1	0	.75

Boston	ip	h	r	er	bb	so	hr	era
Wakefield L	4	5	5	5	1	4	2	4.71
J Wasdin	3	1	1	1	0	1	1	5.09
Swindell	1	1	1	1	0	2	1	3.66
Eckersley	1	0	0	0	0	1	0	4.63

Yankee jerseys await the team in the locker room.

DAILY NEWS Linda Cataffo

SEPT 6	SUN	at Chicago White Sox	6-5	L
SEPT 7	MON	at Boston Red Sox	4-3	L
SEPT 8	TUES	at Boston Red Sox	2-3	W
SEPT 9	WED	at Boston Red Sox	5-7	W
SEPT 10	THU	Toronto Blue Jays	8-5	W
SEPT 11	FRI	Toronto Blue Jays	4-5	L
SEPT 12	SAT	Toronto Blue Jays	3-5	L

In Fargo yesterday, in the capital of Roger Maris, even those who loved Roger Maris knew that one of the magnificent runs in the history of baseball—in the history of sports—comes to an end.

GOING, GOING, GONE

By Mike Lupica, Daily News Sports Writer
September 7, 1998

Mike Lupica

His name is Don Gooselaw, and he has been a Roger Maris guy his whole life, as long as he can remember, long before the world knew about Maris, homers in 1961.

They grew up together in Grand Forks, North Dakota, in the Hampton Apartments on Fifth Ave. and Seventh St. This was almost 60 years ago, the beginning of a friendship that would last all of Maris' life.

"I was as close to baseball history as you could get, I suppose," Gooselaw was saying yesterday. "I used to go to Minneapolis when the Yankees would play there. I was with Roger in Cincinnati for the World Series in '61, the home run year. I thought of him as my best friend. But even here in North Dakota, you have to let go eventually."

Gooselaw is 66 and lives in Fargo now. Maris' family moved there in the 1940s after his father, a railroad man,

Yankee fans enjoy the 1998 season.

DAILY NEWS   Linda Cataffo

was transferred out of Grand Forks. There is a museum in Maris' memory in Fargo, in a shopping mall. Gooselaw runs a Roger Maris golf tournament every year, to benefit a local hospice. In so many important ways, this is the capital of Roger Maris. And even there yesterday, they were ready to let go.

"If [Mark McGwire] breaks it today, God bless him," Gooselaw said. "If he doesn't, I'll be like everybody else these next two days, watching that showdown between him and [Sammy] Sosa when the Cubs go into St. Louis. It'll be like one of those old home run derbies they used to have on television back when Roger was playing. Even I know it's a once-in-a-lifetime thing."

In Fargo yesterday, in the capital of Roger Maris, even those who loved Roger Maris knew that one of the magnificent runs in the history of baseball — in the history of sports — comes to an end.

"We had our turn for 37 years," Gooselaw said. "Now it's somebody else's turn."

There was a pause and then he said, "I'm going to sit

here in front of my television just like everybody else, and get ready to say goodbye."

Maris came out of North Dakota, came to the Yankees from the Kansas City Athletics, and broke a home run record of Babe Ruth's that had lasted for 34 years. Maris' record has lasted longer. Back home they started to think, before McGwire and Ken Griffey Jr. and Sosa came along, that maybe it might stand forever.

"You get spoiled," Gooselaw said. "You take it for granted after a while. You'd see guys make a run, get to 50 home runs, and they'd start talking about Roger, and his pace in '61. Then they wouldn't make it and you'd think, 'Roger's still safe.'"

Safe at home.

The home run record belonged to Maris, and his widow Pat, and his children. It belonged to the Yankees and Yankee Stadium and New York. But it belonged to Fargo, too, even after Maris moved on to Kansas City and, in retirement, to Florida. He always came back in summer, until leukemia killed him young, in 1985, at the age of 51.

He would have dinner with Gooselaw and play golf, and they would talk about how they had to play each other in high school after Maris moved to Fargo. Gooselaw was the quarterback for St. James High, Maris was a halfback for Shanley.

Gooselaw was asked yesterday if Maris ever talked about his home run season of 1961, when he was McGwire and Mickey Mantle was Sosa, chasing him.

"Not unless you asked him," Gooselaw said. "He never brought it up himself. I sometimes got the idea it was a happier memory for the rest of us than it was for him."

Then Gooselaw was talking about that Yankees-Reds World Series in '61 again.

"I saw how happy he was to get on the plane and go home," he said. "I knew how happy he was that the whole thing was over."

Now it ends for good, maybe today or tomorrow, with McGwire and Sosa on a ballfield together in St. Louis for the home run derby Don Gooselaw talked about yesterday, for one of the most amazing games of one-on-one baseball has ever seen.

His man Maris had his run, had all this time. Somebody else's turn, even in Fargo.

DAILY NEWS Mike Albans

The sentiments of Yankees fans worldwide.

STANDINGS AT THE END OF WEEK 24

American League East	W.	L.	PCT.	G.B.
NEW YORK YANKEES	106	47	.693	-
Boston Red Sox	86	67	.562	20
Toronto Blue Jays	82	73	.529	25
Baltimore Orioles	78	76	.506	28.5
Tampa Bay Devil Rays	62	91	.405	44

GAME OF THE WEEK

September 14, 1998 VS. BOSTON RED SOX

A REAL CROWD-PLEASER

El Duque whitewashes fading Sox

SEPTEMBER 15, 1998

By Rafael Hermoso, Daily News Sports Writer

WEEK 25 ● SEPTEMBER 13 - 19

A record-breaking Stadium crowd found itself divided between allegiances to the Yankees and Pedro Martinez last night. New York's large Dominican community turned out to cheer the Red Sox starter, but he was outdone by Orlando Hernandez.

Hernandez pitched his first major-league shutout as the Yankees snapped a three-game losing streak with a 3-0 win. He outdueled Martinez (18-6), who allowed three runs in seven innings for his second straight loss to the Yankees and left to chants of "Where is Pedro?" from the right-field bleachers.

Boston remained three games ahead of wild-card contender Toronto, which lost at Cleveland, 6-3.

Last night's crowd of 42,735 gave the Yankees a home season attendance of 2,657,785. They need to average 38,024 fans in their final nine home games to surpass 3 million, the benchmark George Steinbrenner set to discuss keeping the Yankees in the Bronx. The previous record was 2,633,701 in 1988.

Fans support El Duque.

DAILY NEWS Linda Cataffo

The crowd included two young women who ran toward Derek Jeter at shortstop before being escorted away with two outs in the ninth.

Steinbrenner was in Tampa last night, but his manager was mindful of his words.

"I think it's great," Joe Torre said before the game. "This is a great ballpark. Don't get me in trouble. Probably the next one will be great, too."

Hernandez (10-4), who had a 7.06 ERA in his previous four starts, allowed three hits and struck out nine to give the Yankees five starters with at least 10 wins for the first time since 1942.

Scott Brosius' run-scoring single in the seventh gave the Yankees a 2-0 lead. Brosius went to second on the throw home, moved to third on a groundout and scored when Chuck Knoblauch reached first base on a strike-three wild pitch for a 3-0 edge.

What promised to be a pitcher's duel

quickly turned into a holy war in the right-field bleachers, where fans waving Dominican flags honoring Martinez were greeted by chants of "Pedro S——" and "USA."

But as in their meeting last week, the Yankees' only hit off Martinez through the first three innings was a Paul O'Neill single.

The Yankees finally broke through in the fifth inning. Luis Sojo's sacrifice fly to the right-field corner scored Darryl Strawberry from third base.

Strawberry almost gave it back in the sixth when he let Mo Vaughn's fly ball go off his glove on the left-center field warning track. As Strawberry fell on his rear, Bernie Williams ran over him and slammed chest-first into the wall. Williams fell back into Strawberry's lap as Vaughn ended up with a triple.

Hernandez had his usual cheering section, which added to an El Du-K sign for each strikeout. They roared when he escaped a two-on, no-out jam in the first.

Facing their second four-game losing streak of the season, the Yankees had received subpar performances from their starters recently.

"I think the question is why didn't it happen before now?" Joe Torre said before the game. "I think the reason is the starting pitching has been better than it is now."

Torre dismissed any chances of the lethargy carrying into the postseason. "I don't think so, and this ballclub has been to the postseason before," he said. "They know what it takes to be mentally ready."

Although he was more concerned with his team playing well heading into the playoffs, Torre was cognizant of Boston's wild-card race with the Blue Jays.

"There's more pressure on the Red Sox, but I'm sure Toronto would trade places with them in a heartbeat," Torre said. "They're in a better position."

Torre predicted the Red Sox would hold on because "they've been there all year long."

The Yankees had Chili Davis DH-ing and batting lefthanded for the first time since he strained his right rib cage on Aug. 26. The switch-hitter wasn't concerned about proving to Torre that he can swing from both sides.

FINAL
BOSTON RED SOX 0, AT NEW YORK YANKEES 3

BOSTON	ab	r	h	rbi	NY YANKEES	ab	r	h	rbi
Bragg cf	4	0	1	0	Knoblauch 2b	4	0	0	0
JValentin 3b	3	0	0	0	Jeter ss	4	0	0	0
Vaughn 1b	4	0	1	0	O'Neill rf	3	0	2	0
Garciaparra ss	4	0	1	0	B Williams cf	4	0	1	0
O'Leary lf	3	0	0	0	C Davis dh	4	0	0	0
Stanley dh	3	0	0	0	Strawberry lf	2	1	1	0
T Nixon rf	3	0	0	0	Curtis lf	2	1	1	0
Hatteberg c	2	0	0	0	J Posada c	3	0	1	0
Sadler 2b	1	0	0	0	Brosius 3b	3	1	1	1
a-Cummings ph	1	0	0	0	Sojo 1b	2	0	0	1
Merloni 2b	0	0	0	0					
Totals	28	0	3	0	Totals	31	3	7	2

a-flied to left for Sadler in the 8th.

Boston	000 000 000	— 0
Ny Yankees	000 010 20X	— 3

Boston	ip	h	r	er	bb	so	hr	era
P Martinez	7	7	3	3	0	9	0	2.78
Lowe	1	0	0	0	1	1	0	4.08

NY Yankees	ip	h	r	er	bb	so	hr	era
O Hernandez	9	3	0	0	0	9	0	3.25

Yankees pitcher Orlando Hernandez has some fun in the dugout.

"I know I can hit," said Davis, who tore a tendon and ligaments in his right ankle in the second game of the season. "I came back after four months and hit. I need to get as many games as possible."

REST OF THE WEEK

SEPT 13	SUN	Toronto Blue Jays	3-5	L
SEPT 14	MON	Boston Red Sox	3-0	W
SEPT 15	TUES	Boston Red Sox	4-9	L
SEPT 16	WED	at Tampa Bay Devil Rays	0-7	L
SEPT 17	THU	at Tampa Bay Devil Rays	4-0	W
SEPT 18	FRI	at Baltimore Orioles	15-5	W
SEPT 19	SAT	at Baltimore Orioles	3-5	L

"I don't think anything will stop me from protecting my teammates, because I've always been like that."
—Darryl Strawberry

BRAWL COSTS STRAW

By Rafael Hermoso, Daily News Sports Writer
September 15, 1998

Rafael Hermoso

Darryl Strawberry received a three-game suspension (beginning tomorrow) and a $1,000 fine for throwing punches in last Friday's brawl with the Blue Jays. Rookie second baseman Homer Bush and coach Don Zimmer also were fined but not suspended.

Toronto reliever Bill Risley received a two-game suspension.

Strawberry said he would not appeal. Bush, who was caught undercutting Jose Canseco on video, called his $300 fine "awesome, because it could've been a lot worse."

The Yankees still were quietly steamed that umpires allowed Roger Clemens, who precipitated the brawl by hitting Scott Brosius, not to be penalized.

"Do I have a problem with it? Would it make a difference if I did?" GM Brian Cashman said. "Out of respect for the league office, I'll leave it at that."

DAILY NEWS Linda Cataffo

Darryl Strawberry was fined and suspended for his part in a brawl with the Blue Jays.

"I can't have a reaction," said Joe Torre, who was ejected before the brawl for arguing favoritism toward Clemens.

Strawberry claims he didn't start swinging until Risley pulled him down in the scrum.

"I don't think anything will ever stop me from protecting my teammates because I've always been like that," said Strawberry, who was suspended three games after a May 19 brawl with the Orioles.

DAILY NEWS Linda Cataffo

Don Zimmer was also fined after the brawl.

STANDINGS AT THE END OF WEEK 25

American League East

	W.	L.	PCT.	G.B.
x-NEW YORK YANKEES	113	48	.702	-
y-Boston Red Sox	91	70	.565	22
Toronto Blue Jays	87	74	.540	26
Baltimore Orioles	79	82	.491	34
Tampa Bay Devil Rays	63	98	.391	50

x-clinched division title

y-clinched wild card

YANKEE PROFILE
David Cone

TEN YEARS LATER, CONE GETS 20TH

SEPTEMBER 27, 1998

By Peter Botte, Daily News Sports Writer

David Cone

RHP

The year was 1988, David Cone's first full season in a big-league rotation. He would win 20 games as easily as the Yankees steamrolled through this dream season's schedule.

Despite continuing to embark on a stellar career — which has included a Cy Young Award, vast riches, and a reputation as both a consummate big-game pitcher and stand-up clubhouse presence — Cone figured he might not ever get back to that magic pitching barometer.

And then there was yesterday's 3-1 milestone victory over the Devil Rays at the Stadium. In capping a remarkable return from multiple shoulder problems — which forced him to miss a critical start in last fall's AL Division Series — Cone proudly finds himself healthy again as October and the Texas Rangers loom.

He also finds himself a 20-game winner for the first time since he went 20-3 for the Mets in 1988.

"It's been a long time coming," said Cone, who snapped the major-league record for the longest interval between 20-win seasons, previ-

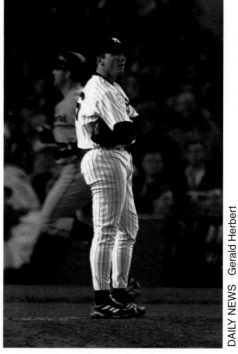

David Cone reacts to giving up a grand slam to Jim Thome during the ALCS.

DAILY NEWS   Gerald Herbert

ously owned by Jim Kaat (seven). "I had 18 wins a long time ago (Aug. 17), and a couple of shots at 20, and I kind of thought I missed the opportunity. That makes it all the more gratifying."

After Mariano Rivera pitched out of a self-induced, bases-loaded situation in the ninth, Cone's teammates exploded in a rare fist-pumping celebration.

Joe Girardi's first order of business was to retrieve the ball from first baseman Luis Sojo and present it to Cone. When his personal catcher hugged him and made the exchange, Cone (20-7, 3.55) could not contain his emotions.

"I didn't expect to react that way, but once it was in the books, I kind of lost it a little bit," said Cone, who allowed four hits on 101 pitches in seven shutout innings. "This is my most gratifying (season), considering where I started and how disappointing last year was at the end."

Cone recalled being so anxious when finally

given clearance to resume throwing that he pitched to bullpen catcher Gary Tuck last November aboard the Yankees team cruise to St. Maarten.

"Sixty feet and throwing them off the deck," Cone joked when someone asked if his velocity was measured in knots. "All I know is I never imagined then I'd be standing here talking about 20 wins. All I wanted to do was be ready on time, be healthy all year and reach 200 innings. Twenty wins, is something I never honestly thought about."

"To accomplish what he did this year, I think is remarkable ," Joe Torre said of David Cone. "This was important to all of us. It's really a great story. He's had a helluva run. Hopefully, we can extend it a little longer."

DAILY NEWS Keith Torrie

David Cone holding the AL trophy.

Shane Spencer — yes, again — and Tino Martinez blasted solo homers in support of Cone, who missed only one scheduled start all year following an offseason shoulder arthroscopy.

Now he will start Game 3 of the AL Division Series next Friday in Texas against the AL West champion Rangers.

"To accomplish what he did this year, I think is remarkable," Joe Torre said. "This was important to all of us. It's really a great story. He's had a helluva run. Hopefully, we can extend it a little longer."

The only scare the 35-year-old righthander encountered was when he had the wind knocked out of him

with a shot to the ribs on Rich Butler's grounder in the third.

After he completed seven innings, Cone watched Rivera's harrowing escape. Afterward a chilled magnum of champagne with a card reading "Congratulations, from The Boss" sat on the chair in front of his cubicle.

Cone later flashed back to the congratulations he received the previous time he won 20 games. "I walked off the mound and I remember President Nixon was in the dugout," Cone said. "I was too young to appreciate it. I guess I took a lot of things for granted back then. That's why this means so much right now."

David Cone Stats

1998 REGULAR SEASON

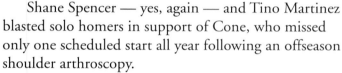

W	L	S	ERA	G	GS	CG	SHO	IP	H	R	ER	HR	BB	SO	HB	WP	BK
20	7	0	3.55	31	31	3	0	207.2	186	89	82	20	59	209	15	6	0

YANKEES 8,   DEVIL RAYS 3

GAME OF THE WEEK

September 27, 1998 VS. TAMPA BAY DEVIL RAYS

YANKS' PLAYTIME IS OVER

Hard-hitting Rangers are first hurdle

SEPTEMBER 28, 1998

By Peter Botte, Daily News Sports Writer

WEEK 26 ● SEPTEMBER 20 -27

The 162-game preseason is over. The time for the Yankees finally has arrived.

"We're about ready to go to war, and I love war," George Steinbrenner said in the clubhouse yesterday after the Yanks' 8-3 victory over the Devil Rays. The team's 114th victory this season served as the final tune-up for the first-round playoff clash beginning tomorrow against Texas.

"I've been reading a new book. 'Whiskey, Women and . . .' something else. It's about General (Ulysses S.) Grant. It's about winning battles and wars. We'll be ready. But not to smoke cigars."

Of course, there were few celebratory cigars to be smoked yesterday, and the only cham-

Bernie Williams won the 1998 American League batting title.

DAILY NEWS   Gerlad Herbert

pagne in the house was a gift from Steinbrenner to Bernie Williams for winning the AL batting title. Instead, the Yankees were shifting their attention from making a mockery of the regular-season schedule to a dangerous five-game showdown with the potent Rangers.

David Wells, whose career-high 18 wins included the first regular-season perfect game in team history, throws the first pitch slightly after 8 p.m. tomorrow.

"We're ready," Joe Torre said of his team, which has won seven straight and 11 of 12 to right the post-clinching doldrums. "We're definitely ready. The players . . . they've been looking forward to Tuesday for a long time.

"You go out there without a safety net now. It's exciting. I wouldn't trade it for anything. There are no guarantees. Patience is short. The blood rushes. It's a wonderful feeling and you're exhausted at the end of the day. But we want to go on like every team in the postseason goes on."

Of course, this has been far from "every team" since the spring, when it was first discussed that anything short of a World Series title would be a disappointment.

"Even when you say you're going to win 100 games you don't even know that. You really need a lot of help to win even 100 games," Torre said. "To win 114 is above and beyond. But now everybody's 0-0, and we start over on Tuesday."

And though Williams edged Mo Vaughn for his first career batting crown, the Yankees all season have been focused on collective goals.

"This is all we were looking forward to when we started in spring training," Williams said. "We never knew how far we were going to get, but we knew we'd have to play hard every day to be in the position we're in right now. And we're not taking anything for granted."

Not against a potent Texas lineup that is capable of winning shootouts and includes MVP candidate Juan Gonzalez and a slew of other dangerous players. While the Yanks took eight of 11 this season and averaged nearly 7.5 runs against the righthand-dominated Texas

rotation, the Rangers averaged 6.8 runs against the Yanks.

"It makes no difference what we did in the regular season. I don't think Texas really cares how many games we've won," Derek Jeter said.

"We don't have one big guy. We have a team full of big guys," Tim Raines said. "Even though we were the wild-card team last year, we felt we should've beaten Cleveland. Knowing what happened to us last year, we're going to do whatever we can to not let that happen again."

FINAL

TAMPA BAY DEVIL RAYS 3, AT NEW YORK YANKEES 8

TAMPA BAY	ab	r	h	bi	NEW YORK	ab	r	h	bi
Winn cf	5	0	1	0	Knoblauch 2b	1	1	0	0
McCracken lf	3	0	0	0	Bush 2b	1	1	1	0
Robinson lf	2	0	0	0	Jeter ss	4	1	1	0
Smith 3b	4	0	1	0	O'Neill, rf	2	0	1	0
McGriff 1b	3	1	3	0	Curtis lf cf	1	1	1	1
McClain 1b	1	1	0	0	B Williams cf	2	1	2	1
Trammell dh	4	1	1	0	Ledee ph lf	1	0	0	0
Kelly rf	1	0	0	1	T Martinez 1b	2	0	0	0
Butler rf	2	0	1	2	Sojo 1b	2	1	1	1
Ledesma ss	4	0	2	0	Strawberry dh	2	0	2	0
Cairo 2b	4	0	0	0	Davis ph dh	1	1	0	0
Difelice c	4	0	2	0	Spencer lf rf	4	1	1	4
Rekar p	0	0	0	0	Posada c	4	0	0	0
					Brosius 3b	3	0	0	0
					Lowell 3b	1	0	0	0
Totals	37	3	11	3	Totals	31	8	10	8

Tampa Bay	000 102 000	—	3
NY Yankees	002 051 00x	—	8

Tampa Bay	ip	h	r	er	bb	so
Rekar	2	2	0	0	0	0
White L	2/3	2	2	2	1	0
Duvall	1/3	1	0	0	0	1
Yan	1 2/3	2	3	3	2	3
Aldred	0	0	1	1	1	0
Lopez	1 1/3	3	2	2	0	0
Tatis	1	0	0	0	0	0
Springer	1	0	0	0	0	1

Duvall pitched to 1 batter in the 4th. Aldred pitched to 1 batter in the 5th.

NY Yankees	ip	h	r	er	bb	so
Bruske W	5	4	1	1	1	2
Irabu	2	4	2	2	0	3
Lloyd	1	1	0	0	0	0
Holmes	1	2	0	0	0	1

> "This is all we were looking forward to when we started in spring training. We never knew how far we were going to get, but we knew we'd have to play hard every day to be in the position we're in right now. And we're not taking anything for granted."
>
> **—Bernie Williams**

SEPT 20	SUN	at Baltimore Orioles	5-4	W
SEPT 21	MON	Cleveland Indians	1-4	L
SEPT 22	TUES	Cleveland Indians	10-4	W
SEPT 22	TUES	Cleveland Indians	5-1	W
SEPT 23	WED	Cleveland Indians	8-4	W
SEPT 24	THU	Tampa Bay Devil Rays	5-2	W
SEPT 25	FRI	Tampa Bay Devil Rays	6-1	W
SEPT 26	SAT	Tampa Bay Devil Rays	3-1	W
SEPT 27	SUN	Tampa Bay Devil Rays	8-3	W

Moments after Chuck Knoblauch grounded to short for the game's first out, the Yankees stepped out of their dugout in unison, tipped their hats toward Ripken in the home dugout and applauded.

THE STREAK IS STRUCK

By Peter Botte, Daily News Sports Writer
September 21, 1998

And in game No. 2,633, Cal Ripken rested.

The quintessential iron man walked into the office of Orioles manager Ray Miller moments before last night's 5-4 loss to the Yankees — and finally asked out of the starting lineup for the first time since May 30, 1982.

The Streak is over after 2,632 consecutive games.

"So that's what a day off feels like, huh?" the 38-year-old Ripken said after he was replaced in the lineup by rookie Ryan Minor minutes before last night's first pitch.

"I guess I just want to say it was time," Ripken said. "Baseball's always been a team game and I've always believed the focus should be on the team. There's been times during the streak where the focus was on the streak, and I've never really felt totally comfortable about that."

Ever since Sept. 6, 1995,

Cal Ripken Jr. ended his consecutive game streak at 2,632 against the Yankees.

DAILY NEWS Linda Cataffo

when he surpassed the 2,130 consecutive games set by Yankees legend Lou Gehrig, Ripken's streak had provided an ongoing source of debate around the Inner Harbor and throughout baseball.

"I just think it reached a point where I firmly believed it was time to change the subject," Ripken said. "Restore the focus back where it should be, back on the team, and then move on."

Miller, like each of his predecessors in the manager's chair here, has been besieged with queries and opinions on how to handle The Streak's ultimate conclusion. Each time, Miller said Ripken had long ago earned the right to make that decision for himself.

While Miller acknowledged Saturday that The Streak would be discussed this offseason, Ripken was cryptic recently when asked if there was a chance he would sit one out before season's end.

"I guess," Ripken was quoted as saying in yesterday's Baltimore Sun, "you'll have to watch and see."

Thus, there were rumors swirling all day that last night would be the night. With the Orioles out of playoff contention and playing their final home game, it seemed like a logical time.

Ripken's name was in Miller's lineup right up until game time; he was to bat sixth and play third base, the position he reluctantly switched to from shortstop for the start of the 1997 season.

Minor, the former University of Oklahoma basketball standout, trotted out to third base when the Orioles took the field. Ripken, who said he was "fidgety and antsy" while sitting on the bench and spending some time in the bullpen during the game — said he had decided in a discussion with his wife on Thursday that this would be the night.

"It was just very important to do it here," Ripken said.

Moments after Chuck Knoblauch grounded to short for the game's first out, the Yankees stepped out of their dugout in unison, tipped their hats toward Ripken in the home dugout and applauded.

Ripken emerged from the Orioles dugout, tipped his hat toward the Yankees and stepped back down to the bench.

With the sellout crowd standing and cheering, Ripken came out again and bowed to his fans.

"This shouldn't be a sad moment. I look at it as a celebration," Ripken said. "Contrary to some reports that I'm on my last breath, I still consider myself an everyday player. I'll be in the lineup tomorrow."

The end came during a magical season that has featured the historic home run chase between Mark McGwire and Sammy Sosa, a perfect game by David Wells and the Yankees' pursuit of the AL record for victories.

And now there is Ripken.

"The streak was born out of my desire to play, and a lot of managers wanting to put me in the lineup," Ripken said. "You're a baseball player. Your job is to play. Nothing will change who I am, or my approach to the game."

DAILY NEWS Linda Cataffo

The 1998 Yankees team prompted comparisons to the Broadway musical.

STANDINGS AT THE END OF WEEK 26

American League East—Final Standings

	W	L	PCT.	G.B.	Home	Road
x-NEW YORK YANKEES	114	48	.704	-	62-19	52-29
y-Boston Red Sox	92	70	.568	22	51-30	41-40
Toronto Blue Jays	88	74	.543	26	51-30	37-44
Baltimore Orioles	79	83	.488	35	42-39	37-44
Tampa Bay Devil Rays	63	99	.389	51	33-48	30-51

x-clinched division title
y-clinched wild card

YANKEE PROFILE
Michael Shane Spencer

SPENCER SHANE-SATIONAL
Rookie OF continues torrid pace

OCTOBER 1,1998
By Anthony McCarron, Daily News Sports Writer

OF

Shane Spencer

Derek Jeter's status as top Yankee heartthrob may be in danger. Shane Spencer has been hotter than a limited edition Beanie Baby lately, slugging eight homers in his last 10 games, including three grand slams in nine days.

He can't even pay for his own dinner when he goes out on the town. "Yeah, people have tried to 'comp' me," Spencer said. "You've just got to remember to leave a big tip."

In the last week of the season, teenage girls in the stands were holding up signs that said, "We love Derek." But the "Derek" was crossed out. In its place — "Shane."

All this was happening before he homered in his first postseason at-bat last night and had two hits and scored two runs in the Yanks' 3-1 victory over Texas. The win gave the Yankees a 2-0 lead in the best-of-five division series.

This from a guy who said, "I wouldn't have imagined making the postseason roster."

What's next, Broadway? Joe Torre already compares him with Joe Hardy, the superstar of the ballclub in the musical "Damn Yankees."

Shane Spencer

DAILY NEWS   John Roca

Spencer's rise to baseball fame reads like an improbable storybook.

Before this season, he was a 26-year-old farmhand who wasn't considered to be a surefire prospect.

But he kept improving and has made the most of his chance in New York. Spencer slammed six homers and knocked in 15 runs during the last week of the season while hitting .440 to earn player of the week honors.

He finished the regular season at .373 (25-for-67) with 10 homers and 27 RBI.

Spencer refuses to believe it's a happy ending already, however. "It won't be storybook until this is over and we win," he said. "I'll enjoy it right now. I was happy to get out there. I'm just riding it right now, cherishing every moment."

Spencer will certainly cherish the second inning of last night's game, when he crushed a solo homer over the 399-foot mark in left-center off of Rick Helling. The 57,360 souls in atten-

"I could hear them get loud out there," Spencer said. "I said, 'Oh gosh. Here we go.'"

DAILY NEWS   Keith Torrie

Rookie Shane Spencer gets doused with champagne in the locker room after the Yankees eliminated the Texas Rangers from the playoffs.

dance cheered so loud and long it forced the bashful Spencer to take a curtain call.

"I could hear them get loud out there," Spencer said. "I said, 'Oh, gosh. Here we go.'"

As he rounded the bases, Spencer said he hoped his homer would jump-start the team. Maybe it gave teammate Scott Brosius some ideas. Brosius homered in the fourth with Spencer on first.

"I'll tell you one thing, he doesn't get cheated up there," Rangers' manager Johnny Oates said of Spencer. "He knows what this piece of wood is made for and it's not for cleaning off his shoes. Where's he been all year?"

Torre was asked if he put Spencer into the lineup last night to get him used to the white-hot glare of playoff baseball. "I wish I could say I have that luxury," Torre said. "I put him in there to hopefully do what he did. I stayed away from him in Game 1 because it was Game 1 and I wanted defense and Chad (Curtis) had some numbers against (Todd) Stottlemyre."

Did Spencer's performance put an end to the Yanks' year-long left-field platoon? "It's going to be tough to get Shane out of there, though I'm not making that

commitment," Torre said.

The left-field choice last night came down to Spencer and Tim Raines, Torre said. Darryl Strawberry might have been in the mix — more likely as a DH, Torre said — but Straw may not play the rest of the playoffs because of an infection in his colon.

"I was thinking Raines, but it's been raining and I was thinking about Raines' leg," Torre said.

Also, with Joe Girardi catching in place of Jorge Posada, Torre said he felt the team could use Spencer's power.

Shane Spencer Stats

1998 REGULAR SEASON

AVG	G	AB	R	H	TB	2B	3B	HR	RBI	BB	SO	SB	CS	SH	SF	HP	SLG%	OBP%
.381	26	63	17	24	57	6	0	9	23	5	11	0	1	0	1	0	.905	.420

DIVISION PLAYOFFS

POWER BELONGS TO YANKEES, NOT RANGERS

Wells, Pettitte, Cone silence high-powered Texas bats to lead Bombers to a sweep

OCTOBER 3, 1998

By Peter Botte, Daily News Sports Writer

SEPTEMBER 29–OCTOBER 3

Going into the American League Divisional Playoffs, many observers wondered if the record-setting Yankees weren't destined to become the greatest flop in postseason history. New York had slumped late in the season and faced the Texas Rangers and their league-leading .289 batting average in the first round of the playoffs.

Never fear. The Yankees received ace pitching from David Wells, Andy Pettitte and David Cone and found just enough runs to sweep Texas and move closer to their place in history.

GAME ONE

The story was David Wells. The Boomer threw a five-hitter over eight innings and Scott Brosius employed some heady base running as the Yanks beat the Rangers, 2-0, at the Stadium on September 29.

"I strive for this type of challenge. I want the ball. This is what it's all about," said Wells.

DAILY NEWS Howard Simmons

Chuck Knoblauch is out as he tries to score in Game 1 of the American League Playoffs.

FINAL

NEW YORK YANKEES 4, AT TEXAS RANGERS 0

NY YANKEES	ab	r	h	rbi	TEXAS	ab	r	h	rbi
Knoblauch 2b	4	0	0	0	Goodwin cf	3	0	0	0
Jeter ss	4	0	1	0	McLemore 2b	3	0	0	0
O'Neill rf	4	1	2	1	Greer lf	3	0	0	0
B Williams cf	4	0	0	0	J Gonzalez rf	4	0	0	0
Martinez 1b	4	1	2	0	Clark 1b	3	0	0	0
Raines dh	3	1	1	0	I Rodriguez c	3	0	0	0
Spencer lf	3	1	1	3	Stevens dh	3	0	0	0
Curtis lf	0	0	0	0	Zeile 3b	3	0	2	0
Brosius 3b	4	0	1	0	Clayton ss	3	0	1	0
Girardi c	4	0	1	0					
Totals	34	4	9	4	Totals	28	0	3	0

HR - O'Neill, Spencer.

NY Yankees	000 004 000	—	4
Texas	000 000 000	—	0

NY Yankees	ip	h	r	er	bb	so	hr	era
Cone W	5 2/3	2	0	0	1	6	0	0.00
Lloyd	1/3	0	0	0	0	0	0	0.00
Nelson	2	1	0	0	1	2	0	0.00
Rivera	1	0	0	0	1	0	0	0.00

Texas	ip	h	r	er	bb	so	hr	era
Sele L	6	8	4	4	1	4	2	6.00
Crabtree	2	1	0	0	0	1	0	0.00
Wetteland	1	0	0	0	1	1	0	0.00

After walking leadoff batter Mark McLemore, the lefty settled down and retired the next 10 batters he faced.

Todd Stottlemyre (eight two-run innings) also pitched valiantly, but the Yankees scraped together just enough offense to get the win.

Because of Stottlemyre's dominance, the Yanks were forced to gamble offensively in the second inning. Leading 1-0 with one out, New York had Brosius on second and Chad Curtis on third with Chuck Knoblauch at the plate. Knoblauch swung through strike three for the second out but Brosius was running on the pitch. As Ivan Rodriguez threw to second, Curtis broke for home.

Brosius stopped midway to second and was tagged out in a rundown to end the inning, but not before Curtis had stomped on home plate. The two runs were all Wells needed.

"Wells was just awesome," Brosius said. "It was a great game to play and a great game to win. Obviously, when you're looking for three (wins), the first one is huge."

GAME TWO

One night after Wells dominated the Yanks, more of the same came from Andy Pettitte.

The 26-year-old lefty threw seven innings of one-run ball in the Yankees' 3-1 victory over Texas, September 30 at the Stadium. Pettitte allowed just three hits and no walks as the Yankees seized control of the divisional playoff 2-0.

"This was a big game for me," Pettitte said. "It was nice to be able to do it for myself and for the team."

Shane Spencer and Scott Brosius homered off 20-game winner Rick Helling to support Pettitte.

Spencer, Brosius and Joe Girardi combined for six of the eight Yankee hits.

"There's no doubt, our pitching's stepped up and they definitely have won these two games for us," Paul O'Neill said.

Pettitte retired the first 12 Rangers he faced through four, mixing cutters and changeups and spotting his pitches with precision.

DAILY NEWS Keith Torrie

David Wells sprays champagne in the locker room after the Yankees sewed up the series with the Rangers.

Spencer and Brosius gave Pettitte all the support he needed. The 26-year-old Spencer launched Helling's meaty 2-2 fastball beyond the wall in left-center in the second.

Two innings later, Spencer was on again with a single. This time it was Brosius who would command the curtain call with a two-run blast to right-center.

GAME THREE

The Yankees got some good pitching and some better news as they rallied behind David Cone to beat Texas, 4-0, October 3 in Arlington. The win completed a sweep of the Rangers and propelled New York into the American League Championship Series against Cleveland.

More importantly, the Yankees learned that Darryl Strawberry was resting comfortably after undergoing surgery to remove a cancerous tumor from his colon. Doctors reported the disease did not appear to have spread.

"Our pitching won this series, hands down," said Paul O'Neill.

"To shut down that offense and limit them to one run, what else can you say?"

AMERICAN LEAGUE CHAMPIONSHIP SERIES

WRIGHT TO THE POINT
Yankees breeze with five in first

OCTOBER 7, 1998
By Peter Botte, Daily News Sports Writer

GAME 1 ● OCTOBER 6

Jaret Wright took it from the top, but only once. He wasn't around long enough to see the Yankees' rejuvenated batting order a second time.

Shane Spencer and his bottom-third brethren were granted a reprieve from supplying the bulk of the offense in the Yanks' 7-2 clubbing of the Indians last night at the Stadium in Game 1 of the AL championship series. The "other" Yankees battered their Cleveland nemesis, Wright, to a swift demise with an ALCS record five-run first inning.

"It sure would be nice to start that way every game," said Chuck Knoblauch, who started a string of four consecutive hits to open the first with a single to right. "Bang, bang, bang and we had three, four and then five runs. . . . We got their pitcher out of the game, and got our pitcher a lead. That's what baseball is about."

From there, David Wells knew precisely what to do. The big-game lefty was masterful yet again, improving to 6-1 lifetime in postseason play with 8 1/3 nearly flawless innings. He didn't lose his shutout bid until Manny Ramirez hit a two-run homer into the upper deck in left with one out in the ninth.

DAILY NEWS Gerald Herbert

Mariano Rivera celebrates with his teammates after winning the ALCS.

FINAL
CLEVELAND INDIANS 2, AT NEW YORK YANKEES 7

CLEVELAND	ab	r	h	rbi	NEW YORK	ab	r	h	rbi
Lofton cf	4	0	0	0	Knoblauch 2b	5	1	1	0
Cora 2b	3	1	1	0	Jeter ss	4	1	2	0
Justice lf	4	0	1	0	O'Neill rf	5	2	2	1
Ramirez rf	4	1	2	2	Williams cf	4	0	2	2
Fryman 3b	4	0	0	0	Martinez 1b	5	1	0	0
Thome dh	3	0	0	0	Raines dh	2	0	0	0
Sexson 1b	3	0	0	0	Spencer lf	2	1	0	0
Alomar c	3	0	0	0	a-Ledee ph-lf	1	0	0	0
Diaz c	0	0	0	0	Posada c	3	1	2	2
Vizquel ss	3	0	1	0	Brosius 3b	4	0	2	1
Totals	31	2	5	2	Totals	35	7	11	6

HR - Ramirez.   HR - Posada.

a-flied to center for Spencer in the 7th.

Cleveland	000 000 002	—	2
NY Yankees	500 001 10X	—	7

Cleveland	ip	h	r	er	bb	so	hr	era
Wright L	2/3	5	5	5	1	1	0	19.80
Ogea	5 1/3	5	2	2	2	2	1	3.38
Poole	1/3	0	0	0	1	1	0	0.00
Reed	2/3	0	0	0	0	0	0	20.25
Shuey	1	1	0	0	2	2	0	0.00

Ogea pitched to 2 batters in the 7th.

NY Yankees	ip	h	r	er	bb	so	hr	era
Wells W	8 1/3	5	2	2	1	7	1	1.10
Nelson	2/3	0	0	0	0	1	0	0.00

KNOBLAUCH'S WRONG TURN

Blunder gives Tribe series tie

OCTOBER 8, 1998

By Peter Botte, Daily News Sports Writer

The Yankees presented their ungrateful visitors with every imaginable chance to increase the crime rate in this town, but the Indians could not steal the game they desperately needed to steal. So the Yankees gift-wrapped it for them.

While Chuck Knoblauch completely vapor-locked and argued what the Yankees believed to be a blatantly bad call at first base, Enrique Wilson scampered and stumbled all the way around from first as the ball rolled away.

This, the winning run in the top of the 12th inning yesterday, allowed the Indians to escape New York with a controversial 4-1 victory and a split of the first two games of the AL championship series.

With Jeff Nelson (0-1) pitching and Wilson on first as a pinch-runner for Jim Thome with none out in the 12th, Travis Fryman laid down a sacrifice bunt, which Tino Martinez fielded near the first-base line.

Martinez' throw hit Fryman square between the numbers on his back practically at the same time his foot hit the base and the ball bounced away. Knoblauch calmly blew a bubble and pointed at Fryman, suggesting that the runner was the outside the designated baserunning box on the play.

MLB Rule 6.05 (k) states if the baserunner is "outside the three-foot line or inside the foul line and in the umpire's judgment interferes with the fielder taking the throw," the batter is out.

Knoblauch waited several seconds before retrieving the ball approximately 25 feet behind the bag.

"I didn't know where the ball was," said Knoblauch, who didn't turn his head to look for the ball for several seconds. "It was so loud and by the time I realized where the ball was, it was too late."

Knoblauch's throw arrived too late to nail

Wilson at home, and Fryman wound up on third. Nelson proceeded to load the bases on a hit batsman and a walk. Then Kenny Lofton greeted Graeme Lloyd with a two-run single to left-center for the final two runs.

FINAL
CLEVELAND INDIANS 4, AT NEW YORK YANKEES 1

CLEVELAND	ab	r	h	rbi	NEW YORK	ab	r	h	rbi
Lofton cf	6	0	1	2	Knoblauch 2b	6	0	0	0
Vizquel ss	6	0	1	0	Jeter ss	5	0	1	0
Justice dh	4	1	2	1	O'Neill rf	5	0	1	0
Ramirez rf	4	0	0	0	Williams cf	4	1	1	0
Thome 1b	5	0	1	0	Martinez 1b	4	0	0	0
Wilson pr-2b	0	1	0	0	Raines dh	4	0	1	0
Fryman 3b	5	1	2	0	Bush pr-dh	0	0	0	0
Giles lf	4	0	0	0	b-Davis ph-dh	1	0	1	0
Alomar c	4	1	1	0	Ledee pr-dh	0	0	0	0
Cora 2b	4	0	0	0	Spencer lf	5	0	1	0
Sexson 1b	0	0	0	0	Brosius 3b	4	0	1	1
					Girardi c	3	0	0	0
					a-Posada ph-c	2	0	0	0
Totals	**42**	**4**	**8**	**3**	**Totals**	**43**	**1**	**7**	**1**

HR - Justice.
a-grounded to shortstop for Girardi in the 9th; b-singled for Bush in the 11th.

Cleveland	000 100 000 003	—	4
NY Yankees	000 000 100 000	—	1

Cleveland	ip	h	r	er	bb	so	hr	era
Nagy	6 2/3	5	1	1	1	5	0	1.23
Reed	2/3	0	0	0	1	0	0	13.50
Poole	1/3	0	0	0	0	0	0	0.00
Shuey	2	1	0	0	2	2	0	0.00
Assenmacher	1	0	0	0	0	2	0	0.00
Burba W	1/3	1	0	0	0	0	0	4.76
Jackson S	1	0	0	0	0	2	0	3.60

NY Yankees	ip	h	r	er	bb	so	hr	era
Cone	8	5	1	1	3	5	1	0.66
Rivera	2	0	0	0	0	2	0	0.00
Stanton	2/3	0	0	0	0	0	0	0.00
Nelson L	2/3	2	3	3	1	2	0	6.75
Lloyd	2/3	1	0	0	0	0	0	0.00

Chuck Knoblauch argues with the umpire as the ball sits on the ground behind him in Game 2.

DAILY NEWS Gerald Herbert

GAME 2 · OCTOBER 7

INDIANS KNOCK THEIR BLAUCH OFF

By Peter Botte, Daily News Sports Writer

OCTOBER 10, 1998

Andy Pettitte could not keep the baseball in the yard, and now the Yankees will rely on an untested rookie to keep them in their dream season.

Pettitte took care of the ball no better than Chuck Knoblauch had done two nights earlier, getting battered for four home runs without surviving the fifth inning, as the Indians forced the Yankees into a hole for the first time since April with a 6-1 thumping at Jacobs Field to assume a 2-1 lead in the AL championship series.

When Orlando Hernandez takes the ball for the first time since Sept. 25 in Game 4 tonight against Dwight Gooden, he takes with him the fortunes of the record-setting Yankees, who suddenly have much deeper problems than debatable umpiring or a second baseman forgetting to pick up a ball.

Pettitte, who will start in Game 7 should the Yankees make it that far, was hammered for six runs on seven hits — including two by Jim Thome and one apiece by Manny Ramirez and Mark Whiten — in 4 2/3 innings.

Three of the moonshots came in a four-at-bat span in the fifth — in which Joe Torre clearly stuck with Pettitte too long — to turn a 2-1 game into a rout.

While Torre's staff carried the Yankees past Texas, his supposedly nine-deep lineup remains eerily silent.

Tino Martinez is making Mo Vaughn's pending free agency look more like a viable option every day, as Mr. Oct-ofer continued his postseason free-fall, going 0-for-4 to extend his hitless string to 13 in this series. Even the great Shane Spencer has one hit in 11 at-bats, but no one expected the folk hero's success to last forever.

"I have to get a hit here and there and take some pressure off the other guys," admitted Martinez, 17-for-90 (.189) as a Yankee in postseason play with four RBI. "But that doesn't really matter to me. We just need to win (tonight) and get the momentum back."

12 year old Michael Jezycki from Staten Island with a note for the Cleveland Indians.

FINAL

NEW YORK YANKEES 1, AT CLEVELAND INDIANS 4

NEW YORK	ab	r	h	rbi	CLEVELAND	ab	r	h	rbi
Knoblauch 2b	3	1	2	0	Lofton cf	5	0	0	0
Jeter ss	3	0	0	0	Vizquel ss	4	0	3	0
O'Neill rf	3	0	0	0	Justice dh	5	0	0	0
B Williams cf	4	0	1	1	Ramirez rf	4	1	3	1
Martinez 1b	4	0	0	0	Fryman 3b	3	1	1	0
Davis dh	1	0	0	0	Thome 1b	4	2	2	3
Spencer lf	3	0	0	0	Whiten lf	3	2	2	1
Brosius 3b	3	0	0	0	S Alomar c	4	0	0	0
Girardi c	2	0	1	0	Wilson 2b	4	0	1	1
a-Posada ph-c	1	0	0	0					
Totals	27	1	4	1	Totals	36	6	12	6

HR - Thome 2, Ramirez, Whiten.

a-lined to first for Girardi in the 8th.

NY Yankees	100 000 000	—	1
Cleveland	020 040 00X	—	6

NY Yankees	ip	h	r	er	bb	so	hr	era
Pettitte L	4 2/3	8	6	6	3	1	4	5.40
Mendoza	1 1/3	3	0	0	0	0	0	0.00
Stanton	2	1	0	0	1	3	0	0.00

Cleveland	ip	h	r	er	bb	so	hr	era
Colon W	9	4	1	1	4	3	0	1.23

Mendoza pitched to 2 batters in the 7th.

DUQUE IS EL LIFESAVER

Sinks Indians, floats Yank boat

By Peter Botte, Daily News Sports Writer

OCTOBER 11, 1998

CLEVELAND—Orlando Hernandez did not need a translator to tell him the Yankees were in peril. The tension was palpable in any language.

For a man who's conquered far more daunting challenges than anything that can come his way on a baseball field, the Yankees' precarious position seemed rather pedestrian.

The Yankees are even now, with David Wells and David Cone due to take the ball here today and back in the Bronx on Tuesday, respectively.

That almost exclusively is because of Hernandez, who lived up to his regal moniker with seven-plus shutout innings to draw the Yankees even at 2-2 in the ALCS with a 4-0 shutdown of the Indians last night at Jacobs Field.

"I had pressure, but I had no fear," Hernandez said through a translator. "I've been through many difficult times in my life on the field and off the field. I knew I would be able to handle it."

Making his first career postseason appearance — and first of any kind in 15 days — the $6.6 million Cuban defector permitted a scant three hits and two walks. And he made the kind of escapes befitting a brave soul who escaped oppression.

Once staked to a 3-0 lead against old friend Dwight Gooden — on Paul O'Neill's first-inning homer, and two runs in the fourth via an RBI double by Chili Davis and a sac fly by slump-busting Tino Martinez (1-for-2 with a walk) — Hernandez was in complete control.

With one out in the home first, Omar Vizquel dunked a bloop single to left and quickly stole second. One out later, Manny Ramirez worked a walk, which brought up Jim Thome, who had blasted two of the four homers the Indians clubbed against Andy Pettitte in Game 3.

It was a telling proposition for Hernandez, against whom lefthanded batters hit more than 100 points higher (.271 to .162) this season than righthanders.

Thome nearly showed why. He rocketed Duque's 3-2 pitch to the fence in right, but O'Neill camped under it to preserve the lead.

"Once he got past that inning, he was basically untouchable," Derek Jeter said.

FINAL

NEW YORK YANKEES 4, AT CLEVELAND INDIANS 0

NEW YORK	ab	r	h	rbi	CLEVELAND	ab	r	h	rbi
Knoblauch 2b	5	0	0	0	Lofton cf	4	0	1	0
Jeter ss	4	0	0	0	Vizquel ss	4	0	3	0
O'Neill rf	3	2	1	1	Justice dh	3	0	0	0
B Williams cf	1	1	0	0	Ramirez rf	3	0	0	0
Davis dh	4	0	1	1	Thome 1b	4	0	0	0
Martinez 1b	2	0	1	1	Fryman 3b	4	0	0	0
Bush pr	0	1	0	0	Giles lf	3	0	0	0
Sojo 1b	0	0	0	0	S Alomar c	2	0	0	0
Posada c	4	0	0	0	Diaz c	1	0	0	0
Curtis lf	3	0	0	0	Wilson 2b	2	0	0	0
Brosius 3b	3	0	1	1					
Totals	29	4	4	4	Totals	30	0	4	0

HR - O'Neill.

NY Yankees	100 200 001	—	4
Cleveland	000 000 000	—	0

NY Yankees	ip	h	r	er	bb	so	hr	era
Hernandez W	7	3	0	0	2	6	0	0.00
Stanton	1	1	0	0	0	1	0	0.00
Rivera	1	0	0	0	0	1	0	0.00

Cleveland	ip	h	r	er	bb	so	hr	era
Gooden L	4 2/3	3	3	3	3	3	1	9.00
Poole	1/3	0	0	0	0	1	0	0.00
Burba	3 1/3	1	1	1	3	4	0	4.00
Shuey	2/3	0	0	0	0	0	0	0.00

Hernandez pitched to 1 batter in the 8th.

Yankee fans go wild outside the stadium after winning the American League pennant.

GAME 4 • OCTOBER 10

WELLS LEADS WAY

Pitches Yanks within win of Series

By Peter Botte, Daily News Sports Writer

OCTOBER 12, 1998

From Chuck Knoblauch's blunder to Andy Pettitte's whiplash to Orlando Hernandez' story-book start, there has been an air of unpredictability surrounding the Yankees in recent days.

On either end of the feeble and the fabled, however, there have been two constants — automatics, really — why the Yankees have seized a one-game lead after Game 5 of the AL championship series.

Meet David Wells, who has proven a puzzle everywhere but on a baseball field come October. Meet Mariano Rivera, who is proving that he no longer needs to Remember the Alomar as long as everyone else finally allows last October to be put to rest.

"This is what it's all about," said Wells, who struck out a career postseason-high 11 batters and walked one. "Fighting all year to get to here, it's been a lot of fun all season and it's a lot of fun now. What we did is we went out there and played hard, but still had fun doing it."

Wells allowed two runs in the first, but only two runs. The only other damage was a Jim Thome solo blast in the sixth, until Wells stubbornly but predictably refused to give up the ball in the eighth. He eventually gave way to Jeff Nelson with one out in the inning and a 5-3 lead.

Rivera, who has not allowed a run in eight playoff innings, relieved Nelson after the righty set-up man hit Travis Fryman and allowed a single to Manny Ramirez.

The righty closer, however, used a 2-2 cutter to induce Mark Whiten to bounce into a double play, started by Knoblauch, to end the eigthth. Rivera finished for his first save of the series and third of the postseason.

"Last year, I never got the chance to pitch after that," Rivera said of Alomar's game-tying Game 4 home run, which came with the Yanks four outs from advancing to the ALCS. "This was my chance."

"I've been very proud of this team," Torre said. "Because every time they've been faced with any kind of challenge, they've responded."

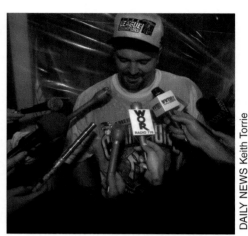

David Wells speaks to the press in the locker room after Game 6.

FINAL

NEW YORK YANKEES 5, AT CLEVELAND INDIANS 3

NY YANKEES	ab	r	h	rbi	CLEVELAND	ab	r	h	rbi
Knoblauch 2b	1	2	0	0	Lofton cf	4	1	1	1
Jeter ss	4	0	0	0	Vizquel ss	3	1	2	0
O'Neill rf	4	1	2	1	Fryman 3b	3	0	1	0
B Williams cf	4	1	1	0	Ramirez rf	3	0	1	1
Davis dh	5	1	2	3	Whiten lf	4	0	0	0
Martinez 1b	1	0	0	0	Thome dh	3	1	2	1
Raines lf	4	0	0	1	Sexson 1b	3	0	0	0
Curtis lf	1	0	0	0	a-Giles ph	1	0	0	0
Posada c	1	0	0	0	Diaz c	3	0	0	0
Brosius 3b	3	0	1	0	b-Justice ph	0	0	0	0
					Wilson 2b	4	0	1	0
Totals	28	5	6	5	Totals	31	3	8	3

HR - Davis.   **HR - Lofton, Thome.**

a-grounded to second for Sexson in the 9th; b-walked for Diaz in the 9th.

NY Yankees			310 100 000	—	5			
Cleveland			200 001 000	—	3			

NY Yankees	ip	h	r	er	bb	so	hr	era
Wells W	7 1/3	7	3	3	1	11	2	1.90
Nelson	0	1	0	0	0	0	0	6.75
Rivera S	1 2/3	0	0	0	1	1	0	0.00

Cleveland	ip	h	r	er	bb	so	hr	era
Ogea L	1 1/3	4	4	4	3	2	0	8.10
Wright	6	2	1	1	7	3	1	9.82
Reed	1/3	0	0	0	0	0	0	11.57
Assenmacher	1/3	0	0	0	0	0	0	0.00
Shuey	1	0	0	0	1	2	0	0.00

Nelson pitched to 2 batters.

ANOTHER WORLD TURN

Yanks rejoice over second in three seaons

By Peter Botte, Daily News Sports Writer

OCTOBER 14, 1998

Tomorrow, the world. Since that chilly and somber night their season died in Cleveland one October ago, the Yankees have lived for this night, have breathed for this moment, have relished this opportunity.

Their destiny finally is upon them. The professional, talented and driven Yankees have one more champagne shower to go. The ultimate one.

For the 35th time — and second time in the past three Octobers — the New York Yankees will play for the World Series title, just as it's supposed to be.

After last night's wild 9-5 elimination of the Tribe consummated their ALCS in six entertaining games, the Yankees will host either San Diego or Atlanta in Game 1 Saturday night at the Stadium.

"I guess it's supposed to happen just like this," Derek Jeter said amid what the Yanks hope would be the third of four champagne-bashes. "In '96 everything was new to me. It seemed like everything happened so fast. Before we knew it we won the World Series.

"Last year, it was real bad when we lost. You get a chance to appreciate this a little more now. . . But here we go."

Yankees' thoughts were also with one who was not there, Darryl Strawberry, recovering from cancer surgery at Columbia-Presbyterian Medical Center.

"I'm going to find a telephone right now and call him," Joe Torre said. "He kept after us,

telling us to 'Go get 'em.'"

Bernie Williams had his biggest game of the 1998 postseason in the 1998 postseason's biggest game, with three hits and two RBI. Scott Brosius belted a three-run homer to juice the crowd early and double a 3-0 lead. Jeter laced a two-run triple, which Manny Ramirez still probably hasn't figured landed behind him, to break open a one-run game in the sixth.

And then the bullpen, a given throughout this series. Little-used swingman Ramiro Mendoza hurled three shutout innings in relief of David Cone, after the consummate big-game pitcher was gassed for a mammoth grand slam by Jim Thome that turned a six-run lead into a 6-5 nail-biter.

Mariano Rivera was automatic in the ninth yet again, rendering Sandy Alomar's 1997 home run a footnote to his career, at least for now.

"Total team effort, man, just like always. We fight, we scrape, we do whatever we gotta do," said David Wells, who won Games 1 and 5 to capture the MVP award. "It's great to win this (trophy), but there's another one I got my eye on."

FINAL

CLEVELAND INDIANS 5, AT NEW YORK YANKEES 9

CLEVELAND	ab	r	h	rbi	NY YANKEES	ab	r	h	rbi
Lofton cf	4	1	2	0	Knoblauch 2b	5	0	2	0
Vizquel ss	5	1	1	0	Jeter ss	5	2	2	2
Justice dh	3	1	0	1	O'Neill rf	5	1	1	0
Ramirez rf	3	0	1	0	B Williams cf	4	1	3	2
Thome 1b	4	1	2	4	Davis dh	3	1	0	1
Fryman 3b	4	0	0	0	Martinez 1b	3	0	1	0
Giles lf	4	0	1	0	Ledee lf	4	0	0	0
S Alomar c	3	0	0	0	Brosius 3b	3	2	1	3
a-Branson ph	1	0	0	0	Girardi c	3	2	1	0
Diaz c	0	0	0	0					
Wilson 2b	4	1	1	0					
Totals	35	5	8	5	Totals	35	9	11	8

HR - Thome.　　　　　　　　　HR - Brosius.

a-flied to center for Alomar in the 8th.

Cleveland	000 050 000	— 5
NY Yankees	213 003 00X	— 9

Cleveland	ip	h	r	er	bb	so	hr	era
Nagy L	3	8	6	3	0	1	1	2.55
Burba	2 1/3	1	3	1	2	4	0	3.97
Poole	1/3	0	0	0	0	0	0	0.00
Shuey	1 2/3	2	0	0	2	1	0	0.00
Assenmacher	2/3	0	0	0	0	1	0	0.00

NY Yankees	ip	h	r	er	bb	so	hr	era
Cone W	5	7	5	5	3	8	1	2.89
Mendoza H	3	1	0	0	0	1	0	0.00
Rivera	1	0	0	0	0	1	0	0.00

GAME 6 ● OCTOBER 13

WORLD SERIES
OCTOBER 17, 1998 VS. SAN DIEGO PADRES

YANKEES OPEN IN GRAND STYLE

OCTOBER 25, 1998

By Peter Botte, Daily News Sports Writer

GAME 1 ● OCTOBER 17

Ridiculed and booed lustily at the Stadium just 11 days before for a costly blunder, Chuck Knoblauch suddenly found himself implored by 56,712 rabid fans to take a curtain call. He giddily obliged.

Openly questioned by the fans and media, and perhaps within his organization, for yet another October swoon, Tino Martinez similarly was summoned to the top step of the dugout several frenzied minutes later. He, too, pumped his fists in relief, then jubilation.

The Yankees exploded for seven runs in the seventh inning on Knoblauch's tying three-run homer and Martinez's upper-deck grand slam to hammer out a 9-6 comeback win over Kevin Brown and the Padres in Game 1 of the World Series at the Stadium.

"I had a little smile on my face because Tino and I had been trying to pump each other up," Knoblauch said as he and Martinez sat side-by-side in the interview room.

"You try to lift each other up. I was probably more excited when he hit his home run

Tino Martinez hits grand slam home run in 7th inning for a 9-6 lead.

Linda Cataffo

DAILY NEWS

than when I hit mine. It was just a great feeling. We've been trying to help each other out for a while."

San Diego hammered hometown five-game prognosticator David Wells for five runs, including two home runs by Greg Vaughn and a two-run bomb by the venerable Tony Gwynn to carry a 5-2 advantage into the seventh.

"They kicked my (butt) tonight," said Wells, who caused headlines earlier in the week when he suggested on Howard Stern's radio show that the Yanks would take out the Padres in five games.

The Yanks had Brown, the Padres' ace, on the ropes throughout his 6 1/3 innings, but had mustered only a two-run double by rookie Ricky Ledee in the second.

With Brown up to 108 pitches after allowing a single to Jorge Posada and a walk to Ledee with one out in the seventh, however, Padres manager Bruce Bochy turned to his usually door-slamming bullpen. His bullpen failed.

First, it was Knoblauch, a Blauch Head no

more for his gaffe that cost the Yanks Game 2 of the ALCS.

Donne Wall fell behind Knoblauch 2-0, and the former Stadium whipping boy made him pay with a towering clout into the left-field seats for his first career postseason homer.

"When it left my bat," Knoblauch said, "I thought it had a chance. I got a little worried when I saw Vaughn jump up on the wall . . . But it was a great feeling to have the whole place up and screaming."

But there was more. Oh, was there more.

Derek Jeter singled to center against Wall and advanced on a wild pitch. One out later, Bernie Williams was walked intentionally by Mark Langston, who then issued a free pass to Davis to load the bases.

Martinez, who entered the inning batting .184 (18-for-98) as a Yankee in three postseasons with only two RBI, delivered when his team needed it most. Finally.

One pitch after home-plate umpire Rich Garcia called a clear-cut strike at the knees ball three, Martinez ripped Langston's full-count offering into the upper deck in right for a monstrous grand slam, his first postseason home run as a Yankee. It was worth the wait.

"I haven't done much, but we've been winning and got to the World Series," Martinez said. "I knew eventually I'd come up in a big situation and get a big hit to help the team win. It's definitely a big relief to do that."

FINAL
NEW YORK YANKEES 3, AT SAN DIEGO PADRES 0

SAN DIEGO	ab	r	h	rbi	NY YANKEES	ab	r	h	rbi
Veras 2b	4	1	1	0	Knoblauch 2b	4	1	2	3
Gwynn rf	4	1	3	2	Jeter ss	4	1	1	0
Vaughn lf	4	3	2	3	O'Neill rf	5	0	0	0
Caminiti 3b	3	0	0	0	B Williams cf	4	1	0	0
Leyritz dh	4	0	0	0	C Davis dh	3	2	1	0
Joyner 1b	3	0	0	0	Martinez 1b	3	2	1	4
Finley cf	4	0	1	0	Brosius 3b	4	0	1	0
Hernandez c	3	0	0	0	Posada c	3	1	1	0
a-G Myers ph	1	0	0	0	Ledee lf	3	1	2	2
Gomez ss	3	1	1	0					
b-Vander Wal ph	1	0	0	0					
Totals	34	6	8	5	Totals	33	9	9	9

HR - Vaughn 2, Gwynn. HR - Knoblauch, Martinez.
a-struck out for Hernandez in the 9th; b-struck out for Gomez in the 9th.

San Diego	002 030 010	—	6
NY Yankees	020 000 70X	—	9

SAN DIEGO	ip	h	r	er	bb	so	hr	era
Brown	6 1/3	6	4	4	3	5	0	5.68
Wall L	0	2	2	2	0	0	1	0.00
Langston	2/3	1	3	3	2	0	1	40.50
Boehringer	1/3	0	0	0	1	1	0	0.00
R Myers	2/3	0	0	0	1	2	0	0.00

NY Yankees	ip	h	r	er	bb	so	hr	era
Wells W	7	7	5	5	2	4	3	6.43
Nelson	2/3	1	1	0	1	1	0	0.00
Rivera S	1 1/3	0	0	0	0	2	0	0.00

Wall pitched to 2 batters in the 7th.

Tiffany Villano of the Bronx holds her prized World Series tickets.

YANKEE PROFILE
Darryl Strawberry

HOME SWEET HOME FOR YANKEE SLUGGER

Straw is upbeat

OCTOBER 17, 1998

By Rafael A. Olmeda and Austin Fenner , Daily News Staff Writers

Darryl Strawberry

A gaunt but grateful Darryl Strawberry was discharged from the hospital yesterday, saying he felt blessed that his colon cancer was diagnosed early and that he was finally well enough to go home.

The Yankee slugger, normally lean but powerful both in the outfield and behind home plate, had sunken eyes and appeared weak. Gone was his long, graceful stride as he stepped carefully to a podium at Columbia-Presbyterian Medical Center, where he had spent the last 14 days.

But his spirits were up as he hugged and thanked the staff for his care — and said he hopes his experience will inspire others to seek medical help for their ailments.

"I thought this day would never come," Strawberry said, standing erect at a podium during a press conference in the hospital lobby before leaving for his New Jersey home. "I'm truly grateful it has arrived."

Strawberry, 36, had 16 inches of his large

Darryl Strawberry with his wife, Charisse, at press conference in the lobby of the Milstein Pavillion, Columbia Presbyterian Hospital.

DAILY NEWS Budd Williams

intestine removed during a three-hour operation Oct. 3. The cancerous tumor had nearly obstructed his intestine.

He was to be discharged last Sunday, but hospital officials said he still wasn't eating normally and needed a few more days to recover.

Yesterday, with his wife, Charisse, at his side, he said he's able to cope with his disease.

"I'm able to face it and deal with it, and not say 'Why me,' but 'Why not me,'" he said.

Strawberry had to watch from his hospital bed as his teammates won their way through two playoff rounds into the World Series. Under doctor's orders to stay home, he said he'll watch Game 1 tonight from his house.

Next, he faces chemotherapy, but doctors said he's expected to recover fully.

"My hunch is he'll get an aggressive chemo

"I'm able to face it and deal with it, and not say 'Why me,' but 'Why not me,'" he said.

A show of support for Strawberry.

DAILY NEWS Howard Simmons

regimen because he's young," said Dr. Paul Basuk, gastroenterologist at New York Hospital-Cornell Medical Center. "Tumors are more aggressive in the young, and he can tolerate more because he's in good health."

Around Yankee Stadium, Strawberry's trip home was good news.

"I would hope to see him throw the first pitch in one of these games," said Adah Carrion, 26, of Manhattan. "If not, we understand. Let him sit back and relax. His World Series ring is coming to him. He earned it."

At his home, Charisse Strawberry said her husband was tired and resting.

"He's glad to be home," she said. "Glad to be out of the hospital."

Darryl Strawberry Stats

1998 REGULAR SEASON

AVG	G	AB	R	H	TB	2B	3B	HR	RBI	BB	SO	SB	CS	SH	SF	HP	SLG%	OBP%
.247	101	295	44	73	160	11	2	24	57	46	90	8	7	0	1	3	.542	.354

WORLD SERIES

OCTOBER 18, 1998 VS. SAN DIEGO PADRES

YANKS PUT UP THEIR DUQUE AND GO UP 2-0

OCTOBER 25, 1998
By Peter Botte, Daily News Staff Writer

OCTOBER 18

GAME 2

Jetting across America on Oct. 18, the Yankees knew full well that the two wins they needed to fulfill their vision quest would not be nearly as easy as any of their previous 123 had seemed.

They traveled, however, with the full knowledge they also could return later that week as validated champions. As conquering heroes.

As baseball legends.

Everything that was right about the summer of '98 in the Bronx finally was back on display in the Yanks' 9-3 outclassing of the Padres earlier that evening. The triumph allowed them to assume a 2-0 World Series advantage before 56,692 frenzied folks at Yankee Stadium.

"Well, we are glad it's a best-of-seven now," Padres manager Bruce Boche said. "This is not the situation we were hoping for, but it's been overcome before."

The 1996 Yankees, of course, were clubbed twice

Jorge Posada celebrates his two-run homer with Scott Brosius.

DAILY NEWS Howard Simmons

at home by Atlanta, only to rebound by taking four straight.

The last team to win the first two games at home and fail to close it out was the '81 Yanks, who dropped four straight to the Dodgers.

"There's still a lot of baseball to be played. I'm sure the people of San Diego are anxious to get in their licks at us now," Paul O'Neill warned.

"We're confident, and we should be, but we're never overconfident," Tino Martinez said.

"That team over there has already beaten some tough teams just to get here, and they're not going to hand us anything."

It couldn't have been much easier than it was in Game 2.

There was the latest storybook chapter for

Orlando Hernandez, who stood where his MVP half-brother (Florida's Livan) stood one October ago and put in his bid to keep the trophy in the family with seven stellar one-run innings.

There was O'Neill making a spectacular leaping catch against the wall in the first on Wally Joyner's blast, saving at least two runs.

And there was offense, droves and droves of actual offense, lighting the scoreboard into overload.

"Obviously, we're happy, but I don't care how many runs you score, you can only win one game at a time," O'Neill said.

Still, there was more than enough cushion to render inconsequential two late runs allowed by Mike Stanton and Jeff Nelson.

Bernie Williams and Jorge Posada belted two-run homers. Former goats Martinez and Chuck Knoblauch combined for five of the Yankees' playoff-high 16 hits. Scott Brosius had three more singles near the bottom of the lineup.

And the talented and respectable NL champion Padres appeared little more than the requisite patsy in a grander Yankees' scheme through two nights.

"It's probably not a good feeling over there right now," said Knoblauch, who went 2-for-3 with two walks.

"But from our standpoint we still have to win two games."

While Hernandez didn't permit a run until he had been supplied his six-run lead, the Yankees bats pounded starter Andy Ashby (seven runs, 10 hits in 2 2/3 innings) from the outset.

Ken Caminiti's throwing error on O'Neill's grounder in the first opened the door for three unearned runs. Williams added a two-run homer in the second.

Ricky Ledee's second straight hit - a double into the left-field corner - added yet another run in the third and finally prompted Padres manager Bruce Bochy to mercifully replace Ashby with Brian Boehringer.

It was still early, but it was far too late. Posada would add his two-run rocket off Boehringer in the fifth.

"We've played well all year to get to this point," Derek Jeter said. "There's no reason now to change how we approach anything."

FINAL
SAN DIEGO PADRES 3, AT NEW YORK YANKEES 9

SAN DIEGO	ab	r	h	rbi	NY YANKEES	ab	r	h	rbi
Veras 2b	5	0	1	1	Knoblauch 2b	3	2	2	0
Gwynn rf	4	0	1	0	Jeter ss	5	1	2	1
Vaughn dh	4	0	0	0	O'Neill rf	5	1	1	0
Caminiti 3b	5	1	1	0	B Williams cf	4	1	1	2
Joyner 1b	2	0	0	0	C Davis dh	3	1	1	1
a-Leyritz ph-1b	1	0	0	0	Bush pr-dh	0	0	0	0
Finley cf	4	0	0	0	Martinez 1b	5	1	3	0
Vander Wal lf	3	0	2	0	Brosius 3b	5	1	3	1
b-R Rivera ph-lf	1	1	1	0	Posada c	4	1	1	2
G Myers c	3	0	0	0	Ledee lf	3	0	2	1
c-Hernandez ph-c	1	0	1	0					
Gomez ss	3	1	2	0					
d-Sweeney ph	1	0	1	1					
Sheets ss	0	0	0	0					
Totals	37	3	10	3	Totals	37	9	16	8

HR - Williams, Posada.

a-struck out for Joyner in the 8th; b-doubled for Vander Wal in the 8th; c-singled for G Myers in the 8th; d-singled for Gomez in the 8th.

San Diego	000 010 020	—	3
NY Yankees	331 020 00X	—	9

San Diego	ip	h	r	er	bb	so	hr	era
Ashby L	2 2/3	10	7	4	1	1	1	13.50
Boehringer	1 2/3	4	2	2	1	2	1	9.00
Wall	2 2/3	1	0	0	3	1	0	6.75
Miceli	1	1	0	0	2	1	0	0.00

NY Yankees	ip	h	r	er	bb	so	hr	era
Hernandez W	7	6	1	1	3	7	0	1.29
Stanton	2/3	3	2	2	0	1	0	27.00
Nelson	1 1/3	1	0	0	0	2	0	0.00

DAILY NEWS Howard Simmons

Paul O'Neill crashes into the wall making the catch for the final out in the first inning.

YANKEE PROFILE

ANDY PETTITTE

FOR FINALE, ANDY SHOWS BRAVE HEART

OCTOBER 23, 1998

By Lisa Olson, Daily News Columnist

LHP

Andy Pettitte

SAN DIEGO—*So take some photographs and still frames for the wall.* That is how the Green Day song, "Good Riddance" goes, the one that was playing when the Yankees won their second World Series in three years, won it with class and style and hears heavy with thoughts of matters much more important than any shiny baseball trophy.

Time grabs you by the wrist, directs you where to go. It tugged and pulled Andy Pettitte every which way last night, from the lonely spot at the loudest of baseball stadiums all the way to Houston, where a certain Yankees fan lay recuperating on his couch, NY cap on his head, a vial of medication by his side.

He would need to be heavily sedated for this, Tom Pettitte had joked. His son hadn't exactly been the steadiest of beacons lately, pitching well only once in his last seven starts, that one coming during the division series with Texas, just days before Tom

Andy Pettitte pitched 7$^1/_3$ scoreless innings in Game 4 of the World Series.

DAILY NEWS   Keith Torrie

would check into a hospital, possibly not to check out.

The son never has been comfortable with drawing attention to himself, even when he outdueled Atlanta's John Smoltz in that fateful World Series Game 5 in '96. So he wasn't about to use his father's health as an excuse when his cutter stopped working, when everyone was calling him the weak link in the Yankees chain.

Besides, didn't the team have enough sadness circulating in the air that was ripe with destiny? There was Chuck Knoblauch's father struggling with Alzheimer's and Scott Brosius' dad dealing with colon cancer and Joe DiMaggio lying in a Florida hospital. And, of course, Darryl Strawberry, never out of his teammates' minds.

"Straw Man, Straw Man," went up the chant in the visitors' clubhouse.

Orlando Hernandez passed around cigars,

Cuban natch. Derek Jeter chased George Steinbrenner with a bottle of Perrier-Jouet and laughed hysterically like a 10-year-old boy when he showered the Boss' perfect gray coif. Someone had the brilliant idea of going back onto the field, back to where they had just beaten the Padres, 3-0, for a clean 4-0 series sweep, and off they went, arm-in-arm, smelling like they had just fallen in a Napa Valley vat.

Pettitte wasn't there, frolicking in the craziness. He was in the kitchen, looking for a phone. Only hours before Pettitte would give up five hits in 7 1/3 innings and make the opposing pitcher Kevin Brown look irrelevant, Tom Pettitte was released from St. Luke's Hospital, his double-heart bypass a tentative success.

It wasn't difficult to figure out what mattered most, a recovering father or clinching the World Series.

"The first two games at Yankee Stadium, I really wasn't thinking about the games. Guys were getting excited and jumping up and down," said Pettitte. "It was almost like I was putting on a show."

This was the show he put on Wednesday night: three straight cut fastballs to leadoff hitter Quilvio Veras in the first inning that told Joe Torre everything he needed to know about omens, about fate. This was Andy Pettitte at his best, relaxed, making adjustments, matching Brown in placement and wits.

"He can match with the best of them," said the Yankee manager. "As soon as I saw the first pitch I knew we were in good shape."

Tom Pettitte was at home, on a couch, too weak to make it here, but his arteries clear. Yes, the son was in good shape. He did what he did to Atlanta in '96, only on a bigger stage, with bigger stakes. "Best game he has ever pitched," said Jeter. "But where is he?"

The party on the field was missing its maestro of the night. "An-dy Pett-itte, An-dy Pett-itte," Jeter yelled,

Andy Pettitte grimaces after striking out in Game 4 of the World Series.

and soon all the Yankees were chanting the name until the cries were louder than any before and Pettitte had no choice but to come join the fun.

"I hope you had the time of your life," they sang along with Green Day, to each other, to Pettitte.

He didn't say much, just blushed and wiped away what appeared to be a tear. Back in Houston, a man on the couch probably did the same. For what it's worth, it was worth all the while.

Andy Pettitte Stats

1998 Regular Season

W	L	S	ERA	G	GS	CG	SHO	IP	H	R	ER	HR	BB	SO	HB	WP	BK
16	11	0	4.24	33	32	5	0	216.1	226	110	102	20	87	146	6	5	0

WORLD SERIES
OCTOBER 20, 1998 VS. SAN DIEGO PADRES

GREAT SCOTT! YANKS 1 AWAY FROM SWEEP

OCTOBER 25, 1998
By Peter Botte, Daily News Sports Writer

GAME 3 · OCTOBER 20

SAN DIEGO— The Yanks seemed down and out in San Diego on October 20. They trailed the Padres late in Game 3 of the World Series until Scott Brosius rode to their rescue. Brosius belted a three-run homer off nearly flawless Padre closer Trevor Hoffman with one out in the eighth inning — his second home run of the game — to propel the Yankees to a 5-4 comeback victory.

While Brosius' blast helped bring the Yanks back from a 3-0 deficit, it also gave them a commanding 3-0 lead in the best-of-7 Series.

"This is the type of thing you dream about as a kid, something I've done in my backyard 100 times," Brosius said. "To come out and to do something to help this team win feels real good."

Brosius' 424-foot blast to dead center, which put the Yanks ahead 5-3 in the eighth, was only the third home run allowed this year by Hoffman,

who had converted 53 of 54 saves. Greg Vaughn's sacrifice fly off Mariano Rivera in the eighth drew the Padres within one. But the Yankees' closer struck out Andy Sheets with runners on first and third to end it and make a winner of Ramiro Mendoza.

David Cone held the Padres hitless through five, but two hits and a walk, combined with a throwing error by Paul O'Neill, led to a three-run inning that snapped a scoreless tie.

Staked to a 3-0 lead, however, Sterling Hitchcock did not record an out in the seventh. Brosius, who is 7-for-13 in the World Series, hit his first career Series homer over the wall in left-center to give the Yankees life.

Shane Spencer followed by roping a double into the gap in left-center, and Padres manager Bruce Bochy quickly turned to Joey Hamilton.

Spencer moved to third on Jim Leyritz' passed

Brosius celebrates his three-run home run off Trevor Hoffman in the eighth inning.

DAILY NEWS Linda Cataffo

ball and scored one out later when pinch hitter Chili Davis reached on an error by third baseman Ken Caminiti.

An inning later, with the Padres leading 3-2 with one on and no out, Bochy turned to Hoffman.

Hoffman, who had not seen action in the Series, recorded one out and then walked Tino Martinez. Next came Brosius, the former Oakland castoff whom Hoffman fanned in this summer's All-Star Game.

Not this time. Brosius crushed Hoffman's 2-2 pitch over the wall in center and pumped his fists over his head as he rounded first.

Offense was rare in the first few innings of the game. Cone held the Padres hitless through five.

Hitchcock was aided by superb defense from the Padres. Center fielder Steve Finley made two acrobatic catches in the first two innings, tumbling and juggling to rob Knoblauch in the first and racing to the fence to make a leaping stab of Brosius' bid for an extra-base hit.

Cone didn't seem to need the same defensive support. After Cone singled to left to lead off the sixth — his third hit in eight World Series at-bats — he had more hits than the Padres.

Cone kept the Padres hitless until Hitchcock's first-pitch single leading off the sixth. Then Cone walked Quilvio Veras to put two runners aboard for eight-time batting champion Tony Gwynn. The .339 career hitter singled to right to score Hitchcock, but O'Neill's off-target throw didn't stop rolling until it landed in the visiting dugout.

Veras was awarded home and Gwynn wound up on third. Caminiti then chased Williams to the track for a sacrifice fly and a 3-0 lead.

FINAL

NEW YORK YANKEES 5, AT SAN DIEGO PADRES 4

NY YANKEES	ab	r	h	rbi	SAN DIEGO	ab	r	h	rbi
Knoblauch 2b	4	0	1	0	Veras 2b	3	2	1	0
Jeter ss	4	0	1	0	Gwynn rf	4	1	2	1
O'Neill rf	4	1	1	0	R Rivera pr-rf	0	0	0	0
B Williams cf	4	0	0	0	Vaughn lf	3	0	0	1
Martinez 1b	3	1	0	0	Caminiti 3b	2	0	0	1
Brosius 3b	4	2	3	4	Joyner 1b	3	0	0	0
Spencer lf	3	1	1	0	Finley cf	4	0	0	0
c-Ledee ph-lf	1	0	0	0	Leyritz c	2	0	0	0
Girardi c	2	0	0	0	C Hernandez c	2	0	1	0
a-Posada ph-c	2	0	1	0	Vander Wal pr	0	0	0	0
Cone p	2	0	1	0	Gomez ss	3	0	1	0
b-C Davis ph	1	0	0	1	Hoffman p	0	0	0	0
Bush pr	0	0	0	0	b-Sweeney ph	1	0	1	0
Lloyd p	0	0	0	0	Hitchcock p	2	1	1	0
Mendoza p	1	0	0	0	Hamilton p	0	0	0	0
M Rivera p	0	0	0	0	R Myers p	0	0	0	0
					Sheets ss	2	0	0	0
Totals	35	5	9	5	Totals	31	4	7	3

HR - Brosius 2 .
a-struck out for Girardi in the 7th; b-reached on error for Cone in the 7th; c-grounded to second for Spencer in the 8th. b-singled for C Hernandez in the 9th.

NY Yankees	000 000 230	—	5
San Diego	000 003 010	—	4

NY Yankees	ip	h	r	er	bb	so	hr	era
Cone	6	2	3	2	4	0		3.00
Lloyd	1/3	0	0	0	0	0	0	0.00
Mendoza W	2	1	1	0	1	0	0	9.00
M Rivera S	1 2/3	3	0	0	0	2	0	0.00

San Diego	ip	h	r	er	bb	so	hr	era
Hitchcock	6	7	2	1	1	7	1	1.50
Hamilton H	1	0	0	0	1	1	0	0.00
R Myers H	0	0	1	1	1	0	0	13.50
Hoffman L	2	2	2	2	1	0	1	9.00

Hitchcock pitched to 2 batters in the 7th.
R Myers pitched to 1 batter in the 8th.

DAILY NEWS Gerald Herbert

Tony Gwynn watches a stadium worker as he paints the World Series logo on the field.

YANKEE PROFILE

ORLANDO HERNANDEZ

RHP

Orlando Hernandez

DUQUE TWIN WIN

Visit from family doubles triumph for Cuba native

OCTOBER 24, 1998

By Tom Raftery, Carolina Gonzalez and Gene Mustain, Daily News Staff Writers

Yankee pitcher Orlando Hernandez' incredible voyage from the dirt streets of Cuba to the Canyon of Heroes in Manhattan was capped with an emotional family reunion early yesterday at a small airport in New Jersey.

The rugged right-hander whose fearsome arm freezes hitters in their spikes melted into a laughing *papi* when —for the first time in nearly a year—he held his beloved daughters in his arms again.

The children—Yahumara, 8, and Steffi, 3—along with El Duque's mom, Maria Pedroso and his ex-wife, Norma Manso, arrived at Teterboro Airport shortly before 3 a.m. on Yankee owner George Steinbrenner's private jet.

Cardinal O'Connor and Cuban leader Fidel Castro joined forces to get them out of Cuba in time to celebrate the Yankees' World Series victory.

Orlando Hernandez' daughters, Yahumara and Steffi (right).

DAILY NEWS   Robert Rosamilio

El Duque hadn't seen his children since he defected from his homeland on a rickety boat in December.

He puffed nervously on a cigarette, paced and fiddled with the buttons on his suit after he pulled up in a limo at the airport, hours early.

When the girls emerged from the jet, El Duque grinned from ear to ear, showered them with kisses and bundled them in blue parkas he bought to protect them from the nippy night air.

"I can't believe they're here," he said, shaking his head. "They got so big."

Which was a greater thrill, winning the Series or the reunion with his family?

"Both," he replied without hesitation.

Only a few hectic hours later, El Duque kept his appointment to appear in the Yankee victory parade.

His daughters were exhausted after the long

trip to the U.S., but the doting El Duque couldn't let them out of his sight and had them with him in the Canyon of Heroes.

Later, he charmed the crowd at City Hall with a little-boy bow then drew a rousing cheer when he apologized for his English and proclaimed: "*Yo amo a Nueva York.*"

It was clear by the ovation that New York loved El Duque too.

If Hernandez also looked a little tired, there was good reason.

It was the wee hours of the morning by the time the champagne-stocked limo whisked the happy entourage from the airport to a Manhattan hotel.

"He was laughing and singing and hugging his youngest all the way," said the limo drive, Sam Johnson.

Hernandez apparently got little sleep later. About 4 a.m., he ducked out of the hotel and into an all-night drugstore for milk. A couple hours later, he returned to the store to buy two Nickelodeon toothbrushes.

The family, here on a 30-day visa, will go to Mass on Sunday at St. Patrick's Cathedral as the specially invited guests of the Cardinal.

Hernandez hopes to personally thank O'Connor and to ask one more favor—to baptize little Steffi.

Praying for a reunion, but in desperate need of help, Hernandez had sent O'Connor a fax Tuesday saying how much he missed his family.

The next day, O'Connor sent an emissary to hand-deliver a letter to Castro asking him to allow

Orlando Hernandez holding his three-year-old daughter Steffi.

DAILY NEWS Howard Simmons

Hernandez' family to visit New York.

It was a touchy request. Two years ago, Hernandez' half-brother Livan—a top pitcher for the Cuban national team, as El Duque once was—defected and joined the Florida Marlins, who won the World Series last year.

Castro, however, decided not to hold a grudge.

"President Castro and his government replied favorably very quickly," said the emissary, Mario Paredes, head of the Northeast Hispanic Catholic Center.

Paredes tried to telephone Hernandez to get the addresses and phone numbers of his family in Boyeros, Cuba. But by that time, Wednesday evening, Hernandez was sitting in the visitors' dugout in San Diego for Game 4 of the World Series.

No one at the Stadium would put the call through. It had to be a prank.

"So finally, I persuaded someone there to call me back in Cuba so they'd know I was real, and finally El Duque got on the phone," Paredes said. "He was so overtaken by the news that he'd be seeing his family he couldn't remember any numbers. Finally, he did."

Paredes arranged for a private plane to fly everyone from Havana to Miami.

"Everyone was pretty nervous and tense on the flight over to Miami," said Paredes. "It was the first time that any of them had flown."

In Miami, the girls were given Yankee caps and shirts and some Cabbage Patch dolls—and seats aboard George Steinbrenner's private jet.

Orlando Hernandez Stats

1998 REGULAR SEASON

W	L	S	ERA	G	GS	CG	SHO	IP	H	R	ER	HR	BB	SO	HB	WP	BK
12	4	0	3.13	21	21	3	1	141.0	113	53	49	11	52	131	6	5	2

WORLD SERIES

OCTOBER 21, 1998 VS. SAN DIEGO PADRES

YANKEES SWEEP INTO HISTORY

OCTOBER 25, 1998

By Peter Botte, Daily News Sports Writer

GAME 4 ● OCTOBER 21

SAN DIEGO—The Yankees, the unquestioned barometer for sports success in this country for decades, have raised the bar yet again.

With a 3-0 victory behind Andy Pettitte at Qualcomm Stadium on October 21—an unprecedented win No. 125 in one calendar year—the Yankees swept through Kevin Brown and the NL-champion Padres much like they have the remainder of their 1998 season.

With class, with precision. With pitching. And with ease.

When Mariano Rivera retired Mark Sweeney on a grounder to third baseman Scott Brosius— named the Series MVP— for the final out, the Yankees were world champions for the second time in three seasons and the 24th time in their history, more than any team in the history of professional sports on this continent.

They were the best anywhere. Just like it was supposed to be.

They did it for Darryl Strawberry, back home recovering from cancer surgery, but with them every step of the way. They did it for George Steinbrenner, the man who always expects to win at all costs, and for Joe Torre, the man who evenly guides them and stays out

Mark McGwire and David Wells before the start of World Series Game 4.

DAILY NEWS Keith Torrie

of their way.

They did it, mostly, though, for themselves.

Pettitte, who was pitching with a heavy heart as his father recovers from heart surgery in Texas, outdueled Brown.

With the Yankees already up 1-0 on Bernie Williams' RBI infield topper in the sixth, a close call by first-base umpire Tim Tschida on Paul O'Neill's grounder to first with none out and one on in the eighth infuriated Brown and the Padres.

It also led to the final two Yankee runs on yet another RBI hit by Brosius and a sacrifice fly by rookie Ricky Ledee.

Pettitte allowed only five hits before giving way to Jeff Nelson with one out and two on in the eighth. The Padres went on to load the bases against Nelson and Rivera in the inning, but the ever-dominant Yankee closer got former World Series hero Jim Leyritz to line to Williams in center to end the threat.

And that was that for a team that won an AL-record 114 games in the regular season, but needed these final 11 for historical validation. So where do they fit? Where will the 1998 Yankees fit in the realm of a franchise that has defined excellence in baseball since the beginning?

"To me, this would be (the best team), because I'm part of this team and I'm very proud of what we've accomplished this year," said Williams.

"When I look back at it, 10 or 15 years from now, I'm going to say I played with probably one of the best teams that ever played in the American League."

Pettitte was handed the ball in Game 4 against the ailing Brown, who was battling a sinus infection, battling an 0-3 hole. Battling the Yankees.

"There are very high expectations when you wear a Yankee uniform," Torre said.

"I'm not putting any other ballclub down, it's just with the Yankees, working for George Steinbrenner, he's a perfectionist, and he always tries to improve on perfection."

FINAL

NEW YORK YANKEES 3, AT SAN DIEGO PADRES 0

NY YANKEES	ab	r	h	rbi	SAN DIEGO	ab	r	h	rbi
Knoblauch 2b	5	0	1	0	Veras 2b	3	0	0	0
Jeter ss	4	2	2	0	Gwynn rf	4	0	2	0
O'Neill rf	5	1	2	0	Vaughn lf	4	0	0	0
B Williams cf	4	0	0	1	Caminiti 3b	4	0	1	0
Martinez 1b	2	0	1	0	Leyritz 1b	3	0	0	0
Brosius 3b	4	0	1	1	R Rivera cf	4	0	3	0
Ledee lf	3	0	2	1	C Hernandez c	4	0	0	0
Girardi c	4	0	0	0	Gomez ss	2	0	0	0
Pettitte p	2	0	0	0	b-Sweeney ph	1	0	0	0
Nelson p	0	0	0	0	Brown p	2	0	1	0
M Rivera p	1	0	0	0	a-Vander Wal ph	1	0	0	0
					Miceli p	0	0	0	0
					R Myers p	0	0	0	0
Totals	34	3	9	3	Totals	32	0	7	0

a-flied to center for Brown in the 8th; b-grounded to third for Gomez in the 9th.

NY Yankees	000	001	020	— 3
San Diego	000	000	000	— 0

NY Yankees	ip	h	r	er	bb	so	hr	era
Pettitte W	7 1/3	5	0	0	3	4	0	0.00
Nelson	1/3	0	0	0	0	1	0	0.00
M Rivera S	1 1/3	2	0	0	0	0	0	0.00

San Diego	ip	h	r	er	bb	so	hr	era
Brown L	8	8	3	3	3	8	0	4.40
Miceli	2/3	1	0	0	0	0	0	0.00
R Myers	1/3	0	0	0	0	0	0	9.00

The Yankees celebrate after winning their 24th World Series.

CELEBRATION!

OCTOBER 23, 1998

BOSS SAVORS SWEET EMOTIONS

Overjoyed by team, crown

OCTOBER 23, 1998

By Bill Madden, Daily News Sports Writer

SAN DIEGO—He had accepted the world championship trophy for the fourth time in his tumultuous and triumphant 26 years as principal owner of the Yankees, and George Steinbrenner was working his way through the sea of pin-striped humanity in the clubhouse at Qualcomm Stadium.

Then Derek Jeter emerged from the masses, pointing a bottle of champagne at Steinbrenner and, in an instant, the Boss was soaked.

"It's okay," he shrieked. "It's *really* okay!"

"That one was for you, Boss," Jeter said. "Just like the other two!"

"This team," Steinbrenner said. "What can you say about this team? I'm not gonna compare 'em with my others. All I'm gonna say is they're as great as any team that's ever been. Nobody can say there's ever been a team better than them."

With that, he reached into a huge ice tub

Balloons being released into the air in front of City Hall to celebrate the Yankees' World Series victory.

DAILY NEWS Pat Carroll

and pulled out a bottle of champagne.

Pointing it at Jeter he began to shake it, only to gasp in surprise.

"What the hell?" Steinbrenner screamed. "There's nothing in this one."

"Stay right there, Boss," Chili Davis said. "I'm gonna make sure to find you one."

They were forming a crowd around him now and as Steinbrenner toweled himself off, the Yankees players off in the distance were chanting, "Straw! Straw! Straw!" and then "Scot-ty Bro-sius, Scot-ty Bro-sius" as the World Series hero was stepping to the TV podium at the other end of the room.

"There are just so many people who deserve credit for this," he said "The people in Tampa who signed and developed so many of these guys. And, of course 'Stick,' Gene Michael. What a job he did."

What about The Boss? Steinbrenner was asked.

"Me?" he said. "All I did was sit there with a yellow legal pad."

As he heard more chanting of "Straw! Straw!" he turned somber.

"We won this for Darryl and for Joe D.," he said. "They're the guys in our hearts and prayers now."

Then it was back to the accolades.

The Padres, he said, deserved credit for giving the Yankees all they had and Padres owner John Moores "deserves that new stadium. I hope he gets it because this field was a disgrace."

Though you wouldn't know from the way the Yankees played on it. And now that Steinbrenner has his fourth World championship trophy and second in three years, how does he feel about selling the team?

"How do I feel now?" he asked. "There's not enough money in the world."

Mayor Giuliani, Joe Torre and George Steinbrenner ham it up for the crowd.

YANKEES HAD STYLE, GRACE OF DIMAGGIO

Bronx Bombers a thrill to watch from the beginning to the end

By Mike Lupica
Daily News Sports Writer

OCTOBER 25, 1998

In the end, this was a DiMaggio of a team. Not just because of the grace of these Yankees. Not just because they played baseball in such a high place from the second week of April to the second-to-last week of October. The '98 Yankees—and that is the way we must think of them now, the way we have always thought of the '27 Yankees—did something much better than that, on their way to 125 victories, on their way to the most splendid season any Yankee team, any baseball team, ever had:

They brought honor to every day, the way DiMaggio did.

The '98 Yankees brought honor to something DiMaggio said once, what feels like a hundred years ago, after what should have been a meaningless September game against the St. Louis Browns. Someone asked DiMaggio why he played so hard, played as if the championship of the world were on the line even if the Yankees had already clinched the pennant:

Joe DiMaggio said, "There might be someone in the stands today who never saw me play before."

He meant he owed everybody his best, every day. Every day was the World Series for him. The way every day was the World Series for these Yankees.

Every day they played as if we were all watching them for the first time, as if we would never see them again, never see Jeter in the hole or O'Neill leaping to the wall or Brosius going deep, or Tino. As if this was the one shot we would ever have to see Bernie running in centerfield the way DiMaggio himself did. If you had a ticket in your hand, if you had paid your money to see the greatest baseball show on earth, you did not have to worry, the Yankees would take care of you. They would make sure that ticket felt like gold.

You would see them at their best.

The glory of baseball has always been the long season. These Yankees brought integrity to that season, playing every game of it until the end, showing even the weakest opponents they were willing to play them right to the steps of the team bus. There was the night against the Phillies, an interleague series at Yankee Stadium, and the Yankees had won the first two games and now in the third and last game, the Phillies were ahead all night.

The Yankees were already a mile ahead of the field, Secretariat at the Belmont, and the game should have meant nothing to them. They played as if it meant everything and came back and came back and finally with two outs and two strikes on him in the bottom of the ninth, Tino Martinez tied the thing with a three-run homer and of course the Yankees won it in the 10th.

That home run Tino hit in Game 1 of the World Series, that grand slam into the upper deck and almost out of the night? He had hit that home run against the Phillies.

Ticker tape coming down on David Wells and other Yankees during the parade down the Canyon of Champions.

DAILY NEWS Howard Simmons

Every day a World Series, all the way until that last ball was in Brosius' glove and he was throwing across the diamond to Tino and the Yankees were four straight over the Padres, were 125-50 forever.

When the Yankees were 40 games over .500, they wanted 50, and when they were 50 they wanted 60. More than anything, more than the history they chased or the history they made, they lit up the summer, they lit up this amazing October, with the fire they brought to the nine innings they had in front of them. Make history today. Win today.

That is why you talk about them with Michael Jordan and the Bulls, who have won six titles, even if there is no Jordan on this team, even if only a handful of Yankees had what you would call a career year. Jordan always accepts the responsibilities of being Jordan, whether he is trying finish off the Jazz in Salt Lake City or playing the Grizzlies in Vancouver at the beginning of a road trip, or the end of one. He never mails in a performance. He always gives the people the show they came to see.

Never does he take off a single game off from being Michael Jordan.

The Yankees were the Yankees every day. Somehow it all came together: O'Neill's fierce pride and Jeter's passion for this kind of stage and this kind of team; David Cone's heart and Bernie's style and the crazy flamboyance of Wells. Finally there was the kind of player you always need to round out a story like this, a surprising star like Scott Brosius, who was nowhere in October of '97, stuck on a nowhere team like the Oakland Athletics, and now has come all the way to the top of the world, playing as if he thought he had to carry his team the last few yards himself.

And overseeing it all was Joe Torre, off Avenue T in Brooklyn, out of all the years of his baseball life when he couldn't make it near a World Series, who now has turned the Series into his office. He is the Brooklyn guy who has a chance now to be remembered as one of the best and most storied Yankee managers of them all.

"They'd be 50 games over .500 and they'd show up mad," Torre said after Game 4 the other night.

Way back in April, on Opening Day at Yankee Stadium in April, Joe DiMaggio was

there to throw out the first pitch, as always, the way he was supposed to throw out the first pitch before Game 1 of the Series until he was taken ill. But he was fine on Opening Day and in such a good mood when he ran into the young women from the U.S. Olympic hockey team, the ones who had won a gold medal in Nagano a couple of months before.

Katie King told DiMaggio that before their games, on the big tour leading up to the Olympics, their coach would always tell them, every game, to have "a Joe DiMaggio Day."

He asked what that was.

And Katie King quoted, as best she could, that line about the St. Louis Browns, from a Yankee season 30 years before she was born.

She said, "He'd tell us we owed the people our best, too."

It is the best way to remember the best baseball season we will ever see. Every day was a Joe DiMaggio day.

Fans along the parade route on Broadway.

STRONG WORDS FROM WHITEY

Sez Yanks best since expansion

"That's the thing that makes it so hard to compare this team with other teams of the past. They're a team in the true sense of the word."
—Whitey Ford

By Bill Madden, Daily News Sports Writer

OCTOBER 23, 1998

So now, in a baseball season of mind-boggling numbers—70 home runs, 2,632 consecutive games—these magnificent Yankees present 125-50 as the epitome of their coronation. If this is not the most stupefying number of all, it is certainly right there with Mark McGwire's 70 home runs or Cal Ripken's 2,632 consecutive games as a number that should stand for the ages.

The debate that will rage for the ages is whether this Yankee team is truly the greatest of all teams or merely the team with the greatest record. Whitey Ford, whose Hall of Fame Yankee career spanned the end of the Joe DiMaggio era to the Mickey Mantle-Yogi Berra-Allie Reynolds-Vic Raschi-Eddie Lopat five straight championship run in the '50s, to the '61 Roger Maris-Mantle modern day Murderer's Row Bombers, is willing to give the '98 Yankees at least this much: "They're definitely the best team since expansion."

Speaking by phone from his home in New York, Ford said that included the '61 Yankees who, until this year, were considered by many to at least be equal to the storied '27 Yankee team of Babe Ruth, Lou Gehrig and Tony Lazzeri. What is most remarkable about the '98 Yankees — as was noted to Ford — is that, right now anyway, there are no definite Hall of Famers on the team.

The '61 Yankees had three Hall of Famers — Mantle, Berra and Ford — but as Ford, the staff ace with 25 wins that year, observed: "We didn't have the pitching depth this Yankee team has. Other than (Ralph) Terry, I have trouble remembering who else we had in the rotation that year. These Yankees can reel out six different quality starting pitchers if they want to.

DAILY NEWS Kim Hughes

The Yankee parade up Broadway near Wall Street.

The Rockettes made an appearance to celebrate the Yankees championship.

There's no dead wood on that staff. Hall of Famers? I don't know. (David) Cone's got some credentials and (El Duque) might if he were 10 years younger."

Undoubtedly, it will be the Hall of Fame issue that will both define and detract from this Yankee team's greatness. Years from now, will people be able to recite the '98 Yankee lineup as they still do with the Mantle-Maris-Berra-Moose Skowron-Elston Howard-Tony Kubek-Bobby Richardson '61 Yankees, the Johnny Bench-Pete Rose-Joe Morgan-Tony Perez-Ken Griffey Sr.-Dave Concepcion Big Red Machine Reds of the mid '70s or even the Reggie Jackson-Thurman Munson-Graig Nettles-Chris Chambliss-Willie Randolph-Lou Piniella Yankees of the late '70s? Will anyone remember that Bernie Williams won the batting title with these '98 Yankees? Or that Tino Martinez led them in homers

with a mere 28 in the year that McGwire hit 70, Sammy Sosa had 66, Ken Griffey Jr. smacked 56, Greg Vaughn clubbed 50 and nine others had 40 or more?

"That's the thing that makes it so hard to compare this team with other teams of the past," Ford said. "They're a team in the true sense of the word. I've had the privilege of working with them in spring training and I've got to say they're as good a bunch of guys as I've every been around. The only wacko in the bunch is (David) Wells, and I especially relate to him."

But when pressed again about the "greatest ever" comparison, Ford hedged.

"I would like to see these guys go into Cleveland and face (Bob) Lemon, (Early) Wynn, (Mike) Garcia and (Bob) Feller three times a year," he said.

NEW YORK YANKEES
1998 Regular Season Statistics

BATTING

PLAYER	G	AB	R	H	TB	2B	3B	HR	RBI	SH	SF	SB	CS	BB	HPB	SO	BA	OBP	SLG
Borowski, Joe	1	0	0	0	0	0	0	0	0	0	0	0	0	0	0	0	-	-	-
Brosius, Scott	152	530	86	159	250	34	0	19	98	8	3	11	8	52	10	97	.300	.371	.472
Buddie, Mike	1	0	0	0	0	0	0	0	0	0	0	0	0	0	0	0	-	-	-
Bush, Homer	45	71	17	27	33	3	0	1	5	2	0	6	3	5	0	19	.380	.421	.465
Cone, David	1	3	1	0	0	0	0	0	1	1	0	0	0	0	0	0	.000	.000	.000
Curtis, Chad	151	456	79	111	164	21	1	10	56	1	6	21	5	75	7	80	.243	.355	.360
Davis, Chili	35	103	11	30	46	7	0	3	9	0	1	0	1	14	0	18	.291	.373	.447
Figga, Mike	1	4	1	1	1	0	0	0	0	0	0	0	0	0	0	1	.250	.250	.250
Girardi, Joe	78	254	31	70	98	11	4	3	31	8	1	2	4	14	2	38	.276	.317	.386
Hernandez, Orlando	2	7	0	0	0	0	0	0	0	1	0	0	0	0	0	5	.000	.000	.000
Holmes, Darren	1	0	0	0	0	0	0	0	0	0	0	0	0	0	0	0	-	-	-
Irabu, Hideki	2	4	0	1	1	0	0	0	0	1	0	0	0	0	0	3	.250	.250	.250
Jeter, Derek	149	626	127	203	301	25	8	19	84	3	3	30	6	57	5	119	.324	.384	.481
Knoblauch, Chuck	150	603	117	160	244	25	4	17	64	2	7	31	12	76	18	70	.265	.361	.405
Ledee, Ricky	42	79	13	19	31	5	2	1	12	0	1	3	1	7	0	29	.241	.299	.392
Lloyd, Graeme	1	0	0	0	0	0	0	0	0	0	0	0	0	0	0	0	-	-	-
Lowell, Mike	8	15	1	4	4	0	0	0	0	0	0	0	0	0	0	1	.267	.267	.267
Martinez, Tino	142	531	92	149	268	33	1	28	123	0	10	2	1	61	6	83	.281	.355	.505
Mendoza, Ramiro	2	0	0	0	0	0	0	0	0	1	0	0	0	0	0	0	-	-	-
Nelson, Jeff	3	1	0	0	0	0	0	0	0	1	0	0	0	0	0	0	.000	.000	.000
O'Neill, Paul	152	602	95	191	307	40	2	24	116	0	11	15	1	57	2	103	.317	.372	.510
Pettitte, Andy	2	4	0	0	0	0	0	0	0	2	0	0	0	0	0	3	.000	.000	.000
Posada, Jorge	111	358	56	96	170	23	0	17	63	0	4	0	1	47	0	92	.268	.350	.475
Raines, Tim	109	1	53	93	123	13	1	5	47	0	3	8	3	55	3	49	.290	.395	.383
Rivera, Mariano	3	0	0	0	0	0	0	0	0	0	0	0	0	0	0	0	-	-	-
Sojo, Luis	54	147	16	34	39	3	1	0	14	1	1	1	0	4	0	15	.231	.250	.265
Spencer, Shane	27	67	18	25	61	6	0	10	27	0	1	0	1	5	0	12	.373	.411	.910
Stanton, Mike	4	1	0	0	0	0	0	0	0	0	0	0	0	0	0	0	.000	.000	.000
Strawberry, Darryl	101	295	44	73	160	11	2	24	57	0	1	8	7	46	3	90	.247	.354	.542
Sveum, Dale	30	58	6	9	9	0	0	0	3	0	2	0	0	4	0	16	.155	.203	.155
Wells, David	1	4	0	1	1	0	0	0	0	0	0	0	0	0	0	1	.250	.250	.250
Williams, Bernie	128	499	101	169	287	30	5	26	97	0	4	15	9	74	1	81	.339	.422	.575

PITCHING

PLAYER	W	L	G	GS	CG	SH	SV	IP	H	ER	HR	BB	SO	ERA
Banks, Willie	1	1	9	0	0	0	0	14.3	20	16	4	12	8	10.05
Borowski, Joe	1	0	8	0	0	0	0	9.7	11	7	0	4	7	6.52
Bradley, Ryan	2	1	5	1	0	0	0	12.7	12	8	2	9	13	5.68
Bruske, Jim	1	0	3	1	0	0	0	9.0	9	3	2	1	3	3.00
Buddie, Mike	4	1	24	2	0	0	0	41.7	46	26	5	13	20	5.62
Cone, David	20	7	31	31	3	0	0	207.7	186	82	20	59	209	3.55
Erdos, Todd	0	0	2	0	0	0	0	2.0	5	2	0	1	0	9.00
Hernandez, Orlando	12	4	21	21	3	1	0	141.0	113	49	11	52	131	3.13
Holmes, Darren	0	3	34	0	0	0	2	51.3	53	19	4	14	31	3.33
Irabu, Hideki	13	9	29	28	2	1	0	173.0	148	78	27	76	126	4.06
Jerzembeck, Mike	0	1	3	2	0	0	0	6.3	9	9	2	4	1	12.79
Lloyd, Graeme	3	0	50	0	0	0	0	37.7	26	7	3	6	20	1.67
Mendoza, Ramiro	10	2	41	14	1	1	1	130.3	131	47	9	30	56	3.25
Nelson, Jeff	5	3	45	0	0	0	3	40.3	44	17	1	22	35	3.79
Pettitte, Andy	16	11	33	32	5	0	0	216.3	226	102	20	87	146	4.24
Rivera, Mariano	3	0	54	0	0	0	36	61.3	48	13	3	17	36	1.91
Stanton, Mike	4	1	67	0	0	0	6	79.0	71	48	13	26	69	5.47
Tessmer, Jay	1	0	7	0	0	0	0	8.7	4	3	1	4	6	3.12
Wells, David	18	4	30	30	8	5	0	214.3	195	83	29	29	163	3.49